LIKE MOTHER, LIKE DAUGHTER?

How career women influence their daughters' ambition

Jill Armstrong

First published in Great Britain in 2017 by

Policy Press
University of Bristol
1-9 Old Park Hill
Bristol
BS2 8BB
UK
t: +44 (0)117 954 5940
pp-info@bristol.ac.uk
www.policypress.co.uk

North America office:
Policy Press
c/o The University of Chicago Press
1427 East 60th Street
Chicago, IL 60637, USA
t: +1 773 702 7700
f: +1 773-702-9756
sales@press.uchicago.edu
www.press.uchicago.edu

British Library Cataloguing in Publication Data
A catalogue record for this book is available from the British Library

Library of Congress Cataloging-in-Publication Data
A catalog record for this book has been requested

ISBN 978-1-4473-3408-8 hardcover
ISBN 978-1-4473-3411-8 ePub
ISBN 978-1-4473-3412-5 Mobi
ISBN 978-1-4473-3409-5 ePdf

Cover design by Double Dagger
Front cover image: Getty
Printed and bound in Great Britain by CPI Group (UK)
Ltd, Croydon, CR0 4YY
Policy Press uses environmentally responsible print partners

To my parents, Eileen and Harold –
because it's the way your parents make
you feel that counts the most.

Contents

List of figures   vi
Preface   vii

one   Mothers, daughters and careers   1
two   Well-mothered daughters?   27
three   A backlash against the way their mothers worked?   57
four   Career choice: like mother, like daughter   73
five   Quiet ambition   95
six   Daughters' aspirations for working motherhood   117
seven   Working motherhood across generations   137
eight   Partners in parenting   157
nine   Making working motherhood work   171

Appendix 1: Study design and method   189
Appendix 2: Table of participants   193
References   195
Index   213

List of figures

2.1	Distribution of the number of children per mother	35
2.2	How much mothers enjoyed their work over time	38
4.1	Daughters' career influencers	78
4.2	Following in the footsteps of their parents' careers	83
4.3	"I am a feminist" – Mothers	89
8.1	Partner is what type of father?	161
8.2	Responsibility for children	166
9.1	"I am a feminist" – combined agreed/strongly agreed	177

Preface

For several decades significant numbers of women have been working in professional and managerial careers, yet women are still far from being equally represented in senior positions.

An unspoken assumption of many is that the example of successful working mothers will, in turn, inspire their daughters and ultimately redress the balance. Two influences motivated me to question this.

First, in my former career in market research, I was continually struck by the many ways in which the women I interviewed – far more so than the men – were still grappling with how to combine a career with parenthood.

Second, although the mother of sons, my personal observations of friends and family caused me to wonder how the millennial daughters of mothers with careers feel about their mothers' careers and how this affects their own ambitions.

Together, these thoughts led me to conduct the research upon which this book is based.

My thanks go especially to the daughters and mothers who participated in this research who were so generous with their time and perspicacious views. It was a pleasure to meet you all.

Thanks also go to Tamsin-Hinton Smith and Lizzie Seal, who supervised my doctoral thesis, to Kay Armstrong, Andrew Sharp and Zoë Young for their valuable contributions to the drafts of this book and to the team at Policy Press.

ONE

Mothers, daughters and careers

Chapter themes

Rachel is in her final year at university. She talks about her interest in her mother's career, growing up with a mother who works relatively long hours out of the home, and how this has influenced her. Her comments illuminate the research question explored in this book, which asks to what extent having a mother with a successful career leads her daughter(s) to want to follow in her footsteps – in terms of both the daughter's career, and how she thinks about combining work with motherhood.

> "I'm really interested in what my mum does; I really admire her career ... If I were to have a career anywhere near as good as hers I'd be very happy. Half as good."

> "She [is involved with] all these interesting projects and there are many things I've looked into ... and she'll be, like, 'Oh, I've worked with them.' ... She knows so many people and it's impressive when you go to [something] with her and there's like a million very important people who know her ... Afterwards I think I always feel more ... engaged in thinking about things, about what I want to do. I dunno how to explain it but it does make me feel inspired to research things that I could do ... When people ask me what I want to do I often talk about my mum's job."

> "My Mum is like, work hard if you enjoy it ... do what makes you happy. I don't see myself as a stay-at-home mum, I guess; I wouldn't want to do that I don't think. I don't necessarily think it's good for the children, well, I don't know, it's up to you. It doesn't harm you in any way to have a working mum and it's probably more enjoyable for your mother. For me, I would want to work."

"I don't think I really realised [about Mum's career] until I was older, in sixth form. I don't think it really occurred to me, or I didn't think about it much ... I think it makes you more independent, which is a good thing. You look after yourself, you cook for yourself, you learn to do things like that. I'd cook for my siblings, and was quite happy to do that. I like having my own space, always have. And it's also quite ... like ... makes you want to do the same sort of things, I guess. I have a lot of friends whose mums stayed at home, and they feel that ultimately they'd be stay-at-home mums after working."

Rachel is typical of many of the daughters interviewed in feeling that having a mother with a career is a benefit to her and that she has not been ill-affected in any way. In the joint interview later, with her mother, Rachel tells her mother, "I don't think it had any negative effect ... I don't know why you'd feel guilty."

Like most of the daughters interviewed, Rachel was proud of her mother's career. Like many of the daughters, she had become interested in her mother's job as she grew older. And, like most, she expected to emulate her mother in working in an interesting career and combining this with motherhood. Rachel's mother, Rose, had started her career in professional services and after having her children she had tried to negotiate working a four-day week. In common with many women of her generation, she was told that this would mean she was no longer on the path to the top level of her career. So Rose switched into a career in the public sector, where she could negotiate some flexibility. Rose then progressed to the highest level of her new profession.

This work focuses on women who work in professional and managerial careers who are also mothers of adult daughters. Twenty-five per cent of women who work have careers classified as SOC 1 or 2 (managers, directors and senior officials, or professional occupations) (ONS, 2010, 2013b). Many women who have reached senior levels in their careers started work in the 1970s and 1980s. Many of these women are also mothers and members of the first generation of highly educated women for whom it was the norm among their peers to work, and to return to work after they became mothers (Wolf, 2013). These mothers are now old enough to have adult daughters in their twenties and thirties, some of whom have children of their own. For this study, 30 mothers – all of whom had consistently worked long hours in demanding careers – were interviewed along with their adult daughters. The daughters belong to a generation of women who, it is often argued, have the potential to achieve professionally as much as men. Yet, as the evidence presented in this book will show, the narrative of progress in gender equality is challenged by the fact that women continue to be poorly represented in positions of power in the UK and other Western democracies, in private and public sector organisations. It is therefore timely for research to explore to what extent having a mother with a successful career leads her daughter to want to follow in her mother's footsteps. This book starts with the words of Rachel and Rose because a question often asked by mothers is whether their children think that their careers have benefited or compromised them. The short answer to this pressing question is that almost all the daughters believed that having a mother with a career that she found satisfying benefited them, or at least did them no damage. This adds to the body of recent research that challenges the prevalent worry expressed by many working mothers that the hours they spend working out of the home leaves their children compromised (Backett-Milburn et al, 2011; Mendolia, 2014; McGinn et al, 2015; Milkie et al, 2015). This is an important finding, because it suggests that the continuing lack of representation of women in the most senior positions at work cannot be accounted for by a backlash of daughters reacting against their upbringing by mothers with a career.

This book will also explore how having a mother with a career influences the daughter's own career ambitions. How likely are these daughters to do as well or better than their mothers in terms of occupying positions of power? This question is relevant to the progress of gender equality in careers. It is often argued that women are encouraged to believe that they can occupy the top jobs in society by seeing other women thrive in their careers (Eagly and Carli, 2007; Carter and Silva, 2010; Tutchell and Edmonds, 2015). Moreover, when successful people are interviewed about their achievements in sport, or business, or any other field, it is very common to hear them talk about being encouraged and empowered from an early age (see, for example, Oakley, 2014). Who better, then, to be a role model of career success, combined with motherhood, than one's own mother?

Mothers as career mentors and role models?

The term 'role model' was first used by the sociologist Merton, who gave the definition as 'the emulation of a peer, parent or a public figure ... restricted to limited segments of their behaviour and values' (Merton, 1968, p 356). People can be role models simply by doing what they do. Mentoring implies a more active role for the more experienced party, according to the definition of 'giving encouragement, advice and guidance to someone less experienced than oneself' (Ragins and Cotton, 1999). Recent work in the field of management studies suggests that mothers can and do play these roles for younger women in the workplace, even though they are more likely to seek mentors working in the same organisation. With few women occupying senior positions in organisations, women often have to look for role models elsewhere (Singh et al, 2006). Kelan and Mah's (2014) discourse analysis of MBAs' role models suggests that women admire other women who have stereotypically feminine qualities, such as having people skills, being emotional and having children, in conjunction with more stereotypically masculine skills, such as knowing what you want and being successful. Nevertheless, it is still the case that becoming a mother affects women's ability to occupy powerful positions, in politics, in business and in the professions, in a way that becoming a father does not (Williams, 2003; Eagly and Carli, 2007; Miller, 2012; Mason et al, 2013; Tutchell and Edmonds, 2015). Therefore, as Kelan and Mah argue, 'being a business woman and having children is seen by many women as being difficult. It is an issue they see as relevant for their future life' (2014, p 99). The combination of careers with motherhood is at the crux of this book.

My research shows that at the start of the daughters' careers their mothers are indeed highly influential. Most daughters thought their mothers were the main influence over their academic success, which provided a gateway to a career. Many also thought that their mothers helped shape their initial choice of career. Indeed, a third of the daughters researched have followed their mothers into the same career or a career with similar values. For example, the daughter of a research and insight manager in a FTSE 100 company became an academic researcher. Many of the daughters also thought of their mothers as successful and described them as role models.

Paradoxically, my research also shows that having a mother as a role model of career success is far less predictive than one might imagine of the daughters progressing as far or further in their own careers. This is particularly surprising given that the majority of these mothers and daughters reported close relationships. This meant that in the interviews I heard many exchanges that could be aptly described as mothers mentoring their daughters. By 'mentoring', what is meant is mothers listening, asking questions and, sometimes, giving advice about and help with situations at work. What seemed to be far less common was mothers communicating the value of ambition. That is, talking within their families or publicly about the value to themselves and others of rising to positions of influence. This is surprising in the context of public debate about women attaining leadership positions (as many of the mothers who participated in this research had). Indeed, several daughters commented directly on the difference between their perceptions of their mother's career in relation to their father's. One example came from Natalie, who had followed both of her parents into law. She said: "I think Mum did well, but she never talked about it as much as Dad did."

Communication happens in many ways, so this book will examine what mothers *say* and what their daughters *hear*. It will also look at what daughters deduce from what their mothers *do*. One key aim of this book is to reveal what lies behind what one daughter aptly described as her mother's 'quiet ambition'.

There are many ways in which people can experience discrimination, including being discriminated against because of gender, social class, ethnicity or sexuality. Of course, many people are subject to biases drawn from multiple sources of inequality, and all are areas that need scholarly inquiry. The intention here is to be single-minded in focusing on the significant problem of gender inequality in the context of professional and managerial work, given that these women represent 25% of working women, that both men and women become parents, and that women are still not included equally at all levels in the workplace. Nevertheless, what gender equality at work means to this author is creating the conditions for individuals to perform well to meet the objectives of their organisation while also thriving at work, being able to be the people they are and being able to make room for facets of life outside work that are vital to them. Defining gender equality in this way means that achieving it is very likely to also benefit those facing other biases and barriers to equality. There is no one path to success; a career does not necessarily take place in one occupational field and we each have our own interests and qualities. So my research defines career success in a general sense of being committed to a career and moving upwards to a senior position.

Generations

Clearly, this is an intergenerational study so it is important to carefully define what is meant by 'generation' – and to account for how it is relevant to the world of work. Three definitions of generations are commonly used: incumbency-based, cohort-based and age-based (Joshi et al, 2010). All these definitions draw on how generation influences one's identity and values, and all have relevance to my research.

Incumbency-based definitions are commonly used to describe position within the family, that is, being a grandmother, a mother or a child. This position within a generational hierarchy can also apply to relative positions of authority in the workplace. Cohort-based definitions focus on the shared experiences of a particular time or situation, for example, becoming a mother for the first time or entering the workplace at the same time. Age-based generations, which are commonly used in corporate organisations, are based on the work of Strauss and Howe (1991). Definitions are different across countries depending on cultural history. The mothers in this study are mainly representatives of the 'baby boomer' generation, born, roughly speaking, between 1946 and 1964. Most of the daughters in this study were born between 1980 and the mid-1990s, and are mainly considered to be members of the 'millennial generation' (Strauss and Howe, 1991; Broadbridge et al, 2007). An implication for my study is that there are differences in the generational cohorts of mothers and grandmothers in their employment opportunities, derived from their age. There are also differences arising from their vertical position in family chains.

The framework for this research has its foundations in several bodies of thought. First, seeing intergenerational relationships through the interaction of both historical and biographical time. Historical time exposes the cultural location of generations at a specific point in time and biographical time focuses on the smaller stories of the interactions of generations within family chains (Kehily and Thomson, 2011). This builds upon Mannheim's (1952) concept that different generations are imbued with values shaped during childhood and adolescence, as well as those of contemporary culture, that combine to define the zeitgeist. By studying families, we are given insight into the interaction of psychological and social factors that lie behind actions and attitudes. Intergenerational research requires consciousness of different relationships between individuals and time, and the impact of that on the interpretive view of the research participants. Temporal issues are embedded in much of the discussion about working motherhood. For example, the 'concerted cultivation' of middle-class children requires the investment of time devoted to helping with their learning and development (Lareau, 2011). The monitoring and protection of children from risk, which Furedi (2002) argues to be a core aspect of current parenting culture, also requires the investment of time. For middle-class mothers, the depiction of decisions about working motherhood as a quest for 'work-life balance' has at its crux mothers' measurement of hours given to motherhood versus hours given to the workplace (Crompton, 2006; Thomson et al, 2011; Rottenberg, 2014).

All of these factors are cultural phenomena that affect those having children today much more than they affected the generation of mothers in this study who gave birth in the late 1970s and 1980s. In the 1970s and 1980s the context for work-life choices was commonly a choice between working or being a stay-at-home mother (Crompton, 2006; Thomson et al, 2011). Attitudes to working motherhood were also different. The British Social Attitudes survey has measured attitudes to gender roles over time and provides evidence of the order of magnitude of change. In 1984, 43% agreed that 'a man's job is to earn the money, a woman's job is to look after the home'. By 2012 only 13% agreed (Scott and Clery, 2013). As Adkins (2002) argues, women, including those who are mothers, are expected by society to work. This is at odds with society's expectations of mothers. Hays, writing in 1996, noted the phenomenon of 'intensive motherhood'. Intensive motherhood is defined as child-centric, expert-guided motherhood that requires the subjugation of the mother's ambitions and desires to that of the child. The cultural trend towards the intensification of motherhood and its responsibilities is often linked to individualisation, and is reflected in the shift in national policy in the UK towards making individual families the site of responsibility for their children's outcomes (Gillies, 2003; McRobbie, 2009; Lewis, 2010; Rottenberg, 2014). Therefore, differences both *in the times* that these different generations were mothering and their different relationships *with* time will be important themes in this book.

Second, I draw upon the work of Morgan (1996) who conceptualises the family as being more than a social relationship and institution. Morgan describes families as a site of social practices and a receptacle for memories. Families are also depicted as fluid and adaptable, with changing needs that respond to changes in the status of adult relationships and to the health and ages of children. The everyday practices that are fragments of everyday life are part of normal, taken-for-granted life for individuals, and are significant because of 'their location in a wider system of meaning' (Morgan, 1996, p 190). Different dimensions of social life are overlaid within family relationships. Finch built on Morgan's ideas in developing her concept of 'display', which focuses on what a family *does*, rather than what a family *is* (Finch, 2007, p 73). 'Display' is defined as the process by which individuals convey to each other that their relationships are family relationships. The significance to my work is that one of the 'tools for display' that Finch discusses is the way that people tell themselves stories through which they 'attempt to connect their own experiences, and their understanding of these experiences, to a more generalised pattern of social meaning about kinship' (2007, p 78). The micro stories told by individual mothers and daughters are woven into a bigger story about social change and transformation in family life (Smart, 2011). These concepts are particularly relevant to the transmission of values and behaviours concerning the combination of work with family life, because they are influenced by personal experience, personal aspirations and the bigger stories of changing cultural scripts on gender roles and the way motherhood is performed. As feminist family scholars emphasise, it is helpful to study the private family and public lives of women as intertwined issues, because of women's unequal positioning as primary carers for children and the implications this has for the position women take in relation to paid work (Ribbens-McCarthy, 1994)

The next pillar underpinning my research concerns intergenerational transmission of values. Psychosocial researchers Bjerrum Nielsen and Rudberg (1994), writing in a Scandinavian context, shine an interesting light on how continuity of values is passed on intergenerationally between mothers and daughters while simultaneously accommodating social and cultural change. They examine the process through which cultural discourse stimulates adjustment to self-identity. They focus on the profound changes in the traditional social definitions of gender roles that are associated with the rise of working women, many of whom are mothers. A key element of their theory is the acknowledgement that changing definitions of and conflicts within gender roles does not mean that gender identity 'dissolves' (Bjerrum Nielsen and Rudberg, 1994, p 8) or loses its psychological significance. They point to the argument of psychoanalytic theory that 'socialisation… works *through* its contradictions – at the same time as those contradictions make change feasible' (1994, p 3). They further argue that girls are both socially and personally motivated, and that each generation of women adjusts to new social roles in a way that influences the formation of their identity on both conscious and unconscious levels. They describe this theory as 'gendered subjectivity' (1994, p 92). Bjerrum Nielsen and Rudberg contend that some aspects of gendered subjectivity, such as traditional models of motherhood, are particularly persistent, and that many of our motivations are unconscious and individual, as well as socially influenced. The significance of these ideas is that when investigating the ways in which daughters emulate their mothers' approach to managing work and family life, we can expect to find some continuity in the transmission of work values and gender roles, but these values are unlikely to be passed down between the generations in a linear fashion. Moreover, in a later work, Bjerrum Nielsen argues that individual feelings of gender can be seen as a central psychosocial link, because the social transformation of gender involves the work of feelings (2017, p 2). Gender norms and practices may be transformed 'from within' and by larger social forces (2017, p 15). This means we can expect to find tensions in the relationships *between* generations and *within* generations of women about their relationship with work.

The intergenerational transmission of values and behaviours concerning work and work-life balance implies the need to consider how continuity and change are mediated through the mother–daughter relationship. At the core of this issue is the question posed by Bjerrum Nielsen and Rudberg: 'how are we to study individuals in change, and not only the change of discourse?' (1994, p 1). This prompts the need to understand the changing social context of work and working motherhood because substantial changes have occurred, over the lifetime of the mothers and daughters in this sample, that could imply a dislocation between the daughters' expectations and the influence of their mothers' experiences. Examples are changes evident in the models and nature of work, attitudes towards women and mothers working, and in the legislative context. One profound change is the switch in emphasis in feminist thinking between these generations and the relationship of feminist bodies of thought to the rise of individualism and postfeminism. All feminisms draw attention to gender politics and see family and mothering as a site of power (Ribbens-McCarthy and Edwards, 2011). The emphasis of second wave liberal feminism and socialist feminism on equality at work and questioning women's primary responsibility in the domestic sphere were the dominant strands of feminism contemporary with the generation of mothers in this study being at the beginning of their careers. The key sites of contested power were conceptualised as the patriarchy and also capitalism in the case of socialist feminists. Second wave feminism was a clear political movement that aimed to achieve structural change to male/female gender relations in public and private spaces (Rowbotham et al, 1979; Ribbens-McCarthy and Edwards, 2011; Bjerrum Nielsen, 2017). Third wave feminism's emphasis on individual identity, agency, practices and freedom of expression is contemporary with the generation of daughters in this study and is not typified by a uniting aim (Lorber, 2010). Linking feminism to the gendered issue of motherhood, Ribbens-McCarthy et al (2000, p 796) identify a 'moral imperative arising out of an ethic of care for dependent children' that implies that the children's interests should come before the adults', which conflicts with the feminist aims of empowering women. Moreover, the feminist vocabulary of empowerment has been subsumed by McRobbie's

(2009) postfeminist era. Gill persuasively defines postfeminism as a sensibility, which comprises interrelated themes such as the 'notion that femininity is a bodily property; the shift from objectification to subjectification; an emphasis upon self-surveillance, monitoring and self-discipline; a focus on individualism, choice, empowerment; the dominance of a makeover-paradigm; and a resurgence of ideas about natural sexual difference' (Gill, 2007, p 147). Postfeminism as a sensibility is a set of discourses, not a distinct theoretical stance, which, like third wave feminism, is not an ideology with a clear aim to which one can subscribe. The ways in which this sensibility manifests itself in the workplace is summed up by Gill and Orgad (2015) as feminism having been made over to make it safe and unchallenging for corporate culture through 'individualising technologies' that suggest women need to be 'fixed' to fit in better with manmade workplace culture rather than advocating a change to corporate culture. Professional women are commonly positioned as needing to work on the self, for example, to build their confidence and assertiveness (Sandberg, 2013; Kay and Shipman, 2014). Therefore, as Lewis describes, women can be blamed for their own exclusion from the workplace, 'with little attention directed at the structural and cultural constraints which act on them' (2014, p 1858). As Beck and Beck-Gernsheim argue, 'it is perhaps only by comparing generations that we can perceive how steeply the demands on individuals have been rising' (2002, p 76).

The fourth and final pillar upon which my research is based brings together concepts concerning the tension between big and small histories and intergenerational transmission of values, and focuses on the intersectionality between gender and generation. This is particularly important to research on the borders of sociology and management studies, because gender differences are enacted daily in the workplace in many distinct ways. Women, in comparison to men, are shown in the next section to be significantly underrepresented in senior positions in society. Women tend to act as primary parent and take unequal responsibility for their family lives (Hochschild and Machung, 1990; Gatrell, 2005; Miller, 2005, 2011; Lyonette and Crompton, 2015). Women's prospects for promotion and career satisfaction are negatively impacted by having children (Stone, 2007; Connolly and Gregory, 2008; Durbin et al, 2010a; Lanning, 2013). Many academics and practitioners also argue that the idea that women will one day become mothers affects their career and promotion prospects (Crompton, 2006; Gatrell, 2008; Sandberg, 2013). In addition, women often feel like they don't fit in in workplace cultures that were made by men, for men, and which contain biases (often unconscious) that inhibit women's career progress. Some of this bias is attributable to employers *anticipating* that women will become mothers (Glick and Fiske, 1997; Eagly and Carli, 2007; Kelan, 2009; Tutchell and Edmonds, 2015). My research builds particularly on the work of Kelan (2012) who, drawing on the cross-temporal research of Twenge and Campbell (2008), discusses the societal changes that inform the values of many women of the millennial generation. Kelan points out that by comparison to their mother's generation, there has been growth in self-esteem and narcissism. These shifts are contextualised by the shifts towards individualism described most notably by Giddens (1991) and also the tendency of the baby boomer generation to encourage their children to work in an area they will enjoy. Twenge and Campbell's (2008) research also shows the fragility of the supposed self-esteem of the millennial generation, because this generation is also more likely to be anxious and depressed. Linked to this is a growth in emphasis on work–life balance, which is partly explained as a response to the increasing competitiveness to achieve in education and the growth in intensity of the workplace as hours get longer, jobs become less secure and technology makes it difficult to get away from work (Kelan, 2012, p 36). Interestingly, Kelan also notes that millennial women are more likely than their baby boomer mothers to be assertive and ambitious, but this has not been accompanied by any shift in traits that are traditionally associated with the feminine, such as being compassionate and nurturing. Societal gender stereotyping and work–life balance issues seem to persist across generations of women. The key question explored here is whether the experience and values of female members of the millennial generation make it more likely that women will become more equally represented in senior positions in the workplace.

Generations of gender progress at work

It is timely to offer an original intergenerational perspective on the progress of gender equality in careers, because it is only recently that a large generational cohort of women who have invested much time and commitment in their careers have grown old enough to have adult children – some of whom have children of their own. Many women starting work in the 1970s and 1980s became mothers in the 1980s and 1990s. The working lives of this generation of women often represented a rupture from the experience of their own mothers, who tended not to work outside the home or worked part-time once their children had started school (Sharpe, 1984; Strauss and Howe, 1991). The marriage bar from continuing careers in teaching and the civil service was not lifted until 1946 in the UK, the 1960s in Australia and 1973 in Ireland (Wolf, 2013). Until the 1960s in the UK it was almost impossible for women to be granted mortgages in their own right. Progress in gender equality had been made by 1981, when 24% of working women held jobs classified as managerial, professional or associated professional (Dex et al, 2006). Many of these working women reached senior levels in their careers (Wolf, 2013). These women are the beneficiaries of equal opportunity policies, influenced by second wave feminism with its focus on achieving gender equality with men in the workplace (Crompton and Le Feuvre, 2000). Many are also mothers and members of the first generation of highly educated women for whom it was the norm among their peers to work, and not unusual to return to work after they became mothers (Wolf, 2013). Wolf describes these women as representing those who merged their careers with their family life, rather than 'having a family life punctuated by jobs' (Wolf, 2006). As demonstrated by McRae's (2003) longitudinal study of working mothers who had their first child in 1988, those with higher occupational classifications tended to work full-time continuously, or mostly full-time. The significance of this is that the absence of the mothers from the home for long periods was visible to their daughters, so they can be expected to comment upon the effect having a career woman as a mother has had upon them.

The millennial generation of women are often said to believe that they will achieve professionally as much as men. McRobbie (2007) described this generation's image of themselves as 'top girls', and Harris (2003) called them 'future girl' and 'can do' girls. Think Future published a survey in 2016 of over 20,000 undergraduate and postgraduate men and women across the UK and found that 74% of women feel confident that they will be able to advance their careers as far as they want (KPMG and 30% Club, 2016). The same survey found little difference between men's and women's thinking about the impact they expected having children to have on their career progress. This expectation of future equality is based on compelling evidence from the UK:

- Women have achieved representational parity with men in SOC 2 (professional) occupations and comprise 33% of SOC 1 (managerial) occupations (ONS, 2013b).
- The gender pay gap is at its smallest between men and women in their twenties in managerial and professional roles (ONS, 2013b).
- Between 2007 and 2012, more than 50% of accepted applicants to university were female (UCAS, 2012).

- 59% of newly qualified solicitors were female in 2010 (Law Society, 2011),
- The General Medical Council (2012) counted 4,250 females out of 6,750 doctors in the first foundation year of training in 2010.

The picture is similar in other Western democratic countries. Economist Wolf (2013) estimated that between 15 and 20% of working women combine higher education, good incomes and high skill occupations, which is almost the same figure as for working men. Women occupy roughly the top fifth of the occupational pyramid in Italy, Canada, France, the United States, Denmark, Sweden and the UK. Davidson and Burke's (2011) review of women in management in 21 countries shows that opportunities for women have opened up particularly in the public, service and third sectors. In many of these countries there are more accepting attitudes towards working mothers and the proportion of mothers in work is growing. For example, in the US, in 2013, 75% of women with children between the ages of six and 17 were working. In Canada over 64% of mothers with children aged under three were working (Catalyst, 2016). In Norway, Denmark and Sweden over 80% of mothers work (Pew Research Center, 2015a). Initiatives to target the proportion of women on boards are in place in all the countries listed above, and women now hold more than 20% of directorships. The exception is Canada, where only 16% of board seats in Financial Post 500 companies were held by women in 2013 (Weisul, 2015).

However, while there is much evidence of progress for women in senior roles, there are also considerable challenges to this narrative of progress. Women's pattern of employment is different to that of men. Women, including those with children, have been moving through all levels of the employment pipeline for decades. However, in many countries, women in professional and managerial positions fare poorly in comparison to men on many measures. While both genders enter the workforce in management and professional roles in similar proportions, their career paths quickly diverge (Burke and Mattis, 2005). Women are concentrated in sectors of the labour market that tend to be lower paid. Women who are mothers are disproportionately likely to work part time. All of which contributes to the underrepresentation of women in senior roles (Davidson and Burke, 2011; Vinnicombe et al, 2013). The Chartered Management Institute's study of more than 60,000 UK managers shows that even when male and female managers stay with their companies for five years, 47% of men but only 39% of women were promoted (CMI, 2016). The same study shows that the problem of gender equality in managers' progression through organisations has persisted for a decade. These facts are well known to educated women, which may explain the finding of the 2016 ThinkFuture research among undergraduates, which reported that only 42% of women, in comparison to 72% of men, were confident that their gender will have no bearing on their career progression (KPMG and 30% Club, 2016).

Underrepresentation of women in senior roles

Looking in depth at gender equality in senior roles in the UK is revealing. The Fawcett Society surveyed a nationally representative sample of 8,000 men and women in the UK in 2016, and found that only 21% of women think that men and women are now equal (Fawcett Society, 2016a). Evidence of prevailing inequalities includes the following:

- 29% of MPs are women and the UK is ranked 10th in terms of representing women at cabinet level compared to other European Governments (CFWD, 2015).
- Only 5% of executive board directorships of FTSE 250 companies are held by women (BoardWatch, 2016).
- Big law firms see a substantial fall away between the women at associate level and those who are partners. The figures for Magic Circle firms are 47% and 19%, and for other London firms, 57% and 25%, respectively (Chambers Student, 2014).
- Women's representation at the top levels in the public and voluntary sectors is patchier than many imagine, particularly in the context of the 2010 Equality Act, which established a general equality duty for public authorities. In the very long list of public sector bodies covered in the 2014 *Sex and Power* report, women achieve parity with men in senior positions in only three instances (CFWD, 2014). Women made up 36% of the senior Civil Service in 2013 but accounted for only 27% of Permanent Secretaries (Baker and Cracknell, 2014).
- Even in careers such as teaching that traditionally attract more women than men, there is evidence that women are underrepresented at the top. In secondary schools, 62% of teaching staff are women and yet they comprise only 36% of head teachers (GOV.UK, 2013).

The depth of the problem becomes apparent when examining the pipeline of women poised to enter positions at the top across many countries. Although many companies have between 20 and 30% of women in middle management, this percentage shrinks the further up the occupational hierarchy one looks. The pipeline is therefore worryingly thin:

- McKinsey's 2012 survey of 235 large European companies shows that within consumer goods companies women account for 30% of middle management, falling to 18% of senior management and vice presidents, and falling again to 11% at executive committee level. The picture is even weaker for the more stereotypically male-dominated finance sector, where women comprise 22% of middle management, but only 13% of senior management and vice presidents, and an even smaller 9% of seats on executive committees.
- US statistics show that women at every level hold fewer of the line roles that are associated with responsibility for profit and loss and tend to lead to promotion, with the gap between men and women holding these roles becoming larger at every stage of the occupational hierarchy (Barsh and Lee, 2012).
- Only 18% of women hold positions at senior executive level in FTSE 250 companies (Vinnicombe, 2015). The UK government-backed Hampton-Alexander review has set targets for 33% of executive committee posts to be filled by women by 2020 (Smith, 2016).

Those who study the numbers behind general equality at work often remark how 'pathetically weak' the delivery of women into positions of seniority and influence is (Tutchell and Edmonds, 2015). It is relevant to the generation of daughters in my study that their expectations of equality at work are likely to be compromised. For example, the proportion of women in the top 10% of earners is 47% between the ages of 25–29 but consistently falls away after the age of 30 (ONS, 2013b). Explanations for this stalled progress towards gender equality at work commonly fall into four key areas:

- the 'motherhood penalty' and the career compromise that comes with *anticipating* motherhood;
- a continuing lack of opportunities for autonomy and flexible working in senior career roles;
- an inhospitable workplace culture that leads women to feel they do not fit in and stands in the way of promotion by merit;
- gender differences in personal qualities such as confidence and ambition that are argued to hold women back.

The chapters to come will examine the role played by these four areas in assessing the likelihood that the daughters of successful working mothers will follow in their mothers' footsteps.

Introducing successful career women and their daughters

This book is based on a total of 88 interviews. Thirty mother and daughter pairs were interviewed separately and subsequently both mother and daughter were brought together for a joint conversation. It is unusual in qualitative research to have as large a sample as this. This was deliberately undertaken to mitigate the difficulties inherent in analysing themes in an intergenerational sample with historically different points of social reference (Thomson, 2014). The larger sample size was also intended to take into account Brannen's argument that interpreting memories inherent to conversations about experiences over a long time span means 'making generalisations may be more risky than usual' (Brannen et al, 2004, p 3).

The definition 'successful working mothers' applied only to the women's careers, not to their mothering. They simply needed to *be* mothers and have careers classified as managers, directors and senior officials, or professional occupations (ONS, 2010). Most felt that, in their terms, their careers were accurately described as successful. I did not seek to represent all working mothers. Nor did I seek out women who were exceptionally successful or high profile in their fields, although about a third of the mothers had reached the highest levels in their careers. The mothers of my sample obviously did have help with childcare, but were not exceptional in that they used many different strategies, including help from grandparents, sharing the care with partners, au pairs, after-school clubs, workplace nurseries and nannies. These qualifications are important because the notion of 'successful working mothers' is highly emotionally charged. This is evidenced by the media response to the publication of Sandberg's book *Lean in* (2013), which sought to offer practical suggestions to women seeking leadership roles in their careers. Criticisms made by media columnists included questioning whether her message had any relevance to the lives of most working women (Williams, 2013). Similarly, the publication of economist Wolf's book, *The XX factor* (2013) was criticised as encouraging the value judgement that ambitious career women were somehow better than mothers who make the choice to work less or not at all (Cosslett, 2013). There is an assumption in these criticisms that writing about women should be applicable to all women, and yet the changes in women's relationship with work since the 1970s mean that women are a more heterogeneous group than was the case when the majority of, particularly middle-class, married mothers did not work out of the home. It is unfortunately still the case that women are well represented at the bottom of organisations but not at the top. That is where one key problem lies – and that is the issue on which this book will focus.

The mothers interviewed lived in different parts of England, worked mainly full-time or close to full-time hours out of the home, and had reached senior levels in their professional and senior managerial careers, in a broad range of occupational fields. They were employed as lawyers, doctors, academics, journalists, secondary school teachers, public servants, social workers, business owners, leaders and managers in finance, IT, retail and marketing. The stipulation about working hours reflects the lack of availability of part-time or flexible hours for those starting work in the 1970s and 1980s (McRae, 2003; Wolf, 2013). A minimum requirement of 32 hours per week was set based on the average numbers of hours worked per week, which for both men and women is 31.5 hours (ONS, 2011a). In practice most had worked much longer hours than this for long periods of their career. As Moen (2005) points out, continuous full-time employment is an outmoded way of thinking about women's careers given that the way women work features 'time outs' (Moen, 2005, p 191) mainly for caring responsibilities, 'second acts' (p 133) and, usually later in careers, 'scaling back' (p 77). It was also important to ensure that the daughters had the opportunity to experience, and comment upon, their mothers' absence from the home due to their jobs.

The focus is on daughters rather than sons because mothers, including those in dual income households and working in high-skill roles, continue to be positioned as having responsibility for the physical and emotional wellbeing of their children (Gatrell, 2005; Miller, 2005, 2012; Lyonette and Crompton, 2015). Also, it is well documented that women, including those in career roles, experience restricted career opportunities based on their *potential for*, as well as their experience of, maternity (Miller 2005, 2012; Crompton, 2006; Gatrell, 2008). Of their adult daughters (which included a set of twins), at the time of the interview, 10 were at university and on the cusp of making decisions about the jobs they wanted to do, 12 were working and nine had at least one child under five years old. Having children under five is important in reflecting the normative view that a preschool child should be looked after primarily by the mother (Miller, 2005; Breitenbach, 2006; Scott and Clery, 2013). All of the daughters were undergraduates or graduates, because the potential to enter career roles now commonly requires a degree. Including daughters at different life stages was based on the hypothesis that views on work-life balance are likely to change in response to observing differences in how men and women experience workplace culture and are affected in the workplace by becoming parents. Among the daughters' generation were those who were applying for or held roles as journalists, dentists, doctors, academics, lawyers, teachers or TV producers, and those who worked in marketing, communications, finance and fashion design. Including in the sample daughters who had also become mothers, offered another level of depth to the narrative accounts, because the transition from daughter to mother to grandmother enhances women's ability and desire to understand their own relationship with their mother (Thomson et al, 2011). For the sake of clarity and brevity, these women are referred to as 'daughter mothers' and their mothers as 'grandmothers'. The occupations of the grandmothers are biased towards teaching and public sector work because women typically had access to a narrower range of employment roles in the 1970s (Institute for Employment Studies, 1995).

In order to protect the identities of those who share their thoughts and stories, pseudonyms are used and only vague biographical information and details of their professions given. Particular care has been taken because it is likely to be easier to recognise a mother and daughter pair than an individual, and because some of the mothers have a public profile. The subjects of my research are all British. Their experience, however, is similar to those in many other countries, as evidenced by the facts discussed in the previous section.

The key findings of this research take account of mothers' and daughters' cumulative perspectives over time about how the mothers' work in career roles is perceived to have affected the daughters interviewed. It is important to clarify this because mother–daughter relationships are complex and fluid (Bjerrum and Rudberg, 1994; Apter, 2001). Also, no mother–daughter relationship is the same – even within the same family. As Giddens (1991) argued, the experience of relationships is constructed in the space between people, rather than in the fixed qualities of either. Interviewing twins demonstrated that the relationship with the same mother did not lead to identical conclusions about the impact of being brought up by a mother with a career. Equally, the mothers reported different views about the impact of their employment upon different children, different daughters or the same children at different times in their lives. The personality of the child and specific events that are particular to each child influenced the way in which the child felt affected by her mother's career. The mothers and daughters whose accounts you will hear had, in varying degrees, close relationships with their mothers, because those who had troubled relationships were not prepared to commit to the joint interviews, as reported by several of those approached. Indeed, several participants commented that they would not have agreed to be interviewed had they had poor relationships with each other. Nevertheless, there are tensions between the views of mothers and their daughters that emerge in the interviews. Inevitably, then, this has shaped the findings because these mothers and daughters tend to be generous in their views of each other's behaviour, achievements and their consequences.

The relative closeness of these relationships meant that both mothers and daughters acknowledged that they tended to be able to deduce what the other was thinking. Even if these thoughts were left unspoken. As academic Verity says of her conversations with her mother:

> "I can tell when we are discussing things if she's not fully vested in her response and then I ask what she actually thought. I'm relatively good at it. And vice versa. She's very good at knowing when I'm worried about something and not talking about it. Or I've talked around the subject and not said the actual thing that I want to discuss. She'll realise that and ask me about it."

Having close relationships does not mean that there is no friction or argument. In fact, arguing is one way in which attitudes have been passed down intergenerationally. As daughter Lily says about her mother: "We've argued about a lot of things so she has shaped a lot of my ideas about the world."

In discussing my research I intend to reclaim the phrase 'career woman'. The phrase is defined by the *Oxford English Dictionary* as 'a course of professional life which affords opportunity for progress'. The currency of the phrase 'career woman' has been devalued because it tends to conjure up a mental image of a woman in a 1990's suit with big shoulder pads and an even bigger briefcase. This mental image triggers a phrase from the past: 'having it all'. This image and phrase have often been used derogatively to suggest that women who work have unrealistic expectations of themselves which encourages feelings of guilt that their children suffer because of their choice to work in a demanding role (Parker, 1995; Hewlett, 2003). However, as evidenced above, in many countries *most* mothers work. Indeed, as argued by Adkins (2002), they are *expected* to work. Many of these mothers have careers they find satisfying, so in my opinion, it's about time we dusted off the phrase 'career women' and used it unapologetically to describe women who have careers, some of whom are also mothers.

Outline of the rest of the book

Chapter Two examines how the daughters felt about having grown up with a mother mainly working full-time or close to full-time hours. In most cases the daughters felt well mothered. The daughters demonstrated this view by recalling far fewer events when they felt compromised by the trade-offs their mothers were making than did their mothers. Most revealing was the five key ways many of the daughters offered to explain how their mothers managed the compromises involved in combining work and family life. This chapter explores five themes: being there for the events where parents (especially mothers) were expected to be, being able to predict their mother's routine, their mother being emotionally present when at home, being cared for at home after school and being taught to be independent. Many of the daughters also appreciated the material benefits to them of their mothers' careers. Emotional benefits were also described, such as being introduced to interesting worlds and people. And, by contrast to some of their peers, having a mother they felt was interested and involved, but not too closely involved, in monitoring their adolescent lives. The views from the generation of daughters were linked to the way their mothers constructed their identities as mothers and workers, and managed their feelings about what this entailed. The accounts of the mothers revealed two types of attitudes towards the management of work and family, described here as 'pragmatic' and 'idealistic'. The main difference between these types is in the way in which they manage (and communicate) feelings of guilt. Most of the mothers who took a 'pragmatic' approach were found among those who had reached the highest levels of their profession. These mothers had constructed an identity that was supportive of their approach to work and motherhood, as described by Garey (1999) in her research among women in employment who were not classified as professional or managerial. Taking a 'pragmatic' attitude presents a path that is more emotionally comfortable than the struggles to be 'balanced' as conceptualised by Rottenberg (2014). The research therefore suggests that the continuing lack of representation of women in positions at the highest level cannot be attributed to a backlash of the millennial generation of women in the workforce against their mothers' approach to combining work and motherhood.

Chapter Three debates the idea that we should expect a backlash from the daughters against wanting to work as long hours as their mothers due to having seen their mothers try to 'have it all', or because of how they feel their mothers' working hours impacted upon them. In fact, as Chapter Two shows, this research did not find much evidence to support this notion of a backlash. This chapter explores other research which argues that mothers working long hours experience greater work–life conflict in the context of societal expectations that women should work part-time when they have primary school-age children (Hochschild, 1983; Blair-Loy, 2003; Gatrell, 2005; Crompton and Lyonette, 2008). The implication of the existing research is that mothers may have transmitted feelings of stress to their daughters. On the other hand, other recent research has focused on the effect on children of maternal employment. The weight of evidence argues that there is little justification for the perception that having a mother who works relatively long hours is damaging to her children. This chapter explores the few exceptions in my research among daughters, where they felt that they were negatively affected by their mothers' working hours. It also considers the few other direct references made to not wanting to work as hard as their mothers had.

Chapter Four will demonstrate that mothers in high-status career roles are, in most cases, the primary influence over their daughters' career expectations. The mothers with careers in my study often acted in ways that fitted the description of mentoring and many were said by their daughters to be role models. Ways in which the daughters' attitudes to work were guided and shaped by their mothers with successful careers included a substantial number of this sample following their mothers into the same or similar careers, having the same work values, and having doors opened to their careers by their mothers. My research suggests that the daughters have absorbed from their mothers that work can be interesting, enjoyable and satisfying, and that they should aim for a career that delivers them these qualities. The knowledge that competitive roles are open to them is also a consequence of the educational achievement that was encouraged by their mothers, as argued by Walkerdine et al (2001). Most of these mothers fostered purposefully a sense in their daughters that they 'could do anything'. This applied equally to their sons, but the mothers felt they particularly needed to help build up their daughters' sense of self-confidence. In some cases, the mothers expressed concern that this lack of self-confidence would be compounded by gender inequality and lead to their daughters not achieving their potential.

Chapter Five shows that many young women are as ambitious for career success as men in the early stages of their career. However, young women quickly lose faith that success will be achievable. Several reasons are given for this, including the effect on careers of parenthood, issues with self-confidence and lack of fit with the dominant culture of the workplace. My research shows that these mothers often acted as career mentors by talking through their daughters' experiences at work, helping them to acquire useful skills and therefore bolstering their daughters' confidence. The daughters characterised their mothers' careers as successful. However, the daughters also described this success as a by-product of hard work and work done well. This is indicative of the finding that the mothers in this study tended to underplay or not talk at all about their career successes. Nor did most talk about the value of achieving positions of influence in terms of personal satisfaction and impact on others. It seems that the temporal relationship of the generations of daughters and mothers in relation to work was focused more in the moment, and less on what the generation of daughters found motivating about what can be achieved by moving up into positions of influence. There are many reasons why it is uncomfortable for mothers to have these kind of conversations with their daughters. However, the research demonstrates the importance of verbal transmission of ambition for career success, and characterises and explains the prevalent absence of this kind of conversation between mothers and daughters as 'quiet ambition'. This chapter also argues that the definition of success be broadened to encompass work values that women feel are aspirational. These conversations will also help the mothers to foster their daughters' self-confidence.

Chapter Six focuses on the aims and aspirations of the daughters with regards to combining work with motherhood. Almost all of the daughters who were child-free anticipated having children and had ideas about how they wanted to shape their careers around motherhood. A clear majority of the daughters also anticipated (or were) working part-time. This chapter discusses the facets of the contemporary culture of motherhood that means many women who have embarked upon professional and managerial careers think about substantially cutting their working hours. A dominant belief is that part-time work gives you the 'best of both worlds'. In essence, good parenting is being measured by time spent at home versus time spent at work – despite the daughters' belief that they were well mothered by career women working much more than part-time hours. This chapter considers why the 'best of both worlds' trope is likely to get in the way of progress towards gender equality in careers. Part-time work may suit some, and for some it may come without career compromise. However, much research has found that working part-time affects the career satisfaction and progress of many in a negative way. Women tend to underestimate the social pressure that influences their individual choices. This chapter therefore considers the need for social and organisational solutions to help working parents, as well as desirability of challenging parental determinism and 'the intensification of responsibility' (Thomson et al, 2011, p 277).

Chapter Seven examines the influence the generations of mothers and grandmothers have upon their daughters' views about combining work with motherhood. The chapter explores the continuities and discontinuities in intergenerational transmission of attitudes about work and hours of work through the lens of differences in historical, biographical and maternal time. The chapter shows that almost all the daughters and 'daughter mothers' intend to emulate, or are emulating, their mothers in continuing to work after motherhood. Many conversations take place about working motherhood between the grandmothers and 'daughter mothers', because female generations become closer when the generational chain acquires another link. This is a moment in the biographies of the daughters when they are most receptive to their mothers' influence. Reasons why the grandmothers encourage or discourage commitment to work are discussed. A more unexpected finding concerns conversations about working motherhood, which take place between many mothers and their daughters who do not have children. A key explanation for this is the mothers' generation's heightened awareness of how different their experience of work is from preceding generations of mothers. Their consciousness of their pioneering role goes hand in hand with liberal feminist views that prompt conversations about the importance of continuing commitment to work. Discussions about possible opportunities to work flexibly also arise as a result of the professional experience of the mothers' generation. Despite this evidence of maternal influence, an examination of generational differences in working hours, in sources of work–life conflict and motherhood cultures leads to the conclusion that the most impactful generational difference driving the aspirations of a majority of the daughters to work part-time are the shifts in motherhood culture. Grandmothers' views on the gains and losses of contemporary motherhood reinforce this conclusion.

Chapter Eight focuses on the crucial role played by partners and fathers in influencing both the positive and negative feelings mothers have about combining work with motherhood. Almost half of the partnered mothers and daughter mothers had a more or less egalitarian parenting arrangement. These mothers tended to feel more positive about their experiences of managing work and family life. Nevertheless, most of the mothers (including many with egalitarian parenting partnerships) shouldered an unequal amount of domestic responsibility. This has persisted across generations, as exemplified by the fact that over half of the daughters had or were planning to adopt the male breadwinner, female part-time model that they perceived as the 'best of both worlds'. Motivations and experiences involved in shared parenting tend to be emotionally complex and full of contradictions (Thomson et al, 2011; Miller, 2012). Contradictions are evident in that 80% of the daughters who do not (yet) have children said in the online questionnaire that they expect or hope to take an egalitarian approach to parenting, and yet in the interviews, when attitudes were explored in depth, more than 50% said they planned to adopt the prevalent male full-time, female part-time model. Also, only 22% of the daughters wanted to be primary parent – even as many said they wanted lots of help from their partners. This sends a mixed message to fathers and suggests that couples have work to do in unpicking and discussing their motivations.

Chapter Nine reflects on the intersections between the accounts of the relationship between mothers and daughters with social changes in the expansion of opportunities for women. The key findings of the research are summarised in the context of the stalled progress of women into the highest level of careers. The implications of the findings are then discussed from the perspective of families, looking in turn at suggested actions for mothers, daughters and partners. The recommendations for daughters centre on challenging feelings of generalised maternal guilt by communicating the finding of this, and other research, that most daughters feel positive about having a mother with a career. The daughters in this research pointed out several ways in which they were protected from feeling any ill effects, which it will be useful to disseminate in order to positively influence the 'emotion management' of work and caring commitments (Hochschild 1983, p 44). Mothers have an important role to play in encouraging their daughters' ambition. However, the broader context for the recommendations starts with the need for fundamental change in workplace culture, in order that women can be fully integrated at the highest level and not just included more, at what is often felt to be too high a cost to themselves and their families. This leads to a discussion of contemporary feminisms in the context of the culture of 'maternal citizenship' (McRobbie, 2013, p 124) and the masked cost to the professional, middle-class women (who are the subject of this study) of the trend towards making individual mothers wholly responsible for their children's outcomes. I argue for a closer link between academic research and public and corporate policy to unmask inequalities hidden by the discourse of choice and 'postfeminist common sense' (Gill et al, 2017, p 241). The intertwined nature of caring responsibilities and work suggests both spheres need to be the concern of public and corporate policy to address gendered inequalities. Recommendations are made for organisations and social policy on redesigning the way in which flexible working is delivered for those in career roles, childcare provision, changing workplace culture and challenging the definition of career success – to advance the achievement of gender equality in careers.

TWO

Well-mothered daughters?

Chapter themes

This chapter explores the way the daughters who participated in this research felt about their lived experience of being brought up by a mother with a career who worked relatively long hours outside the home. Lived experience is defined as self-reflexively ascribing meaning to experiences (Van Maanen, 1988). A key finding of this research is that almost all of the 31 daughters felt well mothered. This is their overall assessment and does not preclude occasionally feeling less positive about their mothers and their childhood experiences. This chapter explains what lies behind this finding. Only two daughters felt that having a mum who worked long hours had affected them badly, and one more was ambivalent in her feelings. This chapter starts by telling the story of mother and daughter pair Eve and Emily, who are an example of the dominant view that having a mother with a career has been a positive influence.

Eve is a mother of three and a doctor working full-time in a hospital. Her hours are often unpredictable but she also reports that she has had considerable autonomy, both now and during the time her children were young. She describes her branch of medicine as being more family-friendly than many. For a short period when all her daughters were young, she worked one day a week at home. Her daughter, Emily, has just graduated and is doing unpaid work internships while applying for a course that will lead to a vocational qualification. Emily says that, "we depend upon Mum for pretty much everything", for both big things, like financial support, and smaller things, like being picked up from the station. She talks about her parents as a unit, and when asked to recall her childhood, she remembers her parents not being around much during the day and enjoying spending time with them when they were at home:

> "I see Mum coming through the door with bags and keys in an evening-y sort of way ... I suppose if you see your parents all the time but divide it by 10 and that's the relationship

27

we had with them, which was fab, it was always fab when we saw them … Yeah, it's worked out pretty well really."

Emily comments that she has never really thought much about having a working mother. It was just how it was. And "how it was", she says, has worked out fine for her and her sisters. Her clear memories of being together as a family came from weekends and holidays. This reflects the view of many of the daughters interviewed. Emily talks about it being impressive to have a mum with a career. It is quite clear from this remark, and others made in the joint interview, that she, in common with almost all the daughters in this study, does think it is better to work as well as being a mother. Emily reflects that she gets on very well with her mother. She talks about the easier transition she experienced in their relationship as she went through adolescence, in comparison with some of her friends. She attributes her ability to get on with things, and not expecting "to be pandered to", to having a mother who did not "mollycoddle" her and treated her as an individual. When thinking about the times at home without her mother, Emily describes hanging out with her sisters and says that they are close and they tend to "deal with stuff" as a trio. She describes her mum as "a rock", says she goes to her mother for solace and advice, and respects her mum's straight-talking opinions – although they don't always agree. When asked, she says that when she was at school her friends' mums seemed to be around more but that her mum was part of the community of mothers and was there for school events. Emily does not say that this was particularly important to her, but this 'being there' for events at school when other mothers were attending was frequently emphasised as important in the daughter's accounts. It seems much more critical to the daughters that their mothers were *not* absent from significant public events than it was to have their mothers present in a more everyday way.

Eve talks about "work being an absolute given, as much as knowing my own name, whereas being a mum is more extraordinary". This sentiment catches a key theme for these mothers. Work is important to them because they find it satisfying, rewarding and necessary. Yet this does not mean that it is more important to them than the emotionally rewarding, extraordinary aspects of their life as a mother. Like many of the other mothers, Eve does not see work and family life as a choice between two poles. Rather, she negotiates the daily demands of both. Neither does she relate to the term 'work–life balance', because "life is so much lived at work as well."

Eve, in common with most of the mothers interviewed, raises many more feelings of ambivalence about compromises made between the time and emotional energy she needs to give to family and work, than does Emily. Eve tells me how hard she found it to leave her daughters when she went back to work after maternity leave – hard in an emotional way and hard in a physical way due to tiredness. Eve talks about an unsatisfactory experience with a nanny and being glad when the children could express any problems. On the other hand, she appreciates the good relationships her daughters had with other nannies and expresses her enjoyment of the family's attachment to those who stayed for several years. Eve recounts incidents when she was late in picking up Emily because of "the equal and opposite duties" of obligations to patients to her family. Eve portrays this as the inability to be in two places at the same time, which symbolised to her daughters that, in that moment, her work was more important than they were. Eve reports that this temporal pressure diminished as her daughters got older, but was replaced by difficulties in "being there" at the infrequent moments at which teenage children decide that they need to talk to their mother. This view derives from conversations with her part-time colleagues about the importance they attached to being at home after school, when their children were in their early teens, to notice and pick up on any problems their children were experiencing. She regrets not knowing whether this would have been beneficial for her daughters. Eve says that all her daughters have volunteered that they are glad she works and think their relationship is better for it because she is not "on their case". She also says that, "They'll relate that they've had a conversation amongst themselves and say that they like the way they've been parented and will seek to do something similar ... because I think we've come through with pretty good relationships on the whole and that seems pretty favourable."

Eve also wonders if this view will hold when her daughter is interviewed. She feels that her daughters knew how much she enjoyed and needed her career and that they could have been sparing her when volunteering that they generally felt well mothered. I observe that this comment indicates some feelings of maternal guilt that is not reflected back in Emily's interview. Eve is typical of mothers I describe as having a 'pragmatic' attitude, in feeling some regret about specific events and also occasionally reflecting on what kind of mother she has been in a way that demonstrates occasional feelings of guilt. However, she does not live her daily life as a worker and a mother with a generalised feeling of guilt or aspire to mothering in a different way.

In common with others of her generation, she took three months maternity leave. Eve also says that she did not enjoy playing with her children when they were young, preferring to cede this role to her husband:

> "I would have gone stark-raving mad actually; I wasn't particularly good. I loved mothering, I loved having them but I wasn't very good at playing with them. I liked to care for them and do laundry and bedtime and bathing and reading and I could colour always but [my husband] was better at Playmobil and Barbie dolls."

Eve's feeling is that she was much better as a mother after her daughters went to school. Many other mothers, too, express that they found being with very young children boring and this reinforced their decision to return to work. Many say that they feel they are better mothers because they work. Eve also reports that she divides her time between family and work and does little else. Emily confirms this view. This is typical of many of the mothers interviewed.

As previously mentioned, the key findings of this research triangulate the accounts of mothers and their daughters, and pays attention to their cumulative perspectives over time about how working in career roles is perceived to have affected their daughters.

The world in which the mothers' generation worked

The social context in which decisions are made about working motherhood was distinctly different for the mothers' generation in contrast to that of their daughters. The frame for decision-making for mothers starting work in the 1970s and 1980s, was most commonly a choice between working or being a stay–at-home mother. Their daughters, by contrast, are making choices in the different context of more mothers working than ever before. Looking at the proportion of women returning to work within one year of childbirth, 24% returned to work in 1979, 45% in 1988 and 67% by 1996 (Walker et al, 2001). Moreover, by 2011, the gap in employment rates between women with or without dependent children had narrowed to 0.8% in contrast to 5.8% in 1996 (ONS, 2011b).

Turning to mothers in full-time work, the proportion of women returning to full-time work within a year of having a baby was 5% in 1979 (Callender et al, 1997). By 2010, the proportion of mothers with dependent children in full-time work was 29% (ONS, 2011b).

('Full-time' is defined as more than 30 hours per week. These figures do not break down the occupational level.) These startling changes have prompted researchers such as McRae to comment that women have 'signaled a strong intention to remain in paid work with only minimal disruptions for childcare' (McRae, 2003, p 321). McRae's longitudinal study adds weight to her observations because she is able to evidence the behaviour of the same cohort of women over different points in time. McRae's study is of particular relevance to this research, because her sample of almost 1,000 working mothers had their first child in 1988, and because she breaks down her findings by the class of the women's own occupation. McRae's sample breaks out those working continuously full-time or mostly full-time between 1988 (their first pregnancy) and 1999, and shows that 40% of these working mothers had occupations classified in their own right as Social Class 1 and 23% were classified as Social Class 2 (2003, p 324). This demonstrates a strong tendency among this generation of career women to combine motherhood with working full-time.

Work-life conflict and maternal guilt

Lyonette and Crompton coined the term 'work-life conflict' to depict the struggles people experience in their everyday lives in managing work and family life (Lyonette et al, 2007, p 283). They argued that mothers who are professional and managerial workers experience particularly high levels of work-life conflict because they work long hours, and tend to be in partnerships with men who also work long hours, and yet the women are more likely to take the major responsibility for childcare and domestic chores (Lyonette et al, 2007).

The alternative term 'work-life balance' is more commonly used. This terminology is controversial because it can be emotionally loaded and can imply a choice between two separate, equal and opposing pulls. Feminist academic Rottenberg (2014, p 147) argued that envisioning progressive middle-class motherhood as balancing has helped create a new gender norm in which women are expected to find satisfaction by combining their responsibilities for both work and the domestic sphere. This represents progress in the sense that women are no longer being asked to choose one sphere of their life over the other. However, Rottenberg pointed out that 'balance' is just as hard to achieve as the 'having it all' notion coined in the 1980s (Gurley-Brown, 1982) because women have still not been liberated from their primary responsibility for domestic life. In addition, the idea of needing to find the ideal balance between work and family life is oppressive to working women because it prompts guilty feelings about not making the right choices. Language matters, and the idea of choosing to have an 'unbalanced' life may encourage women to feel self-critical.

Thomson et al also stated that the phrase 'work–life balance' is inadequate because it fails to convey the 'practical, moral and interpersonal complexities involved' (Thomson et al, 2011, p 175). The choices women make about fitting children around work are characterised by Thomson et al as an emotionally heightened topic that leads to reflexivity about identity, role and relationships with partners and other women. Thomson et al posit that 'the juxtaposition of working and maternal identities can be productive of insights and reflexivity, yet it can also produce troubling feelings, defensive responses' (2011, p 191). I suggest that this line of reasoning could be expanded to cover the 'emotion management' that Hochschild argued comes with the negotiations that take place within relationships, within workplaces and within the heads of women who report their feelings of guilt and stress (Hochschild, 1983, p 44). Hochschild's interactionist theory of emotion posits that, as well as having biological functions, emotions are socially shaped and subject to manipulation. She described the ideological strategies used to manage uncomfortable, even distressing, emotions and applied this to the stresses involved in managing work, domestic roles and motherhood. Hochschild argued that women have reason to construct stories that protect themselves in social situations, such as managing 'the second shift' and the perceived judgement of other women (Hochschild and Machung, 1990). She called this process a 'status shield' (Hochschild, 1983, p 163).

Experiencing work–life conflict links to an element of continuity in 'gendered subjectivity' (Bjerrum Nielsen and Rudberg, 1994, p 92), that is, the resilient notion of maternal guilt felt about mothering well enough (Parker, 1995; Blair-Loy, 2003; Christopher, 2012). These authors argued that guilt emerges as the dominant response when mothers deviate from socially constructed ideas of motherhood norms, and the authors applied their arguments to North America and the UK, in particular. According to Seagram and Daniluk (2002) the notion of maternal guilt is so pervasive as to be considered a natural component of motherhood. How the generation of mothers in my research managed their feelings about working motherhood is an important theme that will be discussed in this chapter.

Gender identity, motherhood and work

Scholarship on gender identity and how it intersects with motherhood and the workplace is also important to understanding these different generations of working women. Crompton (2006) argued that there is no inevitable correlation between female employment and the evaporation of traditional gender roles, because the ways in which childcare is negotiated can either dismantle or reinforce these roles. Many agree that, despite the sweeping changes in the patterns of women's employment over the last 50 years, there still persists a deeply engrained association between femininity and responsibility for the domestic sphere, particularly children. It has long been contended that women's sense of identity is interwoven with their relationships (Gilligan, 1982) and that the idea and experience of motherhood is particularly powerful because 'the child is the source of the last *remaining, irrevocable unchanging, primary* relationship' (Beck, 1992, p 118, his italics). Butler's influential work *Gender trouble* (1990) explained this association by expressing gender as something we 'do', or perform, in keeping with long-established social norms and shaped by habits formed in childhood. Psychosocial academics Bjerrum Nielsen and Rudberg (1994), writing in a Scandinavian context, built upon the work of Butler (1990) and examined the process through which cultural discourse stimulates adjustment to self-identity. They focused on the profound changes in the traditional social definitions of gender roles that are associated with the rise of working women, many of whom are mothers. A key element of their theory is the acknowledgement that changing definitions of and conflicts within gender roles do not mean that gender identity 'dissolves' (Bjerrum Nielsen and Rudberg, 1994, p 8) or loses its psychological significance. They referred to the argument of psychoanalytic theory that 'socialisation ... works *through* its contradictions – at the same time as those contradictions make change feasible' (1994, p 3, emphasis in original). They further argued that girls are both socially and personally motivated, and that each generation of women adjusts to new social roles in a way that influences the formation of their identity on both conscious and unconscious levels. In summary, gender and individuality are both aspects of 'who we are'; our desires and expectations are both socially and personally motivated, and they are subject to change. This theory is described by Bjerrum Nielsen and Rudberg as 'gendered subjectivity' (p 92) and leads to their suggestion that the desire to be a mother is 'quite unimpaired by the fact that so many women today are not at all content with being *just* a mother' (p 8, emphasis in original). These theories are relevant to the generation of mothers of my study because they, in most cases, departed from their mothers' model of being stay-at-home mothers or working part-time hours around the school day.

Thinking about the impact of working upon identity, Bailey (1999) interviewed 30 pregnant women and theorised that women's identities are refracted through the prism of their primary preoccupations as they move through the life course. She described the six key aspects of female identity as mothering identity, the self and the body, the working person, practices of the self, relational self, and experience of space and time. Little has been written, prior to my research, about the way highly skilled working women conceptualise their own identities. Laney et al (2014) interviewed 30 women holding faculty status in US colleges or universities and with at least one child under 18 at home. The women were aged 34–54 and 27 of them were married. Laney et al concluded that 'motherhood emerged to expand the self personally, relationally, generationally and vocationally' (Laney et al, 2014, p 1245). This sample of female academics are not necessarily representative of all professional women, but they do offer an interesting example of professional working women absorbing all their roles into their identities with different aspects coming to the fore, depending upon their specific circumstances at the time. This suggests that the work of Bailey is applicable to the career women who are discussed here. Himmelweit and Sigala (2004) bring together these ideas to define social identity in the context of work and motherhood as 'what I feel like doing' (in my roles as worker and mother) because of 'the kind of person I am'.

This chapter turns now to investigate issues of identity and feelings about the effects of managing work and family life in the accounts of the mothers and daughters in this study.

Identities as mothers and workers

The mothers in my sample (shown in Figure 2.1) had on average 2.4 children. Indeed, many of those who were at high levels of seniority in their professions had 3 children or more. These women had more children than the average of the cohort of women born in the 1960s, that was under two children per completed family. (ONS, 2016b).

Figure 2.1: Distribution of the number of children per mother (n = 30)

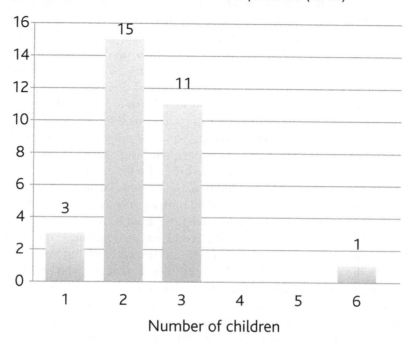

Only two in this sample were examples of 'careerists by necessity' (Crompton and Harris 1998, p 138) who would rather not have worked when their children were pre junior school but felt compelled to, in one case due to the circumstances of her divorce and, in the other case, having a husband who was not earning enough for her not to work. Both these women expressed enjoyment of their careers after their children reached secondary school. All the other women were working in a satisfying career when their first child was born. The grandmothers' generation tended to have taken a longer career break, sometimes of three years or more. Most of the mothers' generation took short periods of maternity leave of, on average, three months. The maternity leave of this generation of mothers was contemporary with policy on statutory maternity leave initiated in 1973. Women were offered the right to return to the same job with the employer for whom they had worked for six months before becoming pregnant. It was not until the 2000s that longer periods of leave became more common. Interestingly, the short maternity leave taken by their mothers both fascinated and shocked most of their daughters. This is indicative of how much the 'cultural scripts' determining views on good motherhood change over time (Miller, 2005, p 11).

In almost all cases the mothers resumed the career path they had started on prior to the arrival of the first child. This confirms the research of Thomson et al (2011) who argued that women's relationship with work tends to dictate their approach to motherhood. What is noticeable about most of the mothers who participated in this research is that all felt work to be an important part of their identity that was *combined* with a strong sense of their identity as a mother. There was no sense of one role being more important to them than the other. Valerie, a senior marketing manager, expressed this vividly as the 'twin pillars' of her life. Many of the mothers, who were already committed to their careers, described being surprised by the intensity of feeling evoked by the birth of their children and the sense that their lives had changed profoundly, as illustrated by Imogen, a lawyer: "Before I had Isabelle my thoughts were rather practical about how ... I would cope with the baby. Her first day in the world was an epiphany – one look at that little face and my life was changed forever with big love."

On the other hand, most felt just as strongly that they did not want to be at home for most of the time. The most frequently expressed fear was of boredom, as illustrated in Eve's account given at the start of this chapter, as well as by Christina, a lawyer: "To be honest I would have gone bonkers doing that. I would really have found it so boring. I couldn't have done it, couldn't. I would have felt sort of pointless."

This view that their work and family lives were interconnected and not separate spheres also resulted in many mothers commenting that they applied their family-rearing skills to work and vice versa. As Eiona, a corporate Chief Executive Officer (CEO), said: "The mixture of settling boundaries and encouragement I do with my children is just the same as the way in which I manage my team."

This research adds evidence from a broad sample of occupational groupings to Bailey's (1999) and Laney et al's (2014) research, in demonstrating that women working in higher skill roles conceptualise their identities in a way that does not set up motherhood and work as binary opposite parts of their identity that are in competition with each other. This adds nuance to what is implied by the phrase, 'work-life conflict' (Crompton et al, 2007, p 283) and to the findings of Thomson et al (2011, p 175) who state that middle-class mothers with careers experience the two as competing projects. However, for all these mothers who identified with and enjoyed work, it was also true that managing work and motherhood involved feelings of compromise. Xanthe, a director in the public sector, summed up the views of most of the mothers as follows:

"I have always liked work ... That doesn't mean I haven't made compromises because I have children because I have, but actually going to work wasn't one of them."

One measure of the mothers' and grandmothers' level of discomfort with the competing demands of work and home was evident in data from the online questionnaire filled in prior to the interviews. It asked them to rate with a number out of 10 how much they had enjoyed their work at different periods of their children's lives. Sometimes, the nature of their job at the time accounted for these scores. More often, though, mothers reported that these scores reflected times of particular stress in managing both pillars of their lives. As shown in Figure 2.2 below, the times of greatest difficulty were prior to secondary school and the older the children got, the more likely the mothers were to give the highest scores to their enjoyment of work. The graph also shows that the mothers experienced a small peak in the enjoyment of their work when their children left home. This was expressed by many as a relief from having to factor their children into what they were doing day by day. These different scores given at different times correspond to Bimrose et al's (2014) research on career transitions, which describes the contextual ways in which mothers make decisions about work in relation to their family circumstances. However, most of the career women interviewed here did not report that they changed their working hours. Explanations for this are that fewer opportunities existed in the 1980s and early 1990s to work less than full-time; it could also plausibly relate to the women's identification with and enjoyment of work.

Figure 2.2: How much mothers enjoyed their work over time (n = 30)

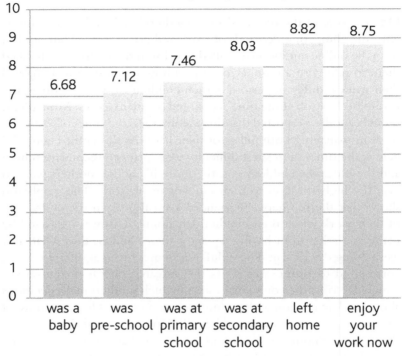

On a scale of 1-10, how much did you enjoy your work at these different stages of your daughter's life

All the mothers experienced challenges or major life changes along the way, and some of these challenges had been profound, such as serious illnesses in the family, the end of relationships and changes of sexual orientation. Procter and Padfield (1998) and Crompton and Harris (1998) attest to the effects of 'fateful events' that cause work-life biographies to change. In all cases, when faced with exceptional problems such as serious illness, these mothers reported that they put their children first without hesitation and, in the words of one lawyer, 'sidelined' work when necessary. It is impossible to fully isolate the effects of the 'fateful events' that change work-life biographies from more everyday challenges. Nevertheless, the mothers in the sample spent most of their time dealing with the challenges of everyday working life, and this will be the focus of this chapter.

These mothers with successful careers mostly enjoyed their work and they worked thoughtfully. By this I mean that day to day they considered and made trade-offs to arrive at solutions they felt comfortable enough with for their daughters. Where differences

between mothers were obvious was in how mothers felt cumulatively about the effects of the trade-offs they had made. This is characterised by Hochschild (1983, p 44) as 'emotion management'. The next section discusses these differences.

Attitudes to managing motherhood and work

The attitudes of mothers to the everyday trade-offs they made were different and specific to their circumstances and also to their thoughts and feelings about motherhood. The word 'attitude' is used in this context to describe a relatively enduring organisation of feelings and behavioural tendencies. These attitudinal differences are important in understanding the views of their daughters about their upbringing. Martha, a CEO in the public sector, expressed elegantly how much of a mother's sense of what is best for her child is a projection of her own values:

> "In my NCT class there were six of us ... all relatively professionally advancing our careers. When we talked beforehand they all planned to go back to work. When the babies arrived they all had a very different narrative. But none of us talked about it in terms of what we wanted. We all talked about it in terms of what's good for our babies. So me: 'Megan's a very sociable baby so she's going to need to be with other children,' whereas my friend Anita would say, 'Well, I don't know, Matthew needs a little bit of extra care, so maybe a few days a week will be enough with a childminder.' Jennifer said, 'It's quite clear that Amy won't thrive if she's not home with me.' And isn't it interesting that none of us had a clue about what our babies personalities were at that point [laughs] so I suspect there's a lot of that rationalisation."

The mothers' reports revealed two dominant attitudes to managing their feelings about motherhood and work, which I label as 'pragmatic' and 'idealistic'. I use adjectives (I behave like this) rather than nouns (I am like this) because the mothers displayed interwoven identities (Bailey, 1999; Laney et al, 2014). These different attitudes were evident not in their level of identification with work, but in the way they thought about mothering. What therefore follows is that differences in attitude are correlated with how much and how often the women felt maternal guilt that made them think they should be mothering in a different way. There is no link between 'pragmatic' and 'idealistic' attitudes and the type of childcare used. For example, those with children in nursery for long hours were found among each type. Nor is there a clear link to working hours. The hours of both types had varied over the course of their careers and included mothers who had been able to flex their hours, who had worked four-day weeks at times or who had, at times, worked 50 plus hours.

Those who were 'pragmatic' in attitude shared the belief that they did not get everything right but their children had not suffered as a result of their career. Some, not all, felt guilt sometimes about specific incidents, as described by Xanthe, a director in the public sector:

> "I sent poor Xenia off to school with quite a cough and cold and she said, 'Miss Jones gave me her gloves because I was so coughy and coldy in the playground.' And I thought, oh no. You shouldn't have gone to school and I should just have stayed at home with you."

My point is that 'pragmatic' mothers did not identify themselves as feeling generalised guilt about being working mothers. As Naomi, a lawyer, put it: "We're all hyped up on this guilt thing but I'm not sure how many of us really feel guilty or should." 'Pragmatic' mothers commented that they were not making a choice between their children and work and that their children were at the centre of their lives. There were difficulties but it was best "just to get on with it". They felt that it was not helpful to see family and work in opposition to each other, because then gain in one area inevitably meant loss in the other. Martha, a CEO in the public sector, said: "I think it is important that young people in the workplace know that you don't have to get it right and perfect all the time and understand it's not a set of binary choices." Orla, a senior manager in finance, explained: "There's a difference between when you measure things relative to perfection or relative to the alternative. I think if you measure the children's experience of growing up relative to perfection then I'm sure that leads to all sorts of regrets."

Some, like Jan, a private sector managing director (MD), explained their position from the point of view of their daughter: "I don't think I compartmentalise very much between home and life and work ... I've never seen those two roles in any way in conflict ... I feel I've always been a bit keener on hanging out with Jessica than she is with me."

Several mothers with 'pragmatic' attitudes reported that they actively negotiated boundaries with their colleagues and employers to allow a level of flexibility to meet the demands of their families. They had first done this early in their careers after they returned from maternity leave, which speaks to a high level of self-confidence. This behaviour at work is described by two of the mothers, both of whom had risen to the highest level in their professions:

> "I have always been clear that I wouldn't sacrifice my kids at the temple of my ambition, which is why I've been very clear with employers about what I will and will not do and that sometimes has been a deal-breaker ... I'm a family person. That's what comes with me." (Rose, CEO in the public sector)

> "I have known lots of women who have invented a dental appointment when they needed to go to the school play. I've always thought it was important to be upfront because it's just as important as work to be at the school play." (Eiona, CEO in the corporate sector)

In part, the attitude of 'pragmatics' seemed to derive from their attitude to life in general and, in part, was a response to the way they felt about having compressed time:

> "I wouldn't feel guilty about it because I think your children will get the benefit of whatever arrangement you made. As long as they're loved and secure I don't think it matters enormously personally ... you just have to make the time and space to make it all work, even if that time is limited." (Christina, lawyer)

> "You don't have time or headspace to rethink what you are doing. You just have to do it. It's fairly relentless. But as long as it stayed relentless in a mostly good way then that's all right." (Bridget, doctor)

A few can also be described as 'pragmatic' because they rarely engaged in a debate with themselves about the way they combined motherhood with work. This was because they felt they had no option financially to make any significant changes. As teacher and grandmother Donna put it: "I had no choice. What's the point in feeling guilty about it?"

Overall, those with a 'pragmatic' attitude felt that, as long as their children felt loved and secure, the trade-offs, that came when work and family life were in competition for their time and attention, were not something to feel guilty or regretful about. Of course, there may be an element of post-hoc rationalisation in these views, given that most of these mothers were no longer in the moment of facing the emotional fall-out of day-to-day problems. However, this position in time was the same for all the mothers participating in this research. Looking backwards, many acknowledged that they had had their fair share of good luck and believed that any problems their children had were not related to their working. This was well expressed by Xanthe, mother of three and a director in the public sector:

> "I'm in the happy position ... of knowing that they are all pretty happy, balanced, independent people and if there are things in their make-up that are less comfortable it's not because I worked. It's for many more complex reasons that ... I always knew there'd be a time when I'd look back and it would be alright because I knew I loved them enough and looking back now I think that's true."

I turn now to the mothers with an 'idealistic' attitude who tended to measure themselves against their ideal in terms of how they would like to behave as workers and mothers. Their language suggests they can be described as perfectionists, which is a quality often associated with women (Gilligan, 2011). They therefore often found themselves lacking and felt guilty. Valerie's description of combining work with family exemplifies this 'idealistic' attitude:

Valerie:	"Feeling I was not doing anything properly. Lurching from crisis to crisis ... never getting it right ... almost never getting it right."
Interviewer:	"What would right have been like?"
Valerie:	"Being the perfect employee and mother. But you'd need 48 hours in a day ... time is one constraint. A bigger constraint is energy and headspace. I have already mentioned my need to do things properly or not at all."

Those with an 'idealistic' attitude held in their heads an idea about the kind of mother and worker they wanted to be. A dominant idea they expressed was feeling that they were not doing either job well enough. Some used highly charged emotional language such as feeling they were 'abandoning' either their colleagues or child. Those with an 'idealistic' attitude talked more often about feeling guilt. Some said this guilt came from within themselves, as reported by Cheryl, grandmother and head of an NHS body: "The only person judging me was myself, but that was enough." Some felt sensitive to cultural judgement. For example, judgement from family members or from other mothers, not for working but for 'working a lot', especially when this entailed 'abandoning' their children to nursery. These women clearly felt that they were not adhering to the dominant cultural script about being a good worker (Williams, 2000) or a good mother (Parker, 1995; Miller, 2012). Both good workers and good mothers are assumed to be available to meet the demands of the workplace or children respectively, which causes obvious conflict.

Situational difficulties also played a part in underpinning the feelings of the 'idealistic' mothers. Those who had experienced relationship difficulties, such as Una, an academic, spoke of 'a generalised sense of guilt' that derived from their emotional situation. Lone mothers were particularly self-critical because all the responsibility was on their shoulders. Of the mothers in this sample, 13 had been lone parents at some time, of whom five had been single for long periods during their daughters' childhoods. Some of the lone mothers used particularly ad hoc childcare arrangements because of their relatively lower salaries, and they also reported guilt about some experiences with childcarers that they felt had put their children at risk, as exemplified by Una again:

> "She ran away from a friend who was supposed to be looking after her after school and went home ... and climbed in through a broken pane of glass in the back door. She was about 10. The friend was a bit mad and didn't let me know what had happened or check that she was ok."

A strong sense comes from the comments of those with an 'idealistic' attitude that they felt they had choices and that there could have been be a better way, if only they'd tried harder to find it. These observations build on the work of Rottenberg (2014) and Stone (2007) who point out the illusory nature of the idea of binary opposites to choose between. Their attitude also references Hochschild's use of the phrase 'cultural cover up' (Hochschild and Machung, 1990, p 22) to describe the cultural oversimplification of the context in which women make their decisions about managing motherhood and work.

Many have discussed the relationship between an 'idealistic' attitude to motherhood and maternal guilt (including Parker, 1995; Miller, 2012). An original contribution of this research is the identification of mothers with a 'pragmatic' attitude to the way they felt they should mother while also working in a demanding career. Moreover, this research offers my definition of the terms 'pragmatic' and 'idealistic' to describe the different types of feelings and attitudes to mothering while also being committed to a career. These definitions derive from my opinion that the often used terms 'Maximisers' and 'Satisficers', coined by Crompton and Harris (1998), to describe the work–life strategies of female members of the banking and medical professions, did not fit the accounts I heard from the mothers in this sample. I also revisit economic theorist Simon's (1956) original definitions of the terms 'Maximisers' and 'Satisficers'. The differences are précised as follows, and demonstrate potential for confusion: 'Maximisers' are defined by Crompton and Harris as women who 'seek to maximise goals in respect of employment and family', whereas Simon's definition is to 'consider and review all possibilities comprehensively to strive to find the best option'. 'Satisficer' behaviour is defined by Crompton and Harris as 'conscious scaling down of employment or family goals in order to achieve a satisfactory outcome', whereas Simon's definition is a 'decision making strategy aiming at an adequate, reasonably satisfying result rather than the optimum outcome' (Crompton and Harris, 1998, p 126; Simon, 1956, p 136). Psychologists (such as Schwartz et al, 2002) also note that 'Satisficers' tend to feel more positive than 'Maximisers'. Crompton and Harris describe as 'Maximisers' those who are most highly agential in effectively making the most of their opportunities and achievements. I theorise that the 'pragmatic' mothers in this sample more closely demonstrate what economists call 'Satisficing', by aiming at an adequate, reasonably satisfying result rather than the optimum outcome. However, most do not feel they are scaling down their goals. 'Pragmatic' seems to be a more apposite term because they challenge the notion of binary choices, are among the most evidently self-confident among the sample and include most of those who had reached the highest levels in their careers. The 'idealistic' descriptor captures these mothers' objective to make the best possible choices for themselves and their children. The word 'idealistic' has a negative aspect given that it describes what is often unachievable. This, however, seems apposite in the context of the notion of illusory choices expressed above.

Whether their attitude to motherhood was more 'pragmatic' or more 'idealistic', most of the mothers tried to mitigate the effects on their children of their working. However, all also thought that because they had worked for long periods out of the home that it was inevitable that this had an effect upon their children. The next section therefore looks at mothers' perceptions of the effects on their children and compares the views of the mothers to those of their daughters.

Was there talk about the effect of working?

The start point for this section is how the mothers arrived at their opinions about the effects of their careers upon their daughters and vice versa. Commentators have theorised that it is not until the second peak in early adolescence that children let go of the safety of parental protection and start to perceive and interact with their parents as people (Blos, 1979; Steinberg, 1990). Some mothers and daughters, such as Eve and Emily who are quoted at length at the start of this chapter, did talk about their feelings about having a working mother. Often, these conversations took place when the daughters reached their late teens or university years and were starting to contrast their own experiences with those of their peers. In many instances no direct conversations had ever taken place about how the daughters felt until, prompted by participation in this research, a direct conversation took place in the joint interviews. The main explanations given for the absence of direct conversation are that the daughters simply did not express any interest, or that having or being a working mother was a normal, unremarkable part of life that both mother and daughter just got on with. Often the mothers had not initiated these conversations. In the case of those mothers with a 'pragmatic' attitude, this tended to be because working was 'an irrevocable choice' for financial reasons and/or because of the satisfaction they got from working. In the case of some of those mothers with an 'idealistic' attitude, feelings of guilt held them back from discussing what would be very hard for them to change. However, even though some had never had direct conversations, it was clear from their accounts that almost all in this sample had close relationships and that they often thought they knew what the other thought or felt, even when topics were not discussed.

Mothers on the effect of working on their daughters

Many mothers, particularly those with a 'pragmatic' attitude, emphasised the positive ways in which they felt their careers had positively affected their daughters. They pointed out that their daughters had benefited from many experiences because of their mothers' salaries. Examples included entertainment and fun such as holidays and making a big event of birthdays and family occasions. As will be discussed in Chapter Four, many felt that it was important to be a role model for their daughters of "a woman having a successful career", as described by Jan, MD of a private sector company. Lawyer Faith said that, "because I was a working mother they identified that as being a possibility for them", and academic and grandmother Stella added: "I think it's good for children to know that women get their satisfaction from different places don't they? From happy families ... from children, but I think it's good for them to know there's satisfaction to be had outside of that environment as well."

When their daughters expressed interest, mothers involved them in their work. This had resulted in introductions and exposure to opportunities that Stella called "bigger and ... interesting worlds". Rose, a CEO in the public sector, echoed this point: "The kids have had exposure to some fantastic things and ... people, an intellectually and culturally rich world. I think it's been really good for them."

Many of the mothers also felt that work gave them satisfaction and a world outside the family, which they believed made them better mothers, as illustrated by lawyer Naomi: "I think intellectually you are more stimulating as a mother if you are working. I don't think I worried so much to that navel-staring degree, so in that way I was a better mother."

On the other hand, *all* the mothers shared stories with me about the trade-offs involved in negotiating their way through the everyday challenges life presented. An overarching theme upon which all agreed was that managing home life and work life takes hard work, as illustrated by these comments: Anita, a teacher and grandmother, said, "Motherhood and work can be mixed successfully. It just takes a lot of hard work and effort." Jan, MD of a private sector company, said, "I think people who are energetic and conscientious tend to be across all of their lives and I think I'm like that and a lot of the working women I know are as well."

The majority of the mothers (both 'pragmatic' and 'idealistic' in attitude) expressed concern that their long working hours outside the home had *sometimes* negatively affected their daughters. Many mothers reported worrying that their children thought that their tiredness or stress led to their doing less or focusing on their children less than they wanted to. An important theme was that work, especially trips away for work, got in the way of being on the spot when their daughter needed them for emotional support. This was more often thought to be an issue for the teen years than when their daughters were younger. Almost all of the mothers recounted a few specific examples from their daughter's childhood and adolescence of complaints about them working or their daughter having reacted badly to separation when younger. Usually only one or two instances had stuck in the mothers' minds over the years, but they recalled these instances as having cut them deeply, as these stories attest:

> "I had been promoted to director and my working day was very long. I often arrived home just before bedtime. I would immediately ask the girls about their homework ... or something they needed to do. I realised later that this ritual was seen by them as my emphasising the irrelevant in their lives ... I had brought my office persona home with me and I was guilty of treating the girls as a project." (Faith, lawyer)

> "When Emily was about five, I spent every day of a two-week holiday with them and came to the shocking realisation at the end of that time that I knew them better at the end of that two weeks ... and that I hadn't known them too well until that point." (Eve, doctor)

Another theme expressed, mainly by the mothers with an 'idealistic' attitude, was concern that their daughters had missed out by not having a parent at home after school. These worries were often the result of mothers comparing themselves with other mothers who participated in activities at the school during the day and were at home after school. This also reflects cultural scripts about what is expected of mothers (Doucet, 2006; Miller, 2012). The worries most often recounted concerned childcare arrangements going wrong, because this went to the heart of the mothers' idea that there was a cost to their children of them not being at home. One of many specific examples given was from Wendy, MD of a STEM business:

> "We found a book behind the sofa and I asked ... 'Why is it here?' and Willow said 'Oh, that's [the childminder's]. I hid it because she would just read and she wouldn't play with me, talk to me.' And again that awful feeling of guilt that there you are thinking your child is happy and looked-after while you're at work and finding out that's not the case."

This confirms the findings of much research that mothers, more often than fathers, take the main responsibility for organising childcare to substitute for them when they are working (Gatrell, 2008; Thomson et al, 2011; Miller, 2012). It therefore follows that mothers shoulder the responsibilities when things go wrong.

How mothers mitigated the effect of working

The mothers' response to the problems they experienced, as opposed to their fears, was to act upon them as far as they were able or thought vital. Mothers had the opportunity to look for more flexible hours in only a few cases (switching, for example, to self-employment) which is unsurprising given that the right to request flexible working only came into force in 2003. One mother, who was 'idealistic' in attitude, decided to leave her job and take a career break for three years. This was an option affordable to her, which was not the case for many.

All the mothers reported that they made every effort to attend school events such as parents' nights and concerts because they thought that important. They did this partly because they were aware that mothers who worked less would be present and so their daughters would be likely to notice the absence of their mothers and feel let down in some way. Another example of this was, if possible with their working arrangements, trying to pick them up from the school gates once a week. Mothers also highlighted that they made the most out of compressed time by establishing stable routines and clear boundaries around family life. This included doing things together every day or at least every weekend as a family, including regular activities such as swimming and taking family trips at the weekend. Lawyer Zadie spelt out her strategy:

> "You do have to maintain a very fine balance ... at weekends and holidays we did compensate for all that running around we were doing during the week and made sure that we did set aside time for the children."

An important finding was that many mothers, both 'pragmatic' and 'idealistic' in attitude, thought that the effect on their daughters of their working had been minimised. This is because the mothers felt they, in the words of senior marketing manager Valerie, "absorbed most of the compromises" themselves. The compromises most frequently mentioned were their relationships with their partners and friends and sleep:

> "I've missed out on friendship, definitely. All the friends I had were to do with the children, parents of their friends." (Karen, teacher and grandmother)

"I think [we] definitely compromised on our relationship ... I think we were too knackered to think about it. I think we were surviving ... and we definitely compromised there without realising it." (Rose, CEO, public sector)

The lone mothers with one child believed they had compromised on having a family (meaning a relationship and other children) in order to devote enough attention to their daughters. Another compromise, mentioned by many mothers, was having missed out themselves on some of the everyday joy of having children, as described by Martha, a CEO in the public sector: "I sometimes look back and think, do I remember enough about when they were little? ... maybe I was always thinking about doing the next thing and didn't spend enough time in the moment."

Despite the specific incidents they recalled, most of these mothers looked back over all their experiences and thought that their daughters did not have a deep-seated problem with their mothers' commitment to work. The main explanations they offered for this view were that having a working mother was a normal and accepted part of their daughters' lives, and having tried to absorb the compromises themselves. Of course, this was not without cost to them. The key question is, how did their daughters feel?

Daughters' stories on the effect of working

All of the daughters had good relationships with their mothers, although they varied in closeness. They epitomised Benjamin's (1995) characterisation of the process of separation between mothers and daughters experiencing favourable conditions and positive emotional development as 'renunciation' rather than 'repudiation'. Benjamin explained that renunciation combines recognition of the daughters' individual difference with feelings of 'identificatory' love for their mothers (Benjamin, 1995, p 8).

It is noteworthy that the daughters recounted far fewer negative incidents or concerns relating to having a mother who worked long hours, either in the pre-tasks that most completed prior to the interviews or in the interviews themselves. In most cases, the incidents they recalled were felt to be transitory, such as their mum being away when the cat was run over, missing their Mum after a trip to the dentist, or (most frequently mentioned) having to sit in their mothers' place of work while they were off school with minor illnesses. The three exceptions will be discussed in Chapter Three. Of the others, only Florence, the working daughter of a lawyer, said she had missed out "a bit":

> "When I think of my childhood I don't think of her being too much in it. Which I think she would be slightly gutted to hear ... I probably did miss out on things just in terms of a bit of face-time and kind of knowing my mum when I was younger ... maybe that feeling of being a mummy's girl."

She went on to tell me she was a "massive daddy's girl", even though her father also worked full-time. Arguably, this indicates that Florence felt that her mother had more responsibility to be there than her father. This again illustrates the resilience of cultural scripts about motherhood. More typically, when asked open questions about any feelings about growing up with a working mother many said, just as their mothers predicted, that they had never given it much thought. This is exemplified by Chloe, an academic, who said: "I can't remember wishing she was around more ... I think your parents are quite incidental." Many daughters thought that their absence of strong feelings was indicative of them having no significant problems with their mother's working. Several explicitly reported that they had no feelings of having "missed out" or feeling "resentful", or "neglected", or "tension as a result of her working". A few of the mothers with an 'idealistic' attitude had expressed their guilt to their daughters. Their daughters told them they had no need to feel guilty. For example, Diana, an undergraduate, said: "My mum's thing about feeling guilty. I don't think she needs to feel guilty. I certainly don't feel damaged because my parents weren't there." Also Harriet, working in education, expressed her guilt about the ad hoc childcare arrangements her daughters experienced. Her daughter Hannah had a more sanguine view:

> "Lots of these things you only piece together when you are older. Like we used to have a lot of sleepovers with our friends, which I thought was amazing fun – it was! But I also realise now that my mum was basically sharing childcare with another friend who was also a single mum. At the time, I was 10, I just thought I had a brilliant social life."

The daughters talked less about problems and more about how their mothers managed their work and home lives in a way that meant their daughters did not feel compromised. Five key themes emerged:

- daughters knowing the routine of when their mothers would be there and how to contact her;
- mothers being there for important events (when other mothers will be too);
- daughters being cared for at home after school;
- mothers being fully present when spending time with them at home (especially on weekdays);
- daughters being encouraged to be independent.

Knowing the routine: Knowing when their mother planned to be away, what time their mother would be home or that they were able to contact her at work helped the daughters feel secure. As recent graduate Gina explained: "We always ring her at work. She never says we can't. She's always available to us unless she is in a meeting." The importance of knowing the routine was also described by Jessica, an undergraduate daughter of a company director:

> "Knowing her routine maybe as a child was very important. We had this woman who came every Wednesday when they were both working ... Tuesday was the day when my dad came back early. I guess that helps. You know Mum is never there on a Wednesday so that's fine."

Important events: It was highly desirable for all the daughters that their mums were there for what the daughters considered to be important events, such as sport or arts performances or parents' nights. The daughters often commented that it was more noticeable and significant to them that their mothers were at their school events than their fathers, which also reflects deep-seated cultural constructs about motherhood. Even if a few occasions were missed, knowing that their mother had wanted to be there was often enough. These were the main things that contributed to the daughters feeling that they were important to their mothers, as illustrated by recent graduate Isabelle:

> "We had nannies and we missed her when she went away for work but ... we were aware that she loved us. So I never felt like she wasn't there even when she wasn't."

There is a link between expectations of other mothers being present and not wanting to feel left out or for these occasions to feel like a public statement that their mothers had something better to do. The growth in fathers' involvement in school is also likely to shift the emphasis to a parent being present rather than it being vital that one's mother is there.

Being at home after school: There was only one significant difference between the accounts of daughters of mothers with 'pragmatic' or 'idealistic' attitudes, in terms of what made them feel fine about having mothers who worked longer hours. Several daughters of 'idealistic' mothers said that they did not want to replicate, with their own children, their experience of being cared for away from home after school. This view seems to have come from a mixture of their own memories and conversations with their mothers who did have concerns about their daughters' after-school care. It did not matter to the daughters who cared for them at home – just that they were at home after school for most of the time.

Being fully present: Most had vivid memories of family holidays and spending time with the family at weekends, regularly doing activities as a family such as going swimming, to the cinema or on walks. Many of the daughters said that they valued their mother being more than just physically present when she was home. They wanted her to be available, to be attentive and not obviously caught up in working while at home with them. Several had noticed that their mother limited the amount of work they did at home or worked when they were in bed or otherwise occupied. Academic Chloe raised the importance of being genuinely present and pointed out that, in contrast to her father:

> "My mum works long hours as well and I had a sense that her work was very important to her ... [but] she was very good at switching off and having evenings and weekends and holidays."

This is challenging to achieve in the age of digital working. Also, in the context of comments about knowing the routine and being there for important events, it is likely that daughters would feel comfortable with having set times in the evening that mothers do not allow to be interrupted by work. Of course, the times children want their mothers to be available will vary by age.

Being independent: Many of the daughters said that they were glad that they had learnt to be independent and self-reliant. They attributed this to having a working mother, observing that they were more independent and confident than their friends who were more 'mummied'. By this they meant that their mothers ran around after them and were very involved in their lives. Gina, a recent graduate described this theme:

> "This girl I travelled with she was really 'mummied' and was just crying all the time and skyped her mum every day ... It wasn't good for her, she just had no confidence at all, not even to get on a bus first."

Moreover, several had noticed since university that their friends felt emotionally responsible for mothers who had prioritised their children over work and were glad not to be in this position. This valuing of independence that correlates with having a mother who worked relatively long hours is confirmed by the work of Aughinbaugh and Gittleman (2004).

My research shows that almost all of the daughters felt that their mothers' work had not affected them negatively, which suggests that the mothers have been successful in absorbing the compromises themselves. Little directly comparable research exists that examines the perspectives of mothers and daughters and that also focuses on mothers with successful careers. However, some corroboration comes from the Timescapes qualitative longitudinal interviews with much younger (primary age) children that inquired about the impact of having working parents. They found that children did not feel ill affected, but also highlighted that many of the children said they disliked not being able to go home straight after school (Backett-Milburn et al, 2011). Thinking about research among older children, psychologist Apter (2001), in her book *The myth of maturity*, discussed the importance to young adults in their late teens and twenties of feeling that their mothers are attentive and supportive of them even as they also strive to separate themselves. She also commented that it is little acknowledged how much young adults remain emotionally invested in their parents.

Conclusions

There is limited literature on which to draw which looks at the effect on children over time of having a mother working comparatively long hours in a career role. This is because it is only since the 1970s that many women have been in SOC 1 and 2 careers, and because research from North America tends to compare stay-at-home mothers with full-time workers and the UK model is more commonly part-time work versus full-time work. An original contribution of my research is to demonstrate that even though a significant proportion of the mothers, particularly those with an 'idealistic' attitude, expressed maternal guilt about trade-offs they had made over time between work and their families, their daughters rarely mirrored their mothers' concerns. Moreover, mothers and daughters were in accord in terms of the benefits of having a working mother with a career.

Almost all the mothers in this research really enjoyed working, but the stories they told made it clear that they did not identify more strongly with work than motherhood. Being a mother was central to their identities. All were thoughtful about the way they managed their careers and motherhood, meaning that they considered the implications of the day-to-day trade-offs they were making. These findings confirm the work of Garey (1999, p 75) who described working mothers as being in the process of constructing a 'mutually supportive' identity in which work and motherhood are interwoven. Garey (1995) also theorised that working mothers construct new definitions of good mothering that work around their work. Her theories are based on night-shift workers, and I perceive that a similar process is happening with the mothers with careers in my study: for example, the priority placed on being present for their children when they are at home and the frequently stated view that they are better mothers because they also have satisfying work. This also accords with Sutherland's (2010) findings about middle-class white mothers in the US. My research identifies two main differences in attitude in the way mothers felt they should mother while also working in a demanding career. My original contribution is the identification of those taking a 'pragmatic' attitude. 'Pragmatics' challenge the notion of binary choices in the trade-offs they make between the demands of their work and families. They share a view that they did not get everything right, treat trade-offs as a fact of life and also feel that their children have not suffered as a result of their working. They feel the decisions they made on a daily basis were usually good enough. This is underpinned by their belief that their children feel loved and secure. Those with a 'pragmatic' attitude include some who had reached the highest levels in their careers, and this is probably related to the fact they did not often feel regretful or guilty about the way they managed their work and life. Another possible explanation for this is that many of those with 'pragmatic' feelings about motherhood had much more support from their partners. This will be debated further in Chapter Eight.

I describe the other dominant attitude expressed in this generation of mothers as 'idealistic', to capture their focus on making the best possible choices for themselves and their children. They report feeling maternal guilt more frequently because they have a clear image of the kind of mother and worker they want to be and feel that they have not lived up to their own expectations in either role. Therefore, they are more uncomfortable in their identities. While many of the 'idealistic' mothers express greater concerns than the 'pragmatics' that their work has sometimes negatively affected their daughters, and sometimes even expressed this view to their daughters, their overall view was that their daughters felt neutral about the effect of their mothers' careers upon them because they had taken many of the compromises upon themselves.

Most of the daughters expressed a more positive view than their mothers. They saw benefits in the role model their mothers presented and in the fruits of their experiences, contacts and salary. They also gave specific reasons why they had not felt disadvantaged by their mothers working, which cohered around five key themes.

Finally, a key original finding is that the views expressed by the daughters' generation shows that they did not need a constant maternal presence in order to feel well loved and well mothered. Almost all did not reject or feel ill affected by their mothers' approach to managing a career. Gina, the recent graduate daughter of a director of a consultancy, summed up these themes well in describing her mother in reference to her own, anticipated, relational identity as mother, worker and partner:

> "She's definitely a very involved mother. She always has been and in no way rejects that role. But I think she does take it on in conjunction with a career and I would want that. I wouldn't want to feel like I'd compromised my role as mother ... but it would be equally horrible to feel you'd compromised who I am or that the responsibility has been delegated to me, in terms of taking care of the family, more than it should be."

Three key points made in this chapter are:

- The continuing lack of representation of women in the most senior positions at work cannot be accounted for by a backlash of daughters reacting against their upbringing by mothers who were also committed to a career, because almost all the daughters felt well mothered.
- A link is shown between mothers who take a 'pragmatic' attitude to managing their feelings about motherhood and work and progressing to positions of influence in a career.

- The daughters' view that they had not been ill affected is based on their mothers being there for the events where parents (especially mothers) were expected to be, daughters being able to predict their mother's routine, their mother being emotionally present when at home, daughters being cared for at home after school when possible and being taught to be independent.

The next chapter will consider the exceptions to these findings: the daughters who did feel critical of the hours their mothers gave to their work.

- would like to have been introduced to the cast
- something about herself in the study & her meth. Tempting but fleet on 'lived exp'
- Quite ~~fine~~ Cinderella-like

THREE

A backlash against the way their mothers worked?

Chapter themes

One of the narratives frequently encountered when discussing my research is that the mothers' generation tried 'to have it all'; they worked hard at work and at home, and that we should therefore expect from their daughters a *reaction against* wanting to do the same. As the previous chapter shows, little evidence was found to support this view. This chapter explores in more depth the reasons why the small minority of daughters in this study (three out of 31) felt that the way in which their mothers had worked had affected them negatively. Comments made by all the daughters about their mothers' working hours are also scrutinised. Given that there were only three daughters who felt ill-affected, this chapter starts by telling their stories.

Yvette has her own consultancy business and a senior position in the public sector. She is a lone mother and recounts that after being left by her partner when her daughter Yasmin was aged three, she became the sole earner. This necessitated full-time working and her requests to work flexibly in order to pick up Yasmin from school on two or three days a week were refused. This had meant that Yasmin was in an after-school club between the ages of six and 10. During this time Yvette reports that Yasmin experienced periods when she suffered severely from anxiety when separated from her mother. This anxiety started during occasional visits to Yasmin's father that she found stressful. Yvette says that her daughter's narrative is that her mother's only option was to work because they needed the money. Yvette says that Yasmin thinks that she would have been home with her if she had not had to go to work for financial reasons. Yvette reports that financial necessity lay behind the hours she worked but that she also derived considerable satisfaction from her job. She often felt guilt. She feels that Yasmin would have preferred her to be at home every day after school and in the holidays, but Yvette's view was that Yasmin's anxiety was rooted in her perceived abandonment by her father, and that even part-time working would not have given Yasmin the level of contact with her mother that she craved. Yvette spent all her time outside work with her daughter. One consequence of this was Yvette did not have the opportunity to meet another partner which, in turn meant Yasmin remained an only child. Yvette reports that Yasmin felt herself to be different from other children of separated parents because her father was hardly in her life and because she was the only child consistently in the after-school club. It was this latter point that Yvette regrets most because it was theoretically (but not in practice) more within her control:

> "I felt that if I'd just been able to spend a little more time with her after school ... I think she would have still struggled but I think it would have helped because she went to an after-school club ... five days a week ... and I think she felt it when other kids got picked up from school."

Her undergraduate daughter, Yasmin, describes herself as suffering from severe anxiety and told me that she feels rejected by her father and that her mother's absences while she was at work also made her feel rejected by her, too. Yasmin reports that she told her mum at the time that she didn't want her to work and be away from her so much. Yvette's view of this was subtly different. She reports being aware of Yasmin's feelings about her working hours due to her actions. It was not until Yasmin was older that they discussed it. Yasmin hated summer camps and the after-school club and says how awful it was to be "in care" until five or six o'clock every day. Yasmin contrasts her experiences with those of her peers, most of whom she believed had "parents that chose to stay at home, and have a lot of life despite that choice". She also describes her family as "different". Yasmin seeks to absolve her mother of blame by saying that Yvette had no choice but to work for financial reasons, matching what Yvette reports to be her daughter's narrative. Simultaneously, she does blame her mother for underestimating how bad her anxiety was and her "continual belief that it was a phase". Yasmin ultimately feels that:

> "She was away so much it was difficult to feel like there was some kind of stability ... If she had worked less, I could have got some of my issues resolved and she would have had time to listen to and understand me. I think a child with mental health problems was not a pressure my mum could afford at that time.... So I think it was equally as hard for

my mum as it was for me, and I think she did feel guilty, and I think I picked up on that."

Unlike many of the other daughters, previously discussed, Yasmin makes no reference to her mother enjoying or deriving satisfaction from her work. Yasmin's ambition for the future is to work and create a "stable family" with her partner, whom she has been with since she was 16. She wants to continue to work and share care with her partner after school so her child can "have the opportunity to play with who they want to play with". This underlines her hatred of the after-school club.

The other daughters who have a lot to say about how they disliked the way their mothers "prioritised" work when they were growing up are Tanya, who has recently started work, and Olivia, an undergraduate. Like Yvette, Tanya's mother, Tara, is a lone parent whose daughter's father was absent. Tara, now a company managing director, says that her "big fear was that by working I'd become an unsuccessful mother" because, after having Tanya in her teens, she had chosen a career that meant she often worked long hours and worked abroad, and therefore did not spend enough time with Tanya when she was younger. She reports that Tanya often told her she hated this and missed her mother. Tanya confirms that she missed her mum when she was away for long periods, feeling very sad about this, and that reflecting on her feelings over the last few years made her realise that she was angry and thought, "it really wasn't OK to prioritise work to that level." She attributes her problems to her unusual situation of only having one parent. When growing up she had many friends with divorced parents, but not with wholly absent fathers. Her ambition for any future children she has is to work part-time, although she is already worried what effect this will have on her career, which she is confident she will enjoy. Tanya's final verdict on growing up with a mother with a successful career is ambivalent:

"I am so proud of her and in a way those travelling opportunities were exactly what made me want to go into [the same field] but I also question whether it is a good idea as I wouldn't want that for my children. I think having a single parent is a big part of that though ... I secretly do think having a stay-at-home mum would be quite boring. I might not be able to look up to [a stay-at-home mum] in the same way and it would feel like a lot of pressure to know

that they had given everything up for you ... so I am glad
I have had a working mother, even if at times it was hard."

Olivia's mother, Orla, feels strongly that one parent should stay at home to bring up the children and that, for her family, the person best fitted for the job by temperament and for financial reasons was her husband. Orla reports that her daughter, Olivia, appreciated the value of having a parent at home but would have preferred it to be her mother. Olivia expresses her issues with her upbringing in emotionally charged language, calling her situation "unnatural" and talking about her Dad's "resentment" of his role even while also saying he was emotionally responsive. In the joint interview Olivia tells her mother that she has not been a good mother because, "if you are working so much you are not a mother." Olivia says that she did not feel as a child that she received enough affection from her mum and that she felt jealous of her friends' stay-at-home mothers, who would pick her friends up from school and do their homework together with them at the kitchen table. Orla attributes some of Olivia's problems to the comparisons she made with her peers at school: "Most of the mothers had worked but given up ... I think the mums coming to the gate ... I think she would have liked that. She's conformist. I don't think she enjoyed being in a non-conventional situation." Orla reports reacting to Olivia's issues by going part-time when Olivia was 13 (although in Olivia's memory she was 15 when this happened).

The accounts of Yvette and Yasmin echo themes that came up for the majority of daughters in this study, as discussed in Chapter Two. First, what many of the daughters had in common was a strong feeling that they wanted to go home after school, although it did not matter who cared for them there. Her mother's circumstances meant that Yasmin experienced longer periods in after-school care than any other daughter in this study. Second, the accounts of Yasmin and Olivia show how important it was to them to feel that they "fitted in" at school and that their mothers were visible at school. Third, both Yvette and Tara expressed guilt about difficulties caused by lack of support from a partner. They had also found it hard to organise any flexibility at work. These are all themes that troubled other mothers in this study. What is exceptional among the group of daughters I interviewed, is Yasmin's lack of contact with her father, her mental health problems and the issue emphasised by both mother and daughter that this, and the years in after-school club, made her 'different'. Olivia also brought up the idea of being different. She was alone in having her father (who had a manual job) waiting at the gate of her public school. This also echoes the finding from the whole sample that the judgement of peers at school events is a heightened moment for daughters when thinking about how their mothers' working lives have affected them.

Women should work – but not too much

Attitudes towards working motherhood have changed considerably over time. The British Social Attitudes (BSA) survey measures responses to the gender separation of roles over time. In 1984, 43% agreed that 'a man's job is to earn the money, a woman's job is to look after the home' and by 2012 only 13% agreed (Scott and Clery, 2013, p 122). This suggests that the mothers' generation in this study were atypical of the general female population. The persistence of the notion that women should be primarily responsible for their children is also shown in research from the US. Pew Research found that 51% of male and female respondents believed children are better off if their mother is at home and not employed, while only 8% believed that the same benefit applies to children whose father is at home and not employed (Pew Social Trends, 2014). The notion of a working mother somehow being a bad mother is culturally resilient, not least because framing working motherhood as an either/or choice between work and the home is a trope often amplified by the media (Hadfield et al, 2007).

However, McRae, who studied new mothers contemporaneous with the mothers in my study, demonstrated that a significant majority of working mothers in the UK, irrespective of their level of participation in paid work, felt that it is possible to combine a career – rather than just work – with motherhood. Of those in her sample who worked full-time, 92% disagreed with the statement 'women can't combine a career and children'. Of those working mostly full-time, 88% disagreed, 71% of those working continuously part-time, 69% of those working mostly part-time, and then showing a sharp fall to 55% among those who were not economically active (McRae, 2003, p 327). Unsurprisingly, women's attitudes towards combining work with motherhood reflected their behaviour. The British Social Attitudes survey does not break down opinion by working status, but does show that the most common social view is that mothers should not work as much as fathers. In 1989 the percentage of nationally representative people who agreed that a mother should work full-time when she has a child under school age was 2%; 26% agreed that she should work part-time and 64% that she should stay at home. This compares with figures from 2012 of 5% for full-time, 43% for part-time and 33% for staying at home (Scott and Clery, p 122). This shows movement between the generations in my study in the idea that women can work when they have children under school age, but continuity in the idea that women should not work full-time. This dominant 'cultural script' provides the context for the views of the daughters' generation (Miller, 2005, p 11). It is therefore remarkable that so few daughters criticised their mothers for working relatively long hours during their childhood.

Intergenerational transmission and working hours

Psychological and sociological literature has long argued that parents of the same sex as their child act as role models in influencing their child's employment pattern (Moen et al, 1997; Risman, 1998; Davis, 2007). Socialisation of gender work roles is commonly said to happen through three main channels: reinforcement by parents of gender-appropriate behaviour, children modelling their behaviour on same sex parents and society at large (summarised by Olivetti et al, 2013). McGinn et al (2015) used national archive data from 2002–12 across 24 countries to compare outcomes among nationally representative samples for the adult children of mothers who work, versus those who stayed at home. They found that the children of working mothers were more likely to be employed, to work more hours, in more supervisory positions, and to earn more if employed. An alternative explanation to parental influence is offered by American research from Olivetti and Patacchini (2013), who found that daughters tended to model the working hours of their mothers when their mother's hours were dissimilar to the mothers of their friends, because when a variety of models are available, the tendency is to look at that which is closest to you. However, in the case of the daughters in this sample who did express a desire to work fewer hours, there was no discernible bias in terms of whether or not the mothers of their friends worked. Research that provides a framework for my findings comes from Cunningham (2001), who showed that when parents model non-traditional gender roles in practice, their behaviour is more likely to be transmitted to their children than the message coming from society about what is gender normative.

Working hours and stress in professional jobs

The work of prominent academic Joan C. Williams made it clear that from the point of view of organisations, 'ideal workers' are those who work long hours (Williams, 2000, p 145). As mentioned in Chapter Two, Lyonette et al (2007) argued that mothers who are professional

*(How
 g b t
w. l.
enhance
ment)
Time*

and managerial workers experience particularly high levels of work–life conflict because their experience of long hours at work is combined with taking on a bigger domestic life load than their male partners. Work–life conflict is linked to feelings of maternal guilt in many studies (Rich, 1986; Blair-Loy, 2003). For example, Gatrell's (2005) qualitative study of 20 heterosexual partnerships argued that working mothers feel guilt because their work is in competition with their parenting, whereas men do not report this pressure. Hochschild's (1983) work made explicit the emotional cost, experienced particularly by mothers, of coping with feelings caused by difficulties in managing the twin pressures of paid work and work at home. The significance to my research is that if a mother is unhappy with compromises made for work and communicates this to her daughter, then it is possible that this will result in a reaction against working as hard as her mother.

A simple measure of 'working hard' is hours devoted to the workplace. Studies have asked questions about the connection between working hours and stress. The work of Barnett et al (2008) found that working hours per se do not seem to have a strong link to parental distress. Focusing specifically on professional and managerial workers, Roxburgh (2004) showed that having a higher income moderates the influence of time pressure on maternal depression. It is also important to take account of how mothers depict their working hours to themselves and others. Jacobs and Gerson's (2004) cross-national quantitative study of working time and families showed that long hours of 40 hours plus per week are often taken for granted by professional and managerial couples. Galinsky's (1999) quantitative study in the US also found that working mothers experienced better health and fewer episodes of depression than stay-at-home mothers. Gareis and Barnett's (2002) work in the US with 98 female doctors working either full-time or reduced hours found that the fit of their schedule around children's school schedules is a more important predictor of maternal distress than the perceived demands of the job or working hours. The weight of the evidence suggests that long hours spent in high-skill jobs is not likely to be damaging to the mental state of the mother, especially if they can exert some control over how their work fits around their family commitments. My qualitative data also suggests that the vast majority of the women in this study enjoyed their jobs, which means that feeling distressed about work is unlikely to be their dominant experience (see Chapters Two and Four). Bostock's (2014) study on the meaning of success for women with careers supports my finding. These factors make it less likely that the daughters' generation would have had a negative view of working hours transmitted to them. The next section therefore examines the evidence on the effect of mothers' working hours upon their children.

Are mothers' longer working hours detrimental to children?

In recent years several longitudinal studies with large samples have provided a convincing challenge to the notion that children of mothers who work are likely to experience mental distress. McMunn (2011) reporting on her longitudinal study of participants in the Millennium Cohort Study in the UK – which looked at emotional symptoms, problems with conduct, hyperactivity and peer group relations – found (in all three sweeps of the survey) that girls with mothers who were not in paid work were six times more likely than other girls to exhibit behavioural problems. These differences are not explained by household income, level of mother's education or experience of depression in the mother. Other studies have examined the views of older children, and this work is even more relevant to my research. These studies cumulatively argue that there is little evidence of damage that can be attributed to the working hours of mothers. Mendolia (2014) worked with British Household Panel Survey data collected from 1994 to 2006, comparing self-reported measures of psychological wellbeing, as well as incidents of smoking and intention to leave school at 16, and found no significant correlation between negative effects and hours worked. The strengths of this study are that there is consistent data for these negative effects and comparisons are made between part–time (fewer than 25 hours, and fewer than 30 hours a week) and full–time working (35 hours a week or more). All the mothers included in the analysis did paid work. Also, the findings are consistent across economic groups. The limitation of this study is that it did not examine what happened in the hours the mothers were not working. Instead, Mendolia drew on the work of Bianchi (2000) and suggested that one reason that long working hours do not undermine outcomes for children is that working mothers do not necessarily spend less time with their children than part–time working mothers. Mendolia theorised that working mothers spend less time on household chores. This theory was verified by McGinn et al (2015) in their longitudinal study discussed above. Similarly, Milkie et al (2015) conducted a longitudinal study in Canada, based on panel data, looking at the effects of parents' investment of time on educational performance and behavioural and social wellbeing, including delinquency. They separated out 12–18 year olds (n=778) from 3–11 year olds (n=1,605). They also addressed the time spent by mothers, fathers and both together, and distinguished between 'accessible time' (when parents were present but not interacting with children) and 'engaged time'. They concluded that there was no significant relationship between mothers (or fathers) spending more time with their children and levels of academic achievement, behavioural or emotional problems for younger children. They did find differences with adolescents. This confirms the opinion of many of the mothers in my study that they needed to be available to their children more in early adolescence. The amount of engaged time spent with the mother alone impacted upon the young person's likelihood to be involved in delinquent behaviour, and time spent with both parents together was related to better overall outcomes in terms of behavioural and emotional health. This is a particularly valuable study in pioneering an attempt to quantify the effects of the time spent with children. Milkie et al (2015) acknowledged that engaged time did not necessarily mean quality time, and therefore cited Galinsky's (1999) work to posit that when parents are not stressed and think they are doing the right thing for themselves and their children, the children are more likely to fare well because the parents' attitude is reflected in their responsiveness to their children.

Galinsky (1999) interviewed over 1,000 children aged 8–18 in the US and asked them to grade their parents on a range of parenting skills. Only 10% said they wished their mothers would spend more time with them and having a working mother was never predictive of children's responses. However, 34% wished their mothers would be less tired and stressed after work. It is particularly relevant to my research findings that Galinsky's conclusion was that parents who were comfortable with their choices about working or not working were more responsive to their children than those who questioned their choices. This positively influenced how well their children fared on measures of social and emotional development and school success. A limitation of Galinsky's research is that 74% rated their mothers positively and yet no explanation is offered for the remaining 26%. Christopher (2012) argued that outcomes for children of employed mothers are influenced by the way the mothers outsource care, arrange their children's social interactions and make themselves available by phone or online when they are not physically present. None of the studies cited above take account of this. Yet, taken cumulatively, all these studies make a powerful case that mothers who work, including those who work full-time, are not compromising their children simply through the act of working. This is relevant to my research in that it corroborates the findings that few of the daughters feel negatively affected by their mothers working hours. However, this is clearly not true of all daughters of career mothers who work long hours, so I now return to explore the views of the small minority discussed at the start of this chapter who did feel unhappy about the way their mothers worked.

Daughters who disliked their mothers working hours – their explanation

Galinsky's (1999) research found that 26% of eight- to 18-year-olds gave their mothers negative scores. In my research it was three out of 31 (10%). Two of the three cases were lone mothers with absent fathers and both of these were 'idealistic' in attitude. The third case was the only one in the sample whose husband stayed at home to raise the children. In this case, the mother had a 'pragmatic' attitude. In all three cases mother and daughter had discussed the daughters' feelings about the mothers' working hours at various periods in their upbringing.

Two out of the three daughters who had a profound problem with the number of hours their mothers worked were in their early twenties and had not yet fully left home. I therefore considered whether there could be a link between these more negative views and recent emergence from childhood, but the eight of the 10 daughters in the sample who were still undergraduates or very recent graduates did not feel that their mothers' working hours had had a negative effect upon them. Therefore, the explanation for the minority of more negative views is likely to lie elsewhere. Another possible explanation is that two of the three daughters with negative feelings were children of lone parents. There were three other daughters in my sample who had grown up with lone parents for most of their childhoods. These daughters had also experienced ad hoc childcare arrangements and reported occasions when they felt sadness or anxiety about losing their mother. 'Daughter mother' Hannah described thinking that her mother had been in an accident and would never come home. However, these three daughters of lone parents did not express a generalised feeling that their mothers' work had affected them negatively. The verdict of recent graduate Ashley was that, "I didn't like her being away but I never saw it as her putting work above me." So, being a child of lone parents is not an adequate explanation. Indeed, Golombok (2015) concluded from her analysis of 35 years of global research that children are more likely to flourish in families that provide love, stability and security, whatever their structure. However, what stands out about two out of the three daughters with negative feelings is they had absent fathers *and* no siblings. They therefore had particularly close relationships with their mothers and when their mothers worked, they felt their absence keenly. Moreover, they had no other company at home when their mothers were at work.

There is little literature written from the point of view of the children of lone parents, but Morris (2013) argued in her PhD thesis that relationships between lone mothers and only children can be particularly intense. Also, Gagnon (2016) conducted doctoral research among 130 children of lone parents who were also the first generation in their families in higher education. She argued that there are many subtle ways in which social pressure is exerted in a way that makes the children of lone parents feel different from their peers in so-called 'normal' two-parent families. Considering all the arguments, I find the most convincing explanation for why these daughters thought their mother's working had affected them negatively was that they all felt different from their peers in a way that troubled them. In the case of Olivia, it was uncommon 10 years ago for a father to be the principal parent (ONS, 2016b). Olivia also perceived other differences because her father was a manual worker at the gates of a private school. Yasmin felt different in having a father who was rarely around and in being in after-school club for longer periods than her peers. Tanya felt that having a completely absent father and a mother whose work took her away from home for long periods made her different. These daughters also felt their mothers' absence particularly keenly in the cases when they had no siblings at home and as a result of suffering from anxiety. As a result, the daughters who were negative about the ill-effects on them of their mothers' working hours, seemed to feel that their mothers had flouted dominant cultural scripts about motherhood, described by Miller (2012, p 41) as 'good mothers' who are assumed to be selfless and available to meet their children's demands.

Daughters emulating their mothers' working hours

The literature raises the question of whether the daughters of mothers who work relatively long hours want to give as much time to work as did their mothers (Vere, 2007; Gerson, 2011). The majority of daughters in this study seemed to accept that the demands of a career comes with the necessity of working long hours, as illustrated by recent graduate Emily: "This seems like a patch where career focus might seem quite natural ... I wouldn't mind it [my job] being the main focus of my life."

Even Tanya, one of the daughters with negative feelings, did not reject the idea of working hard like her mother. Tanya had also picked up from her mother's behaviour the idea that work can and should be enjoyable and interesting and that that is what justifies spending many hours at work. As many said: "It's not just a job." Tanya explained: "I think I've watched her working too hard. But she works too hard because she loves what she does and I think that's what I've taken from her. Trying to find something I love doing too and I want to give my time to and devote myself too."

I did meet several women who said they wanted to cut back on the hours they gave to work so they could have more leisure time. This echoes the findings of Twenge (2010) on the values of the millennial generation. This view was exemplified by Natalie, a lawyer, who reported having conversations with her friends about wanting more time to themselves, and expressed a wish to work part-time to achieve this:

> "I'd quite like to do part-time, sometime. My friends were talking about how ... that whole cliche of work–life balance is becoming quite relevant for us I think regardless of whether you have kids ... just having a day a week to do something for you. It might be more important than working five days a week for more money."

Another example was Fiona, who was two years into her career and working roughly 55 hours a week. She explained that she would like "more balance" between her work and her life. She was concerned that she did not see her friends enough and that she was drifting away from them. She described herself as competitive and someone who thrives on pressure, but also said she knew that her focus meant she could be snappy with her partner. She wanted to work fewer hours so she would feel "happier" and be "a nicer person to be around". Fiona criticised her employer, herself and her colleagues for colluding to feel that long hours are normal, and said that: "There's always someone doing more than you ... People want to work hard and move up, which means everyone's incrementally climbing on each other. If someone works to this time, someone else will work to the next time."

In these cases, the daughters' views about long hours are unrelated to observations about the way their mothers worked. More pertinent to the question posed above are several direct references made to not wanting to work as hard as they had seen their mothers work. The daughters who made these comments were in a small minority.

Florence, who at the time of interview was working extremely long hours (more than 50 hours per week) in marketing, felt that she did not want this to continue. Her hours reminded her how hard both her parents had worked to become "super senior" and she was therefore now thinking, "I don't want to run a big company. If I'm giving up this much of my time now I'd literally have to live in the office." However, this is more a criticism of long-hours culture in the workplace than a criticism of her parents. Isabelle, a recent graduate, was one of the few to say explicitly that she aspired to a career that would not be as demanding of her time as that of her parents: "Both of them have had huge careers ... and they don't have much time ... they have given me a lot of money so I can reject that kind of career." Isabelle also discussed her feeling that her parents had a troubled relationship that had been negatively affected by her father working away.

Interestingly, no reference was made to mothers passing their work stress on to their daughters. Instead, several of the daughters worried more that their mothers, rather than themselves, had suffered from the effects of managing work and motherhood, as exemplified by Willow, a doctor:

> "I know how difficult it was for her then ... one of the things I felt was really positive about ... becoming a bit more of an adult was that opportunity to be supportive of her ... I want to know that she is not too stressed at work, that kind of thing. I tell her to slow down."

In most cases, when daughters knew their mothers were stressed, this was related to relationship difficulties with their partners and to divorce.

Another, perhaps surprising, finding is how few comments about hard work were made in the context of combining work with family life. This confirms the finding of Woodfield that the mothers' modelling of the management of parental and work responsibilities did not 'speak' to participants, who instead saw work as an individual project (Woodfield, 2007, p 217). Overall, far more references demonstrating concern about working hours came in response to factors such as wanting more leisure time and as a reaction against the demands of a workplace that requires intensive hours. It is notable that those in male-dominated professions had more difficulties with their working hours. This confirms Simpson's (1998) study of 221 UK managers. There is much less evidence from the generation of daughters that the way their mothers' worked had influenced a desire to give less commitment to work. An intergenerational difference is that more flexible ways of working are now available in career roles than was the case for the generation of mothers in this study (Gardiner and Tomlinson, 2009). Many of the daughters who were attracted by the possibility of cutting their working hours did not seem to be reacting against their mothers' experience, but rather were drawn to the idea of cutting hours for personal reasons.

Conclusions

The idea that women should work part-time when their children are of school age remains the dominant cultural script in many countries. In addition, much research shows that trying to combine responsibility for young children with work is stressful, especially to mothers. Yet the findings of much research, including my own, present a convincing challenge to the idea that having a mother who works long hours in a career role has a negative effect on children (Cunningham, 2001; Backett-Milburn et al, 2011; Mendolia, 2014; Milkie et al, 2015; McGinn et al, 2015). Research also challenges the notion that most women in managerial and professional careers experience consistent negative health and wellbeing outcomes themselves. Therefore, it is far from inevitable that career women model work as stressful to their daughters, especially when they have jobs they mostly enjoy, some flexibility to work around the schedules of their children and work thoughtfully in terms of absorbing compromises themselves. An important qualification here is that the vast majority of women sampled in all the research cited, including my own, did not consistently work more than 50 hours a week. This is in line with statistics from the UK Department of Trade and Industry (Kodz et al, 2003), which suggest that 4% of working women regularly work over 48 hours a week. (Approximately 66% of these work in managerial or professional occupations.) A very small minority of daughters did make comments about not wanting to work as hard as they had seen their mothers work. This opinion was not expressed as a criticism of how they had been parented; instead, it concerned what the daughters wanted from their own lives. A theme that came to the fore more strongly was resentment of long-hours culture, especially from the women working in professional jobs. Of course, what is true for most is not true for all. Three daughters out of the 31 in my sample were exceptional in their belief that the way in which their mothers had worked had affected them negatively. Their view appeared to derive from their sense of being different from their peers and was compounded, in two cases, by being the only child of lone mothers with absent fathers.

Three key points made in this chapter are:

- The weight of research evidence (including this study) suggests there is no clear correlation between mothers in professional and managerial occupations who work long hours and negative effects for their children.
- There is evidence of a reaction against long-hours culture, but this is not linked to mothers communicating stress about their working hours to their daughters.
- The minority of three in my sample who actively did not want to emulate their mothers' example in relation to working hours were in two cases in intense relationships with their mothers unmediated by having an involved father or siblings. All three daughters seem to be reacting against feeling different to their peers.

Chapter Four explores the influence of this generation of mothers over their daughters' career choices.

Nothing much to say about this chapter.
But ① issue of changing cult rules does need address,
② work lift life enhancement
③ Time

Career choice:
like mother, like daughter

Chapter themes

This chapter focuses on the start of the daughters' working lives and considers the nature of the influence of the generation of mothers over their daughters' choice of career. This chapter also asks whether we should expect daughters to emulate their mothers in choosing to pursue a career.

Jessica is in her final year at university. Her mother, Jan, is at the top of her career. Jessica tells me that both her parents encouraged her academic achievement. She has many discussions about her possible future career with her mother in particular. She describes her mother as "strongly encouraging" her to think about what work she wants to do, to be proactive in getting experience and getting involved with extracurricular activities that could help her develop a competitive CV. Jan's level of involvement has been "a slight bone of contention" between them. Jessica does not feel that she is being directed towards any particular career, but her mother is very involved in helping Jessica make up her mind, by facilitating conversations about careers with her friends and contacts and organising internships. Jessica says: "She wants me to have an idea about what would be good and set out to do it." Jessica had talked to her mother about her work and concludes that: "My mum probably is the biggest influence in terms of talking about my career, I think because ... we are quite similar ... and what she's done I would also find interesting. I think we would go in similar directions." Jessica is one of the few in this study who volunteers that her mother is her role model.

Jan tells me that she loves working and that it gives her a sense of self-worth, fun and intellectual stimulation. She comments that she has often made good friends of her work colleagues and clients. Jan has clearly communicated this to Jessica, who uses very similar words to describe what she wants from work.

This theme of a strong maternal influence over a daughter's career values, and helping her daughter to find her path, is typical of many of those interviewed. Other mothers had been an even more direct influence over their daughters' career choices, as illustrated by the stories told by mother–daughter pair, Tanya and Tara. Tanya is following almost exactly in the footsteps of her mother.

Tara (mother):   "She ended up doing the same course at university that I did ... and going into the same [career]. It's really interesting."

Tanya (daughter):   "We've talked about my career loads ... I feel like she has been a guide telling me you'll have loads of fun doing this ... she's travelled loads and got these amazing stories ... it seems quite normal that I want to do something similar."

Tanya says that her mother had made many friends at work and had brought many of these friends home. Talking to her mother and these friends has influenced Tanya's view that the media sector is for her. Tara arranged work experience placements for her daughter, which Tanya reports were an important factor in her getting accepted on the master's course that led to the job she is just about to start. Despite the direct role her mother has had in influencing her choice of career, Tanya says she feels neither pressurised nor that she is acting to please her mother by following in her footsteps. In my conversation with her mother, Tara tells me that she has been at pains not to be directive. This point is emphasised by many of the mothers I interview. They consider it their role to help their daughters think through their options and to act as supporters, door openers or even protectors when their daughters struggle.

What I observe is that the majority of the mothers have not pushed a particular career. However, almost all have been active in encouraging, advising and shaping their daughters' expectations. Most of these mothers want and expect their daughters to do well, and to find a career they find worthwhile. Significantly, mothers and daughters often express a common belief in the value of hard work and fear of being bored. There is, of course, a fine line between feeling supported and feeling under pressure. This is illustrated by undergraduate Yasmin's comment about her mother: "She's never been academically pushy, but she did just assume that I'd go to university." The pressure on women to 'be perfect', with its cost in terms of self-confidence and anxiety, is a well-worn discussion and one that will be visited later here (see, for example, Gilligan, 1982). Nevertheless, the verdict of most of these daughters is that their mothers have not always got it right, but that they are mainly helpful and encouraging. These daughters are for the most part clear about what they are striving for. Largely, they want an interesting, absorbing career and/or want to do something of social worth.

Standing on their mothers' shoulders

The question I posed at the start of this chapter is should we expect daughters to emulate their mothers in pursuit of a career? Strong academic evidence exists to support the notion of the transmission of work roles and values between generations of mothers and daughters. Work values and occupation choices are linked to one's sense of identity – that is, 'the kind of person I am'. This link between self-concept and work role identity has its foundations in the work of Super, who claimed that, 'in choosing an occupation one is, in effect, choosing a means of implementing a self-concept' (1957, p 196). Gottfredson's (1981) work on occupational choice places individual choice in the context of the social and psychological influences that accrue up to the point of making that choice. She emphasised that the impressionistic nature of knowledge of occupations means that choices are often a process by which a person matches their sense of self with a vague impression of a work role. As Gottfredson stated, 'occupational images deal almost exclusively with the lifestyle that occupation affords an incumbent and the type of person that he or she is' (1981, p 551). Turning to the potential influence of mothers on occupational choice, Gottfredson asserted that a person's impressionist knowledge partly derives from talking about their father's jobs. She was writing in 1981 and therefore it is feasible that, by now, successful working mothers as well as fathers will have given their daughters an insight into their working lives, albeit a vague impression, that will influence their choice of career.

Educational attainment

Eichenbaum and Orbach (1983) and Lawler (2000) argued that a mother identifies with her daughter due to their shared gender and behaves towards her daughter unconsciously as she internally acts towards the daughter part of herself. A mother is also a daughter. Walkerdine et al (2001) linked this idea to work, arguing that the middle-class mother feels the need to push her daughters to defer gratification and reach their potential. Walkerdine et al described this potential as 'their destiny to go to university and become professionals'

(2001, p 161). Lawler asserted that this shaping of their daughters' behaviour by mothers is a particular issue for middle-class children because 'middle class-ness has become synonymous with normality' (2000, p 43). Middle-class mothers are argued to equate a 'good self' with educational attainment that facilitates the daughter's ability to reach her potential (Lawler, 2000, p 4.) Lawler goes on to argue that middle-class mothers are more emotionally and materially equipped than those of other social classes to advise and assist their daughters, both in terms of obtaining the qualifications to give them access to good jobs and in practical help to find them (p 4). The same findings come from the perspective of the daughters studied by Walkerdine et al (2001, p 68). They argued that middle-class girls were more likely than working-class girls to envision themselves as being economically successful in good jobs and to have the internal and external resources to help them achieve a rewarding working life. Evidence of this transmission of attitudes on work aspirations is provided by a longitudinal study using the 90,000-strong National Longitudinal Survey of Adolescent Health in the United States. Using econometric analysis, Olivetti et al (2013) compared the working hours of women born in 1978–84, when they were aged between 22 and 34, with the working hours of their mothers and mothers' friends with whom they were in regular contact, controlled for education, family wealth and location. Their key findings were that the influence of the mothers' experience on the daughters' working hours was strongest when the mothers were college-educated. This body of research underscores the importance attached to encouraging educational attainment, which brings with it an expectation of making the most of these qualifications by embarking on a high-skill career path.

Role modelling the expectation of a career

Further evidence that supports the hypothesis that middle-class mothers do influence their daughters' work orientation is drawn from research that includes both working and non-working mothers in its sample. US researchers Moen et al (1997) sampled a panel of 256 mother–daughter dyads and found that middle-class women create the expectation in their daughters of long-term employment. This is shown to be the case regardless of the mothers' workforce participation, which tends to suggest that attitude is more important than behaviour. Moen et al reinforced their findings by carrying out comparisons of gender and work role attitudes on the same sample in 1956 and 1986. These comparisons showed that a daughter's attitudes are more likely to correlate with the mother's attitudes than her position in the labour force. Moen et al therefore concluded that socialisation processes 'operate through verbal persuasion rather than role modeling' (1997, p 291). These findings are confirmed by the recent research of McGinn et al (2015) who studied national archive data from 2002–12 across 24 countries to compare outcomes among nationally representative samples for the adult children of mothers who work versus those who stay at home. They found that the children of working mothers are more likely to be employed, to work more hours, in more supervisory positions, and to earn more if employed. This suggests (but does not directly address) that the children are not reacting against the example set by their mothers. They argue that these outcomes are partially mediated by the more egalitarian attitudes they identify among the children of mothers who work. The authors also speculate that mothers pass on information and skills to their daughters to help them navigate a career. However, a limitation of the research of both Moen et al (1997) and McGinn et al (2015) is that they compare working mothers with non-working mothers, which does not match the situation of the majority of women in the UK who mainly work, but work a variable number of hours.

On the other hand, evidence that moderates the extent to which maternal influence is significant in daughters' work aspirations comes from Woodfield's (2007) research, which focused on the perspective of girls and young women aged 16–22 and also compared women working as teachers with women working as firefighters (aged 24–62). Woodfield found that girls think their mothers 'have significant, although by no means overwhelming, influence on what careers individuals felt they could *expect support* for' (2007, p 217, emphasis in original).

In summary, academic opinion is divided about the primary way in which mothers transmit their work values to their daughters (either verbally or through role modelling). Most argue that mothers support and shape their daughters' career choices rather than overtly directing them down a particular career path. Most also agree that encouraging educational achievement often translates into an expectation of achievement and commitment to work.

"My mother was my main influence": how daughters characterise their mothers' influence

This section considers how the daughters in my research characterised their mothers' influence. Before I met the mothers and daughters, they all filled in an online questionnaire so I could elicit a spontaneous, unmediated response to some of my questions. I asked the daughters to rate out of 10 how much influence different people had on their choice of career. Figure 4.1 shows how they answered.

Figure 4.1: Daughters' career influencers (n=30)

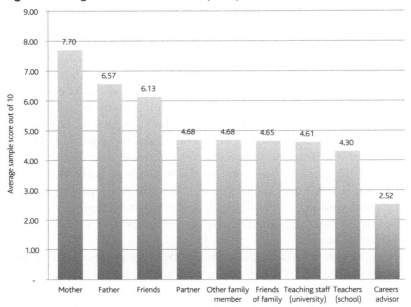

As is clear from this table, most daughters' view is that their mothers are the main influence over their choice of career. The importance of the mothers' influence was directly confirmed in many of the interviews, as illustrated by 'daughter mother' Hannah who had started off in the arts, but later moved into teaching, like her mother:

> "I heard a lot about Mum's job and when I was young I saw a lot of my mum in her workplace when she taught me in after-school classes or when I went to see Christmas plays at her school. Interesting that I became a teacher, and I'm probably a very similar teacher to her. I saw her style."

As I have suggested in the introduction to this chapter, in most cases, the daughters report that their mother did not expect or push a specific career. Instead, many of the mothers were active in guiding their daughter towards or away from choices and in setting expectations of a long-term, satisfying career. The way in which the mothers exerted influence can be described as 'direct' or 'indirect'. By 'direct', I mean actions bearing unambiguously on the outcome, and by 'indirect', I mean 'shaping the context for their daughters' decisions'.

Indirect influence

Starting with examples of indirect influence described by the daughters, these are concerned with educational achievement, communication of a strong work ethic and, reflecting more middle-class assumptions about work, facilitating with money the ability to follow an attractive (and therefore competitive) career direction. Their mothers also modelled the value of enjoyable and satisfying careers.

The first theme concerns the mothers' encouragement of educational achievement, which is linked to aspirations for their daughters to find interesting and rewarding work. Isabelle made this point well: "I knew as a student I should be a really good student and so I was ... I always knew my roles." In some cases this influence is characterised by the daughters as pressure, as exemplified by Zara, who reports that, "My mum is all about 'tough love', especially academically ... We have a joke in our family where we say, 'Mum I got an A,' to which we joke she would reply, 'Why didn't you get an A star?'"

The link between academic achievement and progressing into higher status jobs is well known. It is featured on the websites and in the brochures of most universities. Almost all of the daughters went to Oxford or Cambridge, or to Russell Group universities. Recent figures show that 67% of Russell Group graduates are working in high-skilled roles versus 53% from other universities (ONS, 2013a).

Many daughters talked about their mothers' communication of a strong work ethic that started in relation to schoolwork and extended to a 'mantra' for life. This maternal communication of the necessity to work hard, to 'keep going', to 'have stamina', is also often reported by the mothers' generation about their own upbringing, and amounts to family lore being passed down through the generations – through working class as well as middle class generations. The encouragement of hard work is frequently mentioned by mothers and echoed by their daughters. This was exemplified by mother and daughter pair Alison and Ashley. Alison, a marketing director, talked about passing on to her daughter, Ashley, her parents' focus on hard work: "Ashley has a strong sense of determination. She's not a quitter and I think I instilled that in her ... Both my parents are role models in terms of determination, work ethic and sense of drive. As long as you have tried your hardest, that's all that matters."

Daughter Ashley, a recent graduate, showed in her interview that she has absorbed this message:

> "Well, [Mum's] very hard working ... I guess she's always been quite like driven and she's always wanted me to do really well so she's pushed me quite hard. She's always made me work really hard and stuff so I'm kind of grateful for that as well ... I've got quite a strong work ethic now ... I just think that a lot of people are capable of achieving a lot more so you should try and do what you are capable of because otherwise it's just lazy isn't it?"

This message about work ethic was often accompanied by the communication of the idea that the daughters' could do whatever they strived for as a career, as described by Elly, who has her own business: "[Mum] always said that if you work hard there is no reason why we shouldn't achieve whatever we set our minds to." This confirms the findings of Walkerdine et al (2001) on middle-class mothers advising, equipping and assisting the progress of their children, although far from all of the mothers in this sample were from a middle-class background. Even though it was not articulated, it is possible that this emphasis on educational achievement is intended to preserve for their daughters the middle-class lifestyles that the socially upwardly mobile mothers had achieved through their career success. Ashley speculated that because her mother had not gone to university, perhaps her mother, "wants me to do well and have a nice life like she has".

As other research has suggested, growing up with mothers who went out to work and liked their jobs has led this generation of daughters to expect, almost unthinkingly, that they will do the same. This point is illustrated by 'daughter mother' Sophie, who is a senior manager in education. She said: "As a result of growing up seeing my mum working from as early as I can remember, I simply thought that everyone went to university and all women worked; I still cannot comprehend the idea of not working."

Others, for example, Una, a mother and her daughter, Ursula, who both work in the public sector, described work itself as having social value:

Una (mother):	"You should work to be socially valuable, to contribute to society. We are both amazed by people who don't work."

Ursula (daughter):   "You should make a contribution to society. Everybody should."

Indeed, many daughters expressed the idea that for them *not* to have an interesting career would be reprehensible, either because they felt that their self-respect or respect from others would be compromised, or because of fear that they would be bored or boring to others. As Tanya put it: "It can be the most interesting thing about a person, what their job is ... so I would probably be a bit disappointed with myself or think my life was a bit boring if I didn't go into something interesting."

Tanya also highlighted the balance that many of the mothers tried to maintain between encouragement and pushing their daughters or risking undermining their confidence when they don't succeed at something. Tanya said: "My mum instilled hard work in me somehow without making me feel under pressure. She's always said do what makes you happy and don't put too much pressure on yourself."

A key finding is that almost all of the daughters had been encouraged in their desire to have a career by the fact that their mothers had conveyed their enjoyment of work. Time and time again the daughters stressed how much their mothers "loved their jobs". This had been communicated directly in words, through the stories their mothers told about things that happened at work, and also by bringing home the friends they made at work, as described by Tanya at the start of this chapter. Many daughters also reported that their mothers had cemented this impression by encouraging them to choose a job they would enjoy because it was interesting to them. Xenia, an undergraduate who was aspiring to be a representative of a third generation of successful career women in her family, said: "I always felt this strong sense from both my parents that I had to do something that was interesting to me, not just something that ... made loads of money."

The importance mothers attached to enjoying work is reflected by their daughters' prioritising enjoyment and satisfaction when asked what they wanted from work. This was explained as finding enjoyment in the variety of content within their role and the social side of work, and not wanting to feel bored. Not being bored came up often from both generations. Enjoyment and satisfaction also meant feeling intellectually challenged and that they would be making a contribution to a bigger outcome. This corroborates other academic and business-sponsored studies where enjoyment, intellectual fulfilment and the idea of making a difference are given primary importance across age groups of women working in professional or managerial roles (Bostock,

2014; Opportunity Now, 2014; James, 2015; McKinsey & Company and Lean In, 2016).

The role of money was also significant. All the mothers in the sample had attained a level of security because of their salaries and all but four of the mothers had partners who were also contributing financially to the household. However one feels about the advantage given to the children of relatively affluent parents, there's no doubt that the mothers' incomes acted as a facilitator for the daughters in this study. Financial support from their parents had allowed some of the daughters to take time to travel and decide what they wanted to do. Money also paid for support when doing unpaid internships that were thought to be necessary to get a job in competitive fields, such as advertising; and paid for further education leading to professional qualifications. Indeed, some of the daughters acknowledged that they were lucky to have 'a financial safety net' to enable them to make their career choices without needing to consider money at all. For recent graduate Isabelle, the combined wealth of her parents prompted her observation that to them, coming from working-class backgrounds, making money was "super-important" but "very self-interested" and that this lay behind her desire to "work with the underprivileged" and "do something nice". Another example came from Beth, who had spent several years doing unpaid internships before securing her first rung on the career ladder in the media. She commented that, "[Money] never really crossed my mind ... it was much more important to me that I be happy doing something I want to do."

Direct influence

I turn now to daughters' reports of mothers exerting 'direct' influence over their choices. As a reminder, 'direct' influence is defined here as actions bearing unambiguously on the outcome. Themes that come from the research include daughters entering the same or similar careers to their mothers, direct conversations about career choices and receiving practical help in opening the door to specific careers. Views expressed by the daughters are contrasted with those of their mothers in order to show the maternal influence.

First, a direct measure of the daughters' emulation of the career paths of their mothers is the decision taken by many to go into the same type of career, or a career with similar values. This research finding builds upon Gottfredson's (1981, p 570) observation that information about occupation is strongly influenced by an individual's immediate social setting and that ideas are more easily accepted when no effort is required to access them. Of the 28 daughters who were already in work or knew what careers they wanted, nine were planning to work or actually working in the same field as their mothers or a field with very similar values (such as the daughter of a teacher becoming an educational psychologist). In addition, three were in the same or similar occupations to their father, as shown in Figure 4.2.

Figure 4.2: Following in the footsteps of their parents' careers

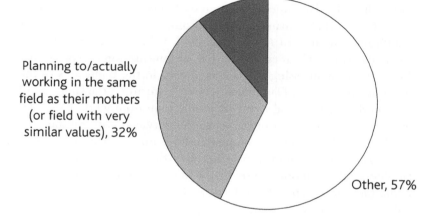

Same/similar occupations to father, 11%

Planning to/actually working in the same field as their mothers (or field with very similar values), 32%

Other, 57%

Following in their mother's career footsteps resulted from the daughters talking to their mothers about their jobs and/or experiencing them first hand through work-experience as illustrated by Gina and Gayle:

Gina (daughter):   "I think I genuinely went into advertising because my mum worked in advertising."

Gayle (mother):   "If I didn't suggest for you to do that first work experience you never would have imagined that it was fun."

Kelly laughingly told me that her mum had frequently described the job she wanted her to do and that was exactly what she had done: "My mum sold me the idea. She used to say to me, 'We've got this lovely educational therapist and it's such a lovely job!' She made it sound so romantic. She totally influenced me and then supported my decision." Kelly was also an exceptional example in reporting that her mother had directly encouraged her to pick a career that would fit around having children, in anticipation that Kelly would have children one day. I also met one other mother who, when her daughter was thinking about changing her career in her late twenties, gave her daughter the same advice to consider how her career could fit around children. In both cases, this seemed driven by the guilt these two mothers felt about working full-time from when their daughters were very young.

Many other daughters felt that they knew something about their mother's job and had decided that it would not suit them. Interestingly, only three of the daughters were following in the career footsteps of their fathers. These daughters tended to have excelled at school in STEM subjects.

Not all of the daughters were interested in talking to their mothers about their work, but many were. This confirms the findings of Lawler (2000) and Moen et al (1997) that work values are transmitted by verbal persuasion. Clear evidence of direct transmission of work values also came from analysing the language used in the transcripts of the individual interviews. Daughters frequently mirrored the language of their mothers when describing what they want from work. Examples given below are taken from the separate interviews with mother and daughter. Both generations emphasised the importance of enjoying work, as discussed above. Another key theme was mothers and daughters talking about careers that give them status. Status is linked by the interviewees to job satisfaction. The example here came from Willow, a doctor, and her mother Wendy, who is the MD of her own company:

Willow (daughter): "I want a career ... I don't want my work to totally define my life but equally I want to be in a job I have satisfaction from. It's nice to do something that is recognised ... I think most doctors do want the status, but they won't readily admit it."

Wendy (mother): "I do have a reputation within the field, which I suppose is a measure of success ... there aren't many [in my field] who become managing directors and run their own profit-making business ... [Success] is external recognition and being able to do what I want, enjoying my work."

Many mothers and daughters also valued specific careers that were perceived to have social value. Both Amy, a 'daughter mother', and her mother, Anita, expressed the same desire to help people that had propelled one into teaching and the other into the health service.

A more practical example of the direct influence of mothers is the help many of the daughters said they received from their mothers at the start of their careers. Examples included arranging internships or helping by finding job advertisements and drafting job applications. Two of the daughters who had mothers who ran businesses had been given projects to work on by their mothers. They reported that this had taught them valuable skills, such as how to manage accounts and how to talk to people. Both daughters said that this experience had increased their confidence in their own abilities.

The depth of their mothers' influence is also evident in comments from several daughters that their mothers did not know or acknowledge just how much influence they have. Recent graduate Ashley showed the contradictory thoughts she has about the way her relationship with her mother plays out when big decisions need to be made:

> "I don't think she realises that she does it but she does tend to try to influence me quite a lot when I've had to make big decisions about my life. I don't know. Yeah. She has quite strong opinions about these things. It makes me always turn to her when I've got a big decision to make, which I think is kind of bad. Sometimes we argue. Like, I wish I could make more decisions for myself rather than always asking mummy [laughs] … But a lot of the time she's right so I should listen to her anyway."

This dance of closeness and separation, rebellion and connection, is typical of mother–daughter relationships, as described by many (Chodorow, 1978; Apter, 1990; Bjerrum Nielsen and Rudberg, 1994; Lawler, 2000).

The balance of the evidence above suggests that mothers with successful careers exercise more influence over their daughters' career aspirations, in both direct and indirect ways, than has been argued by those who privilege individual self-efficacy in motivating career aspiration (O'Brien and Fassinger, 1993). The comments of the daughters illuminate the specific ways in which their self-efficacy is guided and shaped by their successful working mothers – including a substantial number of this sample following their mothers into the same or similar careers, having the same work values and having doors opened to their careers by their mothers.

I turn now to consider views directly expressed by the mothers about how they perceived their influence over their daughters' careers and how those with sons thought their approach to their daughters had differed.

How mothers characterised their influence

Mothers' aspirations were nuanced, complex and differed by child. However, it is clear that most were ambitious for their daughters. Many of the mothers acknowledged that it was important to their parenting strategy that their daughters should achieve their potential and that they should, from a secure and safe base, be encouraged to be independent, as illustrated by Christina, a lawyer:

> "My role is to support her in the world and give her a strong sense of self. But to sort of protect and comfort her as well. There's an absolute assumption that she would always come to me if she needs help or is distressed in any way and yet I feel pleased that she can look after herself."

The notion of working hard came up in this context too, as expressed by teacher and grandmother Patricia: "We just expected them to work hard and achieve … so they did." Xanthe, working in the arts, also articulated this: "Work hard, do things for yourself, achieve."

Many mothers described themselves as encouraging and supporting what they saw as their daughter's own ambition to have a career. The mothers reported that they conveyed these values indirectly, through their actions and by discussing and 'negotiating' around specific situations such as schoolwork and their daughters' ideas about careers. Many, such as CEO Rose, stated they were conscious of not "putting too much pressure about what you have to live up to or do", and also reported intervening when they thought their daughter was putting undue pressure on herself. For example, Bridget, a doctor, told me that she saw her daughter struggling to get a career in the field she wanted and applied "not so subtle pressure to choose an easier career path". Her daughter persisted on her chosen career path and was eventually successful in getting the job she wanted.

Passing on the feminist torch

This mixture of ambition for their daughters to achieve their potential, with encouragement to be independent, applied equally to the mothers' sons. However, many of the mothers also described two views that were of particular relevance to their aspirations for their daughters.

First, even though they acknowledged that the situation of women in the workplace has improved over time, most believed that the odds are still stacked against full gender equality. Second, they thought that their daughters had confidence issues that could get in the way of achieving their potential or cause them to lose out to men in some way.

Seeing their daughters' careers through the lens of gender inequality chimes with Mannheim's (1952) theory about members of active generations who consciously represent themselves by referring to the collective experience of their generation rather than just their individual experience. Many of the mothers felt, in relation to work, that they had been and continued to be in competition with men. Several had achieved career 'firsts' for women or had been among the first to hold the positions they'd reached. Almost all also volunteered examples of personal experience of gender discrimination or sexist attitudes at work, including sexual harassment, sexist assumptions, not having equal access to opportunities and being one of a small minority represented at senior levels. I heard several stories from those working in the private sector about trying to negotiate fewer hours, usually asking to work a four-day week, after the birth of their first child, only to be told that this would mean surrendering their position in the hierarchy of the organisation. Moreover, many mothers spontaneously said that their own decisions about going back to work after the birth of their children were made in conscious reference to feeling the need to represent the progress of women. Doctor Eve was an example of one interviewee who felt this way. She said: "I do feel we had a duty to demonstrate that, yes, we are going to be worth your training." Lawyer Imogen said: "I think it was fear of letting the side down that tipped the balance. I was one of the first female partners to have children as a partner in an environment that was still fairly sexist."

Imogen, like others, went on say that the example of her home-based mother influenced her sense of wanting to change outcomes for women: "I grew up feeling my mother was very frustrated being the person at home all the time, so I think I swung to the other extreme of I'm not going to be bored at home."

Many of the mothers with these views had communicated their desire that their daughter should not limit her horizons because of her gender. Tara, an MD in the media, said: "I think I did say this. That you can do anything you want to do ... I don't think you should let your sex get in the way." Anita, a teacher and grandmother, reported: "I've tried to teach them that being a woman is every bit as valuable as being a man and that anything that men can do, with a few exceptions, women can do."

These attitudes illustrate discontinuity with the past because in many cases the previous generation did not work out of the home or did not work in such high-skill roles. Many of this generation of mothers expressed pleasure that their daughters have easier access to the professional opportunities that they had struggled for. It was clear from the accounts of their daughters that they had absorbed this message about not being subservient to men and their careers, as illustrated by academic Lily: "My mum taught me to value my own ideas. To think that you've got a brain. To use it well. Not to be put down by men."

The mothers who had been lone parents for some or all of their daughter's childhood also emphasised the need to be financially independent, as illustrated by Sophie, a senior manager in marketing:

> "She believed we should never have our backs against the wall in the same way that she did when my dad went. So she believed strongly that we should have a squirrel fund that our husbands can't access. So that in the crisis situation of, 'He's left with the secretary,' ... we'll always be all right."

The mothers' consciousness of gender inequality was also illustrated by the fact that 64% identified themselves as feminists when asked their views in the online questionnaire, as shown in Figure 4.3.

Unsurprisingly, therefore, many of the mothers reported conversations that applied this lens to their daughters' careers. This is consistent with the fact that this generation of mothers grew up with the arguments made by Second Wave feminists about equality of opportunity at work and in the domestic sphere (Greer, 1970; Rowbotham et al, 1979). This correlation suggests that these feminist beliefs underpin the close involvement of many mothers in their daughters' early career choices discussed above.

Figure 4.3: "I am a feminist" – Mothers (n=30)

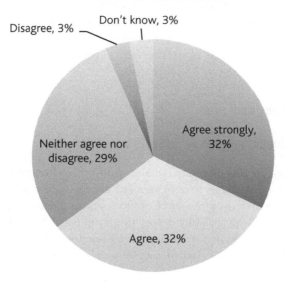

"I am a feminist"

Don't know, 3%

Disagree, 3%

Agree strongly, 32%

Neither agree nor disagree, 29%

Agree, 32%

Self-confidence

The issue of the daughters' self-confidence or self-belief also arises strongly from my research. Every mother was asked what metaphoric gift she thought would be of benefit to her daughter. Of the 30 mothers, 24 (80%) answered self-confidence. Moreover, almost all of those mothering daughters in their twenties wanted their daughters to feel more self-confident. What some meant by this is that the daughters should recognise their qualities and achievements. What most meant by self-confidence is having the strength to achieve what they want to achieve rather than going with the flow or buckling to pressure from others, as described by Jessica's mother, Jan (featured at the start of this chapter): "Jessica is hardly a shrinking violet but I think the forces on you can be quite powerful ... I know lots of very clever women who, I think, haven't fulfilled their potential because they have ... um ... found it easier to go with the flow."

Sense of purpose was the next most frequently mentioned metaphoric quality the mothers wanted to gift their daughters. This, too, related to the mothers' aspirations for their daughters, and was explained in the interviews as the daughter's ability to achieve their potential by realising that no direction is set in stone and that flexibility is important to success.

This chapter has focused so far on the influence of the mothers on the daughters' career choices because of the finding that most daughters thought their mothers were their primary influence. Individual daughters cited a plethora of different influences, including family friends and teachers, but the next section focuses on the other influences that emerged most strongly, namely fathers, self-efficacy and peers.

Other influences

Fathers' influence over early career choice

I have argued in this chapter that the mothers' influence over career choices is stronger than that of the fathers in most cases. This was obviously influenced by the level of close contact daughters felt they had with their fathers. Thirteen of the daughters did not live with their fathers when living at home, but all but four reported that they remained close to their father or were close to their stepfathers and did discuss their career choices with them. Some daughters described their parents as a team. They tended to talk about their parents as a unit (for example, "They pushed us on at school massively"). They had more difficulty separating the role of their father from that of their mother, although their mothers were often described as the "mouthpiece of the team". There appeared to be no obvious link between the daughters who talked in this way and the type of parenting described by both mothers and daughters (for example, egalitarian parenting where both parents took roughly equal responsibility for child rearing). The one daughter who had been brought up by a stay-at–home father identified more closely with her mother and discussed her career options mainly with her mother. Olivia, an undergraduate, said:

> "I always talk to Mum because Dad always says the same thing and it's not what I'm interested in or good at. He made me do a Saturday job as a vet, not taking into account that I'm not good at science."

Some daughters reported that their fathers have been highly involved in their education. Educational achievement, as discussed in relation to the mothers, sets up a transition into a high–skill role. More actively, many fathers have taken a feminist position and have made it very clear that they do not expect their daughters to become housewives. Instead, the fathers gave their daughters the same advice and encouragement to work in jobs they find interesting as they gave to their sons. The daughters also told me that their fathers' career advice tended towards the practical. For example, encouraging them to try for a field where there is less competition or in which the salary offers security – or helping them do the online maths tests prior to interviews! As I have already mentioned, two of the daughters have followed their fathers into a similar career and a few other fathers had particular passions that have influenced their daughters' interests. For example, Willow, a doctor, was very interested in her father's scientific career.

With very few exceptions, the influence of the fathers is more indirect in shaping the context for their daughters' decision-making and is mainly offered as part of a mum-led team. The exceptions are daughters who identify more strongly with their fathers than they do with their mothers. Their mothers tend to collude in this. Natalie, who has followed both her mother and her father into the law, explains:

> "My father and I are quite similar ... my mum always knows what my brother's thinking and my dad always knows what I'm thinking, so we are that way aligned. So maybe he knows how to get through to me more. He's always led those kind of discussions about what to do. And I suppose the fact that I worked at his office had an impact. He would also talk about his work more."

Self-efficacy

The evidence presented here that the mothers' and (to a lesser extent) fathers' influence is strong in shaping and facilitating the early career choices made by their daughters, is only part of the story. The daughters ultimately made the choice themselves about the precise job they wanted to do. This choice was based both on their sense of identity and the circumstances that presented themselves. This builds upon the work of Crompton and Harris (1998), who highlighted the complexity of the interplay of individual and social actors and particular circumstances in determining occupational choices. Self-efficacy and self-image came into play at the early stages of career choice in several ways. Two participants illustrated the idea of fit between an occupation and their personal qualities. Olivia, an undergraduate considering nursing, said: "I've always been a great helper ... at school ... I was voted the nicest girl in the year ... so I'm thinking, why don't I just look at nursing?" Academic Chloe said: "I just noticed that I had a different relationship to the [academic] work than other friends who also did well, in that it felt more personal, more connected to me, to who I think I am."

Several constructed a mental shopping list of the values they wanted a job to have, such as social value and flexibility, and alighted on a job that matched that. Others quite simply chose a career with a clear link to education, such as teaching, or research in a subject that had interested them at university, as in the case of Verity, another academic: "My degree was environmental science and I'm researching management of the environment." Some characterised this as a drift into a career starting with a contact, or a holiday role. This happened to quite a few.

Choices made by the 'daughter mothers' to change career direction were also often made without apparent reference to others, presumably because by then they had far more first-hand knowledge on which to base decisions, as shown by Paula, a dentist and one of the 'daughter mothers' in the sample: "A lot of the skill set from physiotherapy transferred quite well into dentistry."

Interestingly, evidence of *lack* of self-efficacy lay behind the career indecision of three of those who, prior to graduation, had no plan. Belle described being unable to focus either on her degree or on the process of getting a job: "I couldn't cope with exams and doing interviews." Undergraduate Diana articulated her lack of confidence to make a decision: "I'm quite scared of everything … it's like I always wait for the time to be gone and wishing I'd done better rather than pushing myself at the time." Others who had not taken a gap year simply wanted to take time out and go travelling before having to make a decision.

Peer influence

Peers acted mainly to help the daughters develop a clearer sense of who they are and therefore what type of work might best match their sense of self. This was exemplified by Verity, an academic, who reported that: "I've got a friend who is training to be a lawyer and another a doctor, so a lot of people I know want to do something useful." Peers, and sometimes peers who are also partners, were reported to be primary influences by those who were struggling with their sense of self. Meeting like-minded people, at university in particular, helped some to find a direction more comfortable to them. Examples included those whose friends influenced their interest in feminist politics and work in international development. Isabelle said: "I fell into a really good group of friends who helped me learn a lot and are just the coolest group of people … I got very into women's campaigning." This aligns with the revival of feminist debate about gender inequalities post Third Wave feminism, as evidenced by the Everyday Sexism Project (Bates, 2014) and academics such as Phipps (2014).

Conversely, peers, especially in discussion about jobs held at university, helped the daughters articulate what they did *not* want to do, as undergraduate Diana reports: "I don't want to do, like, banking ... any kind of business-related thing is just not me." Megan, working in marketing, said: "It's funny actually, they impacted me massively in a negative way making it so clear what I didn't want to do, the mindset I didn't want to be in."

By contrast, some of the daughters enjoyed the competitive environment they were in at university and felt that their peers spurred them on to try hard to get impressive jobs. Undergraduate Xenia said: "I think Oxford people are quite driven. Everyone wants to do something interesting or impressive in some way." This desire to impress was particularly evident for those in postgraduate, more vocational education who were actively competing with their peer group for jobs. Tanya candidly said: "I guess I want to do something other people think is cool so I can show off." Finally, this research coincided with a recession in job opportunities for young people and an exceptional few reacted to this with a sense of 'why bother?' They tended to seek reinforcement for this attitude from their peer group

Conclusions

The vast majority of the daughters interviewed for this study report that their mothers are the most important source of influence over their choice to embark upon a career path. Simply having a mother who goes out to work and who demonstrates that she enjoys her work sets up the expectation in the daughters that they will do the same. In this way, the generation of women with successful careers act as role models for their daughters' early career choices. In addition, in many indirect and direct ways, the depth of the level of their mothers' influence is clear. The influence and involvement of the mothers seems more profound than the mothers' acknowledge. The mothers think that they have been careful to be supportive, but not to direct their daughters. This is an accurate perception in the sense that few encouraged a particular choice of career – although there were a few examples of mothers who did exactly that. However, most of the mothers I spoke too did not hang back in offering their help and support with their daughters' early career choices. Many mothers actively mentored their daughters in emotional and verbal ways through offering support, discussing their daughters' options and encouraging their feelings of confidence, and in practical ways by facilitating work experience and hunting out job opportunities. This seems to be a way in which the mothers maintain close relationships with their daughters while also going through a period of transition as their daughters leave home. There is clear tension between wanting their daughters to become independent and mothering them in the involved way most, according to their daughters, have done throughout their daughters' education.

What most stands out for me is how much emphasis the mothers put on working hard and for this hard work to lead somewhere positive for their daughters. Many are in a position to help their daughters (and sons), so it's not surprising that they choose to help. The recession of 2008 persisted in affecting the employment of young people at the time of these interviews (Peacock, 2013). It is plausible that this added an anxious imperative to the mothers' desire to see their daughters settled in good jobs at the end of years of effort, exams and education. This was unspoken but may account for the high level of involvement in their daughters' early career choices. The mothers in this study commented that they did not have, or expect, help from their mothers when they were looking for jobs. Filling in application forms, looking for advertised vacancies and facilitating work experience are all examples of types of intervention that represent behaviours started by the baby boomer generation.

Three key points are made in this chapter:

- Almost all of the daughters in this study think that their mothers have been the primary influence over their early career decisions – indeed, a third of the daughters are following their mothers into the same or similar careers.
- Mothers are influential career role models – even more than the mothers realise.
- Mothers with careers mentor their daughters through early career choices. Verbal transmission of attitudes is shown to be a powerful actor in shaping career choices and communicating work values such as hard work and the importance of enjoying your job.

Chapter Five examines what mothers have communicated about career ambition and explores the drivers and implications of 'quiet ambition'.

Quiet ambition

Chapter themes

This chapter explores in which ways having a mother with a successful career influences the likelihood of their daughters aiming to reach the higher echelons of their chosen fields. My hypothesis was that their mothers' career success would normalise the daughters' expectation of doing the same – especially as so many of the daughters were aiming for or working in managerial or professional roles. As argued in the previous chapter, the mothers' generation set up expectations that their daughters would *have* a career. However, the mothers' influence over their daughters' ambitions for their career is less clear. A key explanatory factor is that the mothers are 'quiet' at home about their work ambition and successes. This chapter seeks to explain why this is the case.

Faith, one of the generation of mothers, is a highly articulate lawyer. She became the most senior woman in Europe in her large corporation in a sector heavily dominated by men. When I ask her whether she thinks of her career as having been successful, her articulacy deserts her:

> "Uh ... [long pause] ... I think of it as being me ... but it's ... um ... if I look at it on paper, yes. Um ... because if you're looking at appointments and qualifications ... um, yes. [Long pause] ... But I realise success isn't about paper and qualifications. It's about making a difference in the workplace."

Her daughter Fiona started work a few years ago in a career in finance. Fiona is far less equivocal than her mother in describing Faith's career as successful. This is the case for most of the daughters in this study. Yet many of the mothers are reluctant to describe either their careers or themselves as successful. This includes many who have reached very high positions in their careers. Speaking about her mother, Fiona said:

> "She was the most senior European woman at [a US Fortune 500 company] ... women's progression at the time must have been difficult. Especially considering she's not

the archetypal shout down the phone [boss], she must have got there through pure brilliance. I think of the way she deals with people and also the way she hasn't let anything stop her and she has been very successful ... I think her true virtue is that she'd never want to clamber up to a point where you're incompetent, but do something that matters."

When Fiona and Faith talk later in their joint interview and I ask more about how they think of success and ambition, they instead discuss working hard and producing good quality work:

Fiona (daughter):   "I don't think she's been into progression for its own sake, she's always been quality driven ... to do something that matters. If I make MD because I'm good at it, that sounds fantastic ... that comes very much from Mum."

Faith (mother):   "Anything is possible if you work for it. Yes [laughs]. Work! Work! Work! ... That's my mantra."

What I notice from Faith and many other mothers and daughters, is that they often focus on work 'in the moment'. That is, the importance of working hard and producing good work rather than discussing what their work achieves or the personal satisfaction and ability to influence outcomes that comes with seniority. These are key themes that will be explored in this chapter.

Fiona identifies more strongly with her father than her mother and this was typical of the four out of 31 daughters I interviewed who were the only ones to explicitly talk about upward ambition: "I always thought I would just naturally progress upwards, and it matters a lot to me." Fiona also says that she cannot imagine subordinating her career to that of her partner or any children she may have:

"I don't think I could be happy just with what my other half achieved, because that's his achievements not mine. Kids is obviously slightly different but I don't want to be a dragon mother – 'Look what my kid can do!' [Laughs] I'd want my own things, my own areas that I excel at ... I'd want things where I felt like I was contributing."

Most of the mothers and daughters talk to each other often. Many of the daughters who are working recount conversations with their mothers about the day-to-day issues they face at work. These conversations can easily be characterised as mentoring. A mentor is defined here, as in the *Oxford English Dictionary*, as someone who gives advice and guidance, usually to someone younger and less experienced than themselves. Fiona describes her mum as unflappable and therefore finds it easy to talk through the issues she is experiencing at work. Faith, her mother, tells me about the way she approaches these conversations:

> "She asks me for advice about work ... She's often expressing a problem with something. [Pauses] I don't believe in telling people what to do. I like to listen and then ask questions and get her to realise what she feels she needs to do. Like, 'What do you think it would look like if you did that?' So I never use the 'should' word. I don't like to give her direct advice ... I hope it helps them [both her children] to draw out their thinking around whatever it is."

This is typical of the careful approach of many of the mothers. Even though Faith's advice is indirect, it is of clear help to Fiona in her career. However, the absence of conversation about the satisfaction and purpose of making upward progress in a career is noticeable.

Do women aim for the top?

Recently, there has been much attention paid in public and academic debates to women attaining leadership positions (see, for example, Harris, 2003; Lanning, 2013; Wolf, 2013). Various explanations are given to explain the clear differences in the proportions of men and women reaching senior positions despite many examples of gender parity at the lower rungs of the career ladder. These explanations can be clustered as follows. First, gendered structural constraints such as women turning away from many career fields, especially in STEM subjects, from an early age; the lack of availability and the cost of good childcare; and the lack of flexibility offered by workplaces (see, for example, Stone, 2007; Wolf, 2013; WISE, 2014). Second, workplaces are often depicted as less hospitable to women than to men, around whom workplace culture was originally designed. This results in inequalities in recruitment and promotion and also unconscious bias in daily interactions between men and women that inhibit women's career progress (see, for example, Vinnicome et al, 2013; Bohnet, 2016). Third, arguments also coalesce around gender differences in the qualities of individuals, particularly in the literature coming from the corporate world. For example, a prevalent theme in these studies concerns gender differences in feelings about confidence, resulting in reticence among women when it comes to putting themselves forward for promotion or high-profile roles (see, for example, Sandberg, 2013; Kay and Shipman, 2014). Women are also often depicted as having fewer of the qualities associated with leadership, including being more resistant to taking risks (see, for example, Eagly and Karau, 2002). Some of the factors behind all these explanations of gender equality are related to systems used by organisations. Many of the explanations summarised here rest on the idea that gender differences in the qualities of individual women disadvantage them at work. Having noted the importance of other factors influencing workplace gender equality, my focus in this chapter is on the individual values and attitudes that are transmitted intergenerationally between mother and daughter.

Starting with the evidence relevant to the question of whether women, in comparison to men, are ambitious for career success, studies tend to draw different conclusions about ambition based on age and career stage. Many academic and business-sponsored studies argue that women under the age of 30 have the same attitudes as their male cohort to job advancement. Woodfield's (2007) academic qualitative study was based on five group interviews with university students and a sample of 89 firefighters and teachers. She reported that 'nearly all the participants who talked about their occupation ambitions described a desire to climb far in their chosen career' (Woodfield, 2007, p 181). Think Future, a KPMG-sponsored survey of university students, argued that young women are just as confident in their own abilities as men but are far less confident, even before they start work, that the workplace will treat them equally and nurture their success (KPMG and 30% Club, 2016). In fact, more than half of female students polled believe that their gender may hold back their careers. The Think Future study drew on other studies of women within the workplace to explain these findings. The report argues that women's reservations about being able to experience successful careers are based both on external factors (for example, women's performance being assessed less positively than that of men) and individual factors (for example, women waiting longer than men before they feel ready for promotion). This study was based on more than 20,000 interviews with mainly undergraduate students of 21 universities in the UK and Ireland. Almost twice as many responses came from women as men.

The *Cracking the code* corporate study (YSC et al, 2014) argued that women are ambitious for senior leadership roles but have a different temporal relationship with ambition in comparison to men. They showed that women become more ambitious the further up the career ladder they climb. By the time women reach senior management level, the scale of ambition they express is higher than that of men. This report was based on qualitative interviews and a quantitative survey among cross-industry sectors and employee grades. Opportunity Now (2014) investigated the career motivations of more than 22,000 women and 2,000 men and also concluded that women were not lacking in ambition, based on comparisons between men and women. However, it should be noted that what all these surveys have in common is they are highly skewed towards responses from women, which may compromise their ability to make reliable gender-based comparisons.

Some prominent theories from academic researchers present different perspectives. Mainiero and Sullivan's (2005) individualist career theory research argued that women tend to want three different values from their careers at different stages of their life. These stages are 'challenge' (which is most likely to describe women just starting out in their career), 'balance' (which is most likely to describe women with young children) and 'authenticity' (which is more important in the later stages of women's careers). The 'authenticity' phase does not rule out career ambition, but suggests different drivers. Bimrose et al's (2014) cross-national study of women's career transitions stressed the importance of context to the way in which women make decisions about what success in personal, family and work domains means to them at different points in time. The median age at which women with higher degrees have children tends to be around 30 in countries such as the US and the UK (Wolf, 2013; Pew Research Centre, 2015a). Therefore, Bimrose et al's argument is consistent with the idea that women in senior management are more ambitious, by implicitly suggesting that women are more able to focus on their careers as their children get older.

The confidence gap becomes an ambition gap

There is logically a link between ambition and confidence. A US corporate study showed that women's confidence that they can get to the top declined after only two years in the workplace (Coffman and Neuenfeldt, 2014). This research showed that young women entering careers are more likely than their male counterparts to aspire to a top position (43% versus 34% of men). However, after only two years the percentage for men stayed the same, while the percentage for women exhibited a sharp fall to 16%. Women's level of confidence that they can achieve top positions also halved during the same period. Coffman and Neuenfeldt attributed this to lack of support from work supervisors.

An alternative explanatory factor is the persistence of social notions about gender roles – the behaviours and attitudes that society expects of women – which have been extensively researched by many scholars. Most argue that these gender role differences are socially constituted.

Bem (1981), in her seminal work, posited that the gendered coding of ambition and achievement is typically coded as masculine. Psychologists Kray et al (2001) showed that women perform less well than men in a negotiation task, unless they are told that this often happens, in which case they outperform men. This illustrates that reluctance to 'win' by being competitive is culturally conditioned rather than being explained by biological essentialism. Facebook's Chief Operating Officer (COO) Sandberg quoted studies in multiple industries that show that women consistently underestimate themselves, and coined the phrase 'ambition gap' (2013, p 29). Horner (1972) suggested that women exhibit more anxiety than men about competitive achievement when their success seems to be at the expense of someone else. She identified a female tendency to fear success based on women's perception of conflict between femininity and success. Sluis et al (2010) researched sex differences in motivations to achieve and showed too that women were less actuated by competition than men. Fels (2004) argued that ambition requires the support of an audience and whereas the male presumption is that their achievements will be valued, the female presumption is that they will do the valuing. This is due to the persistent gendered notion that females provide recognition to males. She further contended that gendered norms in behaviour expected from women mean that women tend to shy away from asserting their achievements and instead claim a principled modesty and look for satisfaction from the work itself. Journalists Kay and Shipman's (2014) high-profile book *The confidence code* asserted that confidence can be learned by choosing to eschew the people-pleasing and perfectionism that women are socialised to exhibit and, instead, being prepared to take action that may risk failure. The relevance of this body of research to my study is that it helps explain why mothers are concerned about the lack of confidence exhibited by their daughters. Moreover, the finding that many career women focus on doing a good job and being modest about their achievements suggests that many mothers may not be talking to their daughters about their successes or what ambition means to them.

Workplace culture

A focus on debating women's confidence and ambition may be missing an important point. A compelling alternative argument is that workplace cultures are manmade and inhibit women's progress. Several studies have found that women working at executive level in professional and managerial roles look above them to the top strata in the hierarchy and observe that they do not want to have the levels of stress and long hours associated with senior positions (Opportunity Now, 2014; McKinsey & Company and Lean In, 2016). Much research argues powerfully that day-to-day experiences of gender bias cause women to lose out on promotions and gradually sap their appetite for advancement. Women cite problems such as being sidelined by men's networks, being interrupted or talked over in meetings and being judged by different standards to that of men (Eagly and Karau, 2002; Eagly and Carli, 2007; Williams and Dempsey, 2014; Kelan, 2015). Women can even find themselves sidelined from the frontline roles and prominent projects that lead to promotion, by men with benevolent motives who assume that their childcare responsibilities mean that they will not want to make themselves available for these roles (Glick and Fiske, 1997; Becker and Wright, 2011). Opportunity Now's 2014 survey of more than 20,000 women aged 28–40 highlighted that women are critical of the culture in their workplace. The survey showed that over 60% of these women believe that they have faced overt barriers to their career development because of their gender. 43% do not feel that the opportunities to progress are equal between men and women. 42% believe it is hard for women at their level to network with the most senior staff in their organisation. These are all examples of subtle bias, but the same study also found that over half the respondents report experience of harassment and bullying. This is defined as overbearing supervision, unfair treatment, being constantly undermined by criticism and feeling excluded. 12% more report that they have experienced sexual harassment. It is therefore little wonder that when asked, half of women at junior or middle management levels said they did not want the lifestyle of senior people in their organisations. The prevalence of these worrying findings are confirmed by other big sample studies, such as Women in Whitehall (Hay Group, 2014).

This level of discontent among women working in managerial and professional careers is perhaps surprising in the light of the many equality policies that have been introduced in the workplace. This may be explained by the finding of research that there is a gap between the existence of policies and their implementation (McKinsey, 2012; Bohnet, 2016; Armstrong, 2016). The cumulative weight of this research evidence suggests that it would predict that a significant proportion of the working daughters in my study are ambivalent about career ambition. This is indeed what I found.

Women's view of success

Several studies argue that women conceptualise success in a different way to men. *Cracking the code* (YSC et al, 2014) reported that, when looking at the qualities that they consider to be very important to their sense of success, women ranked more highly than men attributes such as personal and professional growth, work-life balance and having positive relationships. This survey shows little gender difference in wanting to contribute to something that matters or doing something intrinsically interesting. Looking at how women define success, Bostock (2014) interviewed 126 women working at various levels at the University of Cambridge who were nominated by their peers as 'successful'. The average age of those interviewed was 50. Bostock's main conclusions were that women draw their sense of success from a variety of sources. Key among these were doing interesting, high-quality work that they enjoy and work that has a positive impact upon others. Women in Bostock's study stressed the use to which they could put their power and influence. It was important to many women to work collaboratively and facilitate the success of others. It was also important to maintain a happy and healthy family life as well as a career. Bostock suggested that challenging the definition of success in modern workplaces to encompass these broader factors would be useful both for women and men, given that neither gender wish to be locked into one way of defining success. Equally, neither men nor women want to be forced to choose between prioritising either work life or home life (Gatrell et al, 2014).

I now explore how the mothers and daughters of my research talked to each other about work and how they characterised success, ambition and confidence.

Work talk

As discussed in Chapter Four, the vast majority of the mothers in my study made it a priority to encourage their daughters to feel more self-confident, because they saw lack of confidence as a particular issue for their daughters but less so for their sons. Some of this encouragement to be confident applied directly to work. For example, Martha, a CEO in the public sector, talked about her own lack of confidence when she was younger, which had motivated her to encourage confidence in her daughter:

> "I always thought there were things that I couldn't do and I wanted her to know that she could do practically anything she wanted to. Like when she had to raise sponsorship money for a world challenge thing, there were points when she said, 'I can't,' and I was like, 'Of course you can do it. What's stopping you?'... I think I fretted more about her than her brothers. I think there was something about, is she going to be all right as a girl? Is she going to find it harder? But in a way that made me want to toughen her up even more. I suppose to give her some of the skills which I think she got quicker than the boys did, like building relationships even when you don't think you need to. She's got a great capacity for making those relationships, which is hugely valuable. It will stand her in great stead."

Martha's comments illustrate that these kind of conversations are expressions of the mothers' hope that their daughters achieve their potential. There is also a link between the mothers' identification with liberal and socialist second wave feminism and its emphasis on the importance of seeing careers for women as just as important as they are for a man (see, for example, Rowbotham et al, 1979). When asked to be more specific about what achieving potential meant to them, the mothers explained that they want their daughters to be committed in following their interests. Martha has tried to help her daughter by equipping her with skills she will find useful at work. This was one of many examples of mothers trying to help their daughters in this way.

Many of the daughters commented on how they talked more as equals to their mothers having left home – even temporarily. The closeness of their relationships were illustrated by those daughters who were at university and those who were working:

> "I rely on her quite a lot for emotional support ... more so than I have before. Previously I have kept my private life away from her, but as I've got older I talk more about those things with her. So she's someone to bounce ideas off and to go to for advice. I talk about a lot with her. Definitely."
> (Jessica, an undergraduate)

"She is very much my mother. She looks after me and supports me. But I also like it that now I'm older she talks to me like a friend. She's very honest ... I need her for advice and guidance and someone to talk to about my life. I really like spending time with just the two of us. I think she still needs me too. I don't think there will ever be a time when I don't want to speak to her twice a week." (Tanya, recently started work in media)

The talk of many mothers and daughters was often about issues faced at work and can therefore be described as career mentoring. Moreover, many daughters were enjoying the change in the status of their relationships, which often meant that they dispensed advice too. Kelly, a 'daughter mother' said:

"It got to a point when I was about 22 where we can go in and out of that mother–daughter relationship. She can give me advice and be a supportive mother, like with my doctorate. Then somewhere in my twenties I learned I could flip that around and sometimes be supportive to her ... Whereas some of my friends have very fixed relationships with their mothers. Always mother supporting daughter. Now I feel I can help her as well."

These accounts from the daughters about the exchange of advice were echoed by some of the mothers, including Faith (already quoted): "I think as she gets older, or perhaps as I get older, the more we discover that there are things that we like about each other, and that she's got skills and experience that I find really useful and am learning from."

Martha and a few of the mothers who also had sons wondered aloud about the differences in conversations they'd had about work with their daughters. The consensus was that they tended to have more conversations and get into more depth with their daughters. Valerie, a senior marketing manager, considered why this was the case for her and concluded that she has more insight into the kind of issues a woman tends to face at work:

"Verity comes to me more because my experience of [work] is closer to hers. I was also around more during the first five years of her life so I think that probably means we had a closer bond. I was working full-time by the time of [her son's] first birthday and it's hard to separate this out. Is it personality? Is it gender? Or is it that I wasn't around so much that means we are not as close? It could be gender. I feel more attuned to Verity and her work issues."

On the other hand, I also met a few mothers who told me their daughters were not interested in hearing about their work, although I rarely heard this echoed back by their daughters. These findings about everyday work-related conversations taking place between mothers and daughters who both have careers treads new ground. There are, however, parallels with mother and daughter research that focuses on the encouragement to achieve their potential in education that middle-class mothers give to their daughters (Lawler, 2000; Walkerdine et al, 2001).

Also significant, is what was not discussed about work. There seemed to be little awareness that young women continue to experience difficulties caused by workplace culture originally shaped by men, for men. Therefore, there was little said between mothers and daughters about dealing with culturally inspired gender differences in the workplace, such as being judged by different standards to men over the way they speak or look. There was also an absence of conversation about the value to themselves and others of advancing upwards to positions of influence. This suggests the need to explore mothers' and daughters' views on success and ambition.

How mothers talked about ambition and success

A small minority of the mothers characterised their careers as unsuccessful for a variety of reasons. These women mainly they felt that they had taken unconventional paths so would not be thought by others to be as successful as someone with a professional career such as a lawyer or doctor. Another example was one of the grandmothers who was 'a careerist by necessity', having been divorced and then obliged to enter a career that was available, rather than one she wanted to do (Crompton and Harris, 1998, p 138). Most of the mothers did feel successful or proud of their achievements but were uncomfortable with describing their careers as successful. This ambivalence about saying they have had successful careers is illustrated by Faith (quoted at the start of this chapter) and other mothers. For example, Karen, who works in education, said: "Somehow I've been able to go up the ladder. Not because I've constructed it that way. It's sort of been, not exactly, thrust on me." Even those women who have reached particularly high levels in their careers were hesitant in the way they defined career success. Martha, a CEO in the public sector, said:

"If you get to do big jobs, in some people's eyes you must be successful. In my own head, though, all I see are things I didn't do well enough or things I could have done better. I think, from talking to friends and colleagues, that's something women do more than men."

Orla, who worked in finance, sighed at my question about how she would sum up her career and said:

"... Um ... [sighs] ... successful I suppose. Um. Well. I think it was successful because the work itself was enjoyable to me. Stimulating etc. It turned out to be financially rewarding. A little bit more than I expected and it happened also to be a career where success was externally measured and therefore it would be deemed by others that I did well."

This ambivalence shows that women find it difficult to define or talk about their success, and this corroborates research already quoted above which highlighted issues of self-confidence, focusing on the day-to-day content of work and a tendency towards perfectionism (see, for example, Sandberg, 2013; Bostock, 2014; Kay and Shipman, 2014).

When talking about what they valued about their careers, most of this generation of mothers described the winding paths they have taken, not just the level they have reached. In most cases they did not talk about what they have achieved. Instead, they tended to talk more about the impact they have on others, especially their families in terms of combining work with family life. Two accounts illustrate these themes well. First, Tara who is MD of a media company:

"I don't define myself as successful at work every day ... there are times I think, oh God, what am I doing here? How do I define success? It's financial reward. I think that's really important for women, that you negotiate a decent salary for yourself ... Ultimately I think I am successful [long pause]. It's really interesting isn't it. I'd far rather be a successful mother [laughs]. When I got pregnant I thought I don't want Tanya to get to 18 and for me to say, 'I gave up my life for you.' I didn't want her to feel ... [long pause] ... you have to take responsibility for yourself."

A second example came from Barbara, one of the grandmothers, who was one of the first women in her role in broadcast media:

"There was a bit of ambition just slightly lacking in me. I think I could have pushed harder. I was working with women who really hit the high spots and I think that actual fire wasn't in me because I was in the right place. But I was happy with my own little triumphs, which were lesser ones. I think I was successful because it worked for me … I was aiming for a good work-life balance that kept me feeling fulfilled. And I think money always comes into it."

It was clear from the accounts of many that being financially independent was also important to many of these working mothers. This seems to be an underestimated factor in research into what women define as career success (see, for example, Bostock, 2014; YSC et al, 2014). I also observed that comparisons with a man's career often crept into the conversation. This is consistent with Mannheim's (1952) concept of a generation who feel they represent the zeitgeist, not just their individual lives. Some of these comparisons were overtly feminist, like Tanya's assertion that it is important for women to negotiate a good salary. Some of these comparisons were more covert and based on the women's experiences of making compromises because they had taken the role of primary parent.

Some mothers said they had deliberately traded-off their ambition for a career that worked around their family life. These mothers tended to have reached middle management positions. Valerie, a senior marketing manager, talked about "having leftover energy from the job to be with the kids or pursue other interests". She concluded: "I took the decision that I'd take my ambition elsewhere." Xanthe, a director in the public sector, talked about "drawing boundaries in my job … there are just some things I would not do that people with more career drive and direction would have done." The things she described as necessary to getting to the top in her field were evenings spent networking or attending events. She depicted not engaging with these events as a conscious choice based on being the primary parent and having a husband who earned more in a role with unpredictable hours. A few explicitly said that they were reluctant to describe their working lives as successful because they felt they should be focusing on their role as mothers. Karen had held several senior leadership positions in education, and reacted this way to my question about whether she thought she was successful at work:

"No. I always say I'm just pretending ... I always, because, I suppose, of that ... because I felt I made my choices not based on how wonderful it was for my career or how much it suited my skills, I felt a lot of them were accidental ... I still can't figure out how I did that [senior role] [laughs] ... Somehow it didn't ever seem to stay with me that sense of, 'You've achieved something,' because really my heart was always telling me I should do the mother bit."

A larger group of women pointed out that they accelerated their careers once their children were at school. Bridget, a doctor, defined success as "being able to continue building up a career while bringing up my family knowing that you could then expand it further. I guess success is still being in the job, having three happy children." This is consistent with the work of Bimrose et al (2014) and the career theory of Mainiero and Sullivan (2005). Overall, what is clear is that the majority of these women did not talk in terms of being ambitious to reach positions of influence. Their temporal focus stayed mainly in the present, not the future.

How daughters talk about ambition and success

Many of the daughters made reference to women in senior positions when talking about the public debate about women and work, but did not use the language of 'getting to the top' and 'success' when talking about their personal career aspirations. Instead, all but four talked in terms of wanting an interesting career that would develop and continue to interest and satisfy them over time. The daughters described personal career 'success' in ways that were inwardly focused on their self-image, for example, knowing that they excelled at something and feeling satisfied that they were doing a job well or doing something of social value. As discussed in Chapter Four, when the daughters talked about what they wanted from work, they often mirrored the same kind of language used by their mothers. This was evident in the conversation between Fiona and Faith reported at the start of this chapter. Another example came from mother Gayle, who held a senior position in a consultancy business, and her daughter Gina, who was looking for a job in the field in which her mother had previously worked. Both prioritised being interested in their work:

Gayle (mother):   "I don't think of myself as particularly ambitious;
                   it's not that what drove me was getting to the top
                   of things. It's more an interest in things, in what
                   I was doing."
Gina (daughter):   "I want enjoyment and satisfaction from going to
                   work."

Xenia, who was just about to graduate from university, was explicit in expressing her reservations about being ambitious, even though she thought of her mother as having a successful career. Xenia contrasted the views a male friend's father expressed about success with her views about her mother's career:

"One of my friend's dad's mantra for his three sons is 'ambition is everything, success is everything'. And I don't feel that way ... I don't need to be the best ... I'm more ambitious for doing something I think is worthwhile and makes me happy rather than being the most important person in the room. [On her mother's career] I think she is respected by a lot of people, probably more than other people. I think she's prone to ignore that. I think maybe as a woman you're not expected to be too proud; it's expected that you are modest. But yeah I think she's successful."

A small minority of the daughters did indeed express reservations about having a high-ranking position based on equating success with a culture of long hours and/or stress. They questioned whether their physical or mental health would be equal to the strain. This was exemplified by Verity, a postgraduate researcher two years into her career: "I wouldn't want a very high-ranking position if it was stressful and involved a lot of extra hours. And where there is a lot resting on me. I just wouldn't."

This confirms the findings of studies such as Opportunity Now (2014), which showed that 49% of senior and 53% of women in junior or middle management positions (who formed the majority of the 23,000-strong sample) did not want the lifestyle and hours that the workplace culture demanded of senior people in their organisation.

Almost all the daughters described their mothers' careers as successful. This was the case irrespective of whether their mothers had reached middle or higher positions. When explaining why they saw their mothers as successful, their language mainly described external measures of success, such as the status conferred by job titles or describing their mothers' chairmanship of charities or social enterprises.

Willow, a doctor, described her mother's success as "being able to give an important-sounding job title when asked, 'what does your mum do?'" Many also described with pride their mother's career success in relation to men. For example, educational psychologist Kelly defined success as "Getting to a high place, then earning a salary that is perhaps equivalent to a man … if you are a woman, being successful is getting to a position that a man would have got to as well."

A few explicitly described their mother as role models of success. Those that did this described success from their own point of view of feeling well mothered. They invoked both their mother's success at work and as a mother in response to my question about defining a successful working woman. An example of this point of view came from an exchange in the joint interview between Bridget and her daughter, Beth, who said: "My mum is my role model. She is a successful working mother. You might not think you are Mum, but you are successful in your job and you are a successful mum."

Another example came from Jan's daughter, Jessica, who said: "What I've got from my mother is the possibility of doing what I want to do. I shouldn't limit my horizons in any way. I think she'd like me to think that I could be very successful and have a family and that would be OK."

In summary, what is clear from this research is that many of the mothers have left their daughters with a sense that their career success was mainly a byproduct of hard work and being good at what they do. Even though the daughters think of their mothers as having successful careers, they see this success almost as accidental. This point was illustrated by Isabelle, the daughter of one of the mothers who was at the highest level of her profession: "My mum just did really well by accident … she always talks about … just needing to do it because it was happening and she was doing well." Isabelle went on to describe her mother's relationship with career success as "quiet ambition".

Explaining quiet ambition

There are several possible reasons for this tendency of these mothers to downplay their success. It could be related to their own insecurities – the confidence issues discussed above. As Tara, MD of a media company, said: "sometimes I can feel quite guilty about my salary. I think, 'Do I deserve that?' … Moments of self-doubt when you think, 'I'm terrible.'" Another commented that she had listened to the women who were on the BBC Radio 4 Woman's Hour Power List being interviewed, and many had said they did not feel powerful and were waiting to be found out in some way. This phenomenon has been recognised often enough to have a name, 'imposter syndrome', and many researchers have linked this to high-achieving women (for a discussion, see Gibson-Beverly and Schwartz, 2008). Other motivations could be a response to how women have been socialised to feel that they should project a certain sense of self, by, for example, appearing modest. Women's ambivalent relationship with the stereotypically masculine definition of ambition as overt competition to reach the top is also likely to be a factor contributing to 'quiet ambition' (Horner, 1972; Sluis et al, 2010). Another plausible explanation for downplaying success is a desire among some not to bring their work life into their home life. This was most associated with those with an 'idealistic' attitude to motherhood (as discussed in Chapter Two) who felt more generalised guilt about working long hours. Those who felt guilt about working were unlikely to talk about their jobs at home. However, other mothers were motivated by not wanting to bring work stress home with them. 'Daughter mother' Denise, who runs her own marketing business, said:

> "I hate bringing work home and I hate talking about work at home. I very rarely discuss my working day, issues at work or what I've done because ... it's quite stressful ... when you're working to deadlines and having to get things done and I think I consciously didn't want to bring that home."

A few mothers also expressed their concern that the value of the role as parent is being downgraded in the light of the prevailing social narrative that mothers should work (as described by Adkins, 2002). Orla talked about this in economic terms:

> "I think that the process of bringing up children is hugely undervalued. To the point that you've got mainly women going out to do low-value jobs in order to pay someone else to do a high-value job that they could be doing ... Being a parent is an extremely demanding job. It's logical that you would want a parent to do it because it's very unlikely that both of you would have a higher economic value than that."

It is also plausible that the mothers underestimated their daughters' interest in their careers and the importance of their role modelling success at work to their daughters.

An implication of 'quiet ambition' is that while, when asked, the daughters described their mothers' careers as successful, they have not really internalised what this means. The generation of daughters also acknowledged, explicitly and implicitly, that as women they are expected to be modest about their achievements. Therefore, their mothers' career success does not lead the daughters to say that they hope to achieve similar, high positions themselves. In addition, despite their view that their mothers had successfully combined a career with motherhood, many of the daughters expressed a lack of confidence that it will be possible for them to combine a career with motherhood. This corroborates the findings of much academic and empirical research that will be discussed in more depth in Chapter Seven (see, for example, Gatrell, 2005, 2008; Stone, 2007; Opportunity Now, 2014; KMPG and 30% Club, 2016).

It is also noteworthy that several daughters told me that they believe it is unlikely they will be as successful as their mothers. They offered two main reasons in explanation. First, they thought that external circumstances would get in their way. The UK recession of 2008–13 slowed down rates of appointment to jobs and promotions, so they expected not to be in as senior position as their mothers had been when having their first child. The daughters thought that this would present an impediment to career progress. Second, rather than feeling that because their mothers made it to the top, they could too, they tended to take the opposite point of view. They said that few people reach the top so the chances of them doing so were slim. This perhaps demonstrates the female tendency to feel under-confident, as argued by many (Gilligan, 1982; Kray et al, 2001; Kay and Shipman, 2014).

In summary, most of the mothers, including many who have reached very high levels in their professions, seemed to downplay their career success to their daughters. The majority of mothers who have been successful at work did not talk to their daughters about getting to the top or ambition. Neither did they talk about the benefits of career seniority to themselves and others that are argued by writers such as Bostock (2014) to be a more female way of defining success. Getting to the top did not often seem to be presented as a possible career outcome. It is therefore unsurprising that the daughters expressed an appetite for hard, enjoyable and fulfilling work but rarely talked in terms of ambition to reach the top. There were four, revealing, exceptions.

Clear ambition

Two of the mothers who have built successful businesses and have public profiles described themselves as ambitious. They were the mothers of two, out of the only four, daughters who described themselves as ambitious when talking about their own careers. These daughters also credited their mothers with communicating that they can achieve their ambitions. Daughter Jessica reported: "My mum has taught me to be ambitious, to know what I want from work and life and know I can get it." Her mother Jan was one of the few who described herself as "hard-working, determined and ambitious". Elly, working in her own business, said: "I am ambitious. I don't just want to be an artisan, I want to build a big brand." Her mother Eiona was the only mother who spoke directly about her ambition to get to the top from the early stage of her career:

> "Every year my aim was to get promoted and every year I did get promoted ... I've never actually been motivated by money. I've been motivated by the desire to grow businesses and for them to endure ... I want people to say, 'Gosh, that's an amazing thing you have built.' ... I'm a very ambitious person. I always wanted to get to the top and I didn't see any reason why I wouldn't be able to get to the top."

In both cases the mothers had also offered the daughters direct practical help in giving them experiences relevant to their future careers. This suggests that when mothers do have direct conversations with their daughters about being ambitious, helping them to acquire skills and open doors (in the way I have described as 'direct influence'), this does encourage their daughters' confidence and ambition. Mothers modelling career success alone does not seem to be as powerful as talking about success and ambition and encouraging their daughters in practical ways.

importance of talk

The father factor

The two other daughters who talked about their own ambition were Willow and Fiona. Fiona (quoted at the start of this chapter) talked about her mother's "perfectionist gene". She identified more strongly with her father, and it was her father who suggested the career field she entered. He encouraged her to take an analytical approach to her career and to think ahead. Fiona was explicit about wanting his approval. She consulted him more than her mother for day-to-day career advice because his career field is closer to her own. Willow, a doctor, described herself as being "driven by achievement ... When I achieve something I just want to go on to the next thing." She ascribed this to the influence of her father, who was also a scientist and who she described as being very ambitious.

Significantly, the few mothers in this sample with a high public profile and several of those who had reached the highest level in their career reported that they identified more with their fathers than their mothers. Eiona, a private sector CEO, told me that women with robust self-belief tended to have had this instilled by their fathers: "Somehow girls believe it more if it comes from their dad." This builds on the findings of the American researcher Nielsen (2012), who found that daughters whose fathers were actively engaged throughout childhood in promoting their academic or sports achievements and encouraging their self-reliance and assertiveness were more likely to graduate from college and to enter higher-paying, demanding jobs. She also pointed out that girls who have no brothers are overly represented among the world's political leaders. She related this to receiving more encouragement from their fathers to be high achievers. This again raises the notion that ambition and achievement is typically coded as masculine (Bem, 1981; Sluis et al, 2010). Tutchell and Edmonds (2015) also argued that a father's active support seemed to give some of the 100 successful women they interviewed permission to be ambitious and to admit to their ambition.

Conclusions

Many of these daughters, with their good educational qualifications, who are starting out on managerial and professional career paths, have the potential to get to the top of their careers. This is not to say that this should be the aim of everyone. Individual women, just like individual men, have different ambitions and priorities. Yet researchers continue to find evidence of inhibitions felt by women about appearing competitive and ambitious in organisational careers (Kray et al, 2001; Eagly and Carli, 2007; Sluis et al, 2010). My argument is that it would be useful to individual women and to the achievement of gender parity in careers if 'getting to the top' was presented as an achievable and *desirable* outcome. My argument is also that barriers that disadvantage women more than men should not be put in the way. Confidence is linked to ambition in the sense that communicating confidence in one's potential to take on more responsibility or challenges is important to being given the opportunity to rise to new challenges. Therefore, it is also helpful to continue to address the persistent gender imbalance in feeling under-confident.

The generation of mothers and grandmothers in this study have achieved career success. Some to director or department head level, many to higher levels of seniority. My research shows that many act as mentors to their daughters (as defined by Ragins and Cotton [1999]). These mothers also act as role models of what it is possible to achieve. This research also shows that the mothers exert profound influence on their daughters' early career expectations. Yet the accounts of their daughters also suggest that most mothers underplay their own success: through what they say about their jobs, what they show they value and what they *don't* say about the advantages of seniority. One daughter, Isabelle, whose mother was at the top of her profession, described this as 'quiet ambition'. It is certainly the view of some of the mothers at the top of their professions that self-belief is more convincingly instilled in their daughters by their fathers. Moreover, the finding that many mothers focus on doing a good job and being modest about their achievements suggests that many mothers are unlikely to be communicating ways of acquiring and displaying confidence at work. Nor are they communicating their successes and what success means to them, such as what can be achieved when one has a powerful position in terms of personal satisfaction, for social good or through facilitating the achievements of a team. These career outcomes better match the way women define career success (Bostock, 2014; Hewlett and Marshall, 2014). This leaves intact the classic definition of ambition as winning the competition to 'get to the top', and this definition is closer to stereotypically masculine traits.

The evidence from the four daughter–mother pairs who did talk about being ambitious suggests that verbal transmission of ambition has a more powerful influence on the millennial generation of daughters than modelling career success alone. This corroborates the work of Moen et al (1997) who argued that the attitudes expressed by mothers are more strongly influential on their daughters than the mothers' position in the labour force. If mothers with successful careers talked more about what they have been able to achieve through having status and seniority, this would broaden the definition of success at work to something young women would find more motivating.

Of course, it will require more than the intervention of mothers to plug the 'leaky pipeline' from roles at the highest level of careers, but mothers with careers have an important role to play. This comment is made in the light of research evidence that shows a link between women in leadership positions and encouraging fathers. The last words in this chapter are given to Isabelle, the recent graduate daughter of one of the mothers who had reached the highest level in her career. Isabelle reached the conclusion that she would have liked to hear more about her parents' jobs and achievements as she was growing up:

> "I think I would talk to my kids a bit more ... about adult stuff. Like there was always adult stuff that we weren't involved in, their jobs and news basically ... I would have liked to hear more about jobs and news ... because it's only now that I look back on their lives and think wow! I was looking at Dad's CV and he was amazing. And I never knew because he was just always silly, bumbling, fat old Dad, and Mum is amazing too. And that's a shame I think."

Three key points made in this chapter are:

- Most mothers do not talk about their career successes or the values that tend to motivate women's careers, such as what reaching positions of influence can achieve in terms of personal satisfaction and social value. The term I am using to describe this is 'quiet ambition'.
- There are several reasons why it feels uncomfortable to many women to talk about career ambition, yet encouragement from fathers has a positive impact on women getting to the top of their careers.
- The influence of mothers on their daughters' careers could be even more powerful because, in comparison to men, women exhibit broader criteria for career success and are in a good position to advise about gendered impediments to career progress that come from workplace culture and motherhood.

Chapter Six will consider the aims and aspirations of the daughters concerning combining work and motherhood, and the changing culture of motherhood.

Daughters' aspirations for working motherhood

Chapter themes *Focus on daughters*

This chapter switches the focus onto the daughters and examines how they expect to combine working with motherhood. The extent to which the daughters who are currently child-free are anticipating motherhood is explored, as is the effect this may have on their career progress. Their views are compared with the nine 'daughter mothers' in the sample who have at least one child under five years of age. This chapter develops a key finding of this research that over half the daughters are currently working or planning to work part-time hours. This is a surprising finding given that, in the eyes of most of the daughters, their own mothers have modelled their experience of combining enjoyable, satisfying and largely full-time work with being a 'hands-on', encouraging and emotionally involved parent.

Most daughters intended to a more work p/t

Ursula is working in the health service, although she hopes to get the funding to train in the professional career she aspires towards. She is not currently in a relationship and is clearly in the formative stage of her career and yet, tells me she has thought quite a lot about having children:

> "I'm desperately, desperately broody. Yep. Yep. Very much so. I just think it would be really nice to have children. I think part of it, truthfully, is that as a woman ... probably throughout history and still to this day ... I don't feel like a proper grown-up without a child. It's a big thing about womanhood."

Ursula has quite a few friends who are having babies and she reports that her instinct to have children is redoubled by feeling the pressure coming from her Facebook friends. The response to social media, Facebook in particular, of the daughters' generation is a significant phenomenon for those daughters with peers who have children and, especially, those who have children themselves. Ursula says:

"I feel like Facebook is bullying me to have children. It's just constant. The majority of my friends have kids. I do have friends that haven't as well but every different group has been infiltrated now. Their [Facebook] status implies that their children are the meaning of life and you are nothing without children. I mean most of the time it's, 'I've just put the kids to bed,' or 'I just cooked the kids dinner,' and I think, 'Oh great – that's not interesting.' It's all quite mad isn't it?"

Ursula considers that having a child is more important to her than work, but wants to work as well. As she puts it: "it's just two pillars of your life." However, when she thinks about having a child, she thinks in terms of working part-time. Her view is that you don't have time to be a good parent unless you work part-time.

"I'd definitely take the year [maternity leave] and then maybe another year depending upon whether I got bored. I think maybe ... going back part-time just to keep yourself interacting with grown-ups and getting out of the house a bit but at the same time, not suddenly having to go back to full-time work and not having any time."

Most other daughters say the same. Good motherhood is equated with how many hours are spent at work and at home. Ursula is typical of many of the daughters who are child-free, in anticipating having children and thinking about how they will shape their careers around motherhood. Of the 22 child-free daughters, 11 are thinking actively about having children and what this could mean for their careers, and seven more are having vague thoughts about this. Only four have given no thought at all to having children or feel that they probably do not want children. In addition, three of the nine 'daughter mothers' have consciously factored having children into their choice of career. Two of these had swapped careers after they were married.

Denise has two children. She is founder and director of a marketing business and the only one of the 'daughter mothers' to be the main breadwinner. She founded her second business recently, in order to have more flexibility to be available for her children. She believes that, "as they get older they need you around more ... to encourage them to do their homework and go to school plays and parent's evening." This desire to be able to take more control over their work schedules in order to be there for important events, and sometimes be visible at school, is a common theme. Unlike most of the other 'daughter mothers', Denise took short maternity leaves of six months and five months. She says that she never even thought about not going back to work after she had children because, "work gives me a purpose outside of being a mother." Her children were in full-time nursery before starting school. Her work is also about striving to give herself and her family a good lifestyle, which she defines as having a house, a car and money to do enjoyable things like going on day trips, eating out and holidays. She says that she wants to be a "role model" for her children as she feels her mother was for her. Her mother, Donna, lived abroad and had to retrain and get work as a teacher to support her daughters after getting divorced and returning to this country. Denise is unique in my research in making an overt link between her opinion that she had not been ill affected by having a mother who worked long hours and her own expectation that her working long hours will also work out fine for her children: "I didn't have that 'mother's guilt' thing of thinking, 'Is my daughter going to be okay?' because my mum worked and I was personally fine. I didn't have that separation anxiety."

What is remarkable, therefore, is that, for a significant majority of the daughters, knowing they feel well mothered by women working full-time or close to full-time hours seems not to be strong enough to withstand the cultural concept that being a successful mother means working fewer hours in order to be physically present for much of the time.

Gender identity and the anticipation of motherhood

The idea that women without children factor motherhood into their decision-making is framed by the argument that motherhood is seen as part of the feminine role. Of the 22 daughters who did not have children, 19 said that they wanted children. There are acknowledged issues with the elision of motherhood and femininity because not all women want to be mothers. However, Chodorow's (1978) insight that the wish to be a mother is one of the more persistent strands of female subjectivity is relevant to my research. Chodorow (1978), Bjerrum Nielsen and Rudberg (1994) and Crompton and Harris (1998) all argued that notions of motherhood impinge upon most adult women because the association between femininity and motherhood applies at the level of identity, even when identity is in a state of change in response to changing social roles. It has long been claimed that women's identity is interwoven with their relationships (Gilligan, 1982) and that the idea and experience of motherhood is particularly powerful because 'the child is the source of the last *remaining, irrevocable, unchanging, primary* relationship' (Beck, 1992, p 118, his italics). This self-identification of women with motherhood is also an externally, socially imposed construct. The philosopher Battersby put forward the view that 'whether or not a woman is a lesbian, infertile, post-menopausal, or childless, in modern western culture she will be assigned a subject-position linked to a body that has perceived potentialities for birth' (Battersby, 1998, p 16). This links with Gatrell's (2008) assertion that embodied gendered social norms influence women to take decisions about work, in anticipation of combining work with motherhood, long before they are mothers. She gave the example of medical students being guided to make decisions about their training regarding medical specialisation on the basis of being more family-friendly, saying that they experienced decisions 'being imposed upon them at a point before they were ready to make decisions about childbearing' (Gatrell, 2008, p 3). Relevant here also is the fear young women express that their progress in the workplace will be impeded by their gender, as discussed in Chapter Five (KPMG and 30% Club, 2016).

A qualitative study conducted in the US by Orrange (2002) also demonstrated that professionals are thinking about the potential impact of parenthood on their careers. Orrange interviewed students, in their mid to late twenties, who were well advanced in their courses in law and business, and found asymmetry between the views of men and women, in terms of how they hoped their family lives would be constructed. Most women wanted a 'strong form of egalitarianism', which Orrange described as fully sharing in career opportunities and handling family responsibilities (2002, p 292). However, some conveyed ambivalence about how realistic were their aspirations for the future because, unlike men, they were actively grappling with issues involving work and family life. They thought it was possible that their male partners may not want to share opportunities and responsibilities equitably with them. Orrange also found a subgroup of women, among this 'strong form of egalitarianism' typology, who entertained the possibility of remaining single as a consequence of their career ambitions (2002, p 313). This research suggests that the generation of women starting work in the 2000s are sceptical about whether the more egalitarian approach to family life (which Crompton [2006] argues to be a more optimum model) will be achievable for them and that they are making choices accordingly. However, I discovered that decisions made about

working part-time are motivated more by equating part-time working with good motherhood and, for some, a positive desire to take on the role as primary childcarer, rather than as a reaction against fearing that their partners may not want to be, or be able to be, equally involved.

The notion of 'choice' about working motherhood

Middle-class women who are becoming mothers frequently talk about it now being possible to make any choice about how they will combine work with motherhood (Stone, 2007; Thomson et al, 2011). This generational difference was explicitly connected by some daughters to the legacy of the feminism of their mothers' generation, as described by Megan, working in marketing services, as "normalising gender equality". These views reflect what McRobbie (2009) identified as 'the illusion of equality'. McRobbie (2007, 2009) described the ways in which young women expect to be treated as a genderless worker and highlighted the changing 'horizon of authority' away from the idea of competing against men and towards the idea of the self as a project to work on. Many academics have argued that the notion of choice is illusory and contradicted by women's lived experience (Hochschild, 1990; Thomson et al, 2011; Rottenberg, 2014). Stone, who studied why high-flying career mothers leave their jobs in the US, explained that:

> Choice rhetoric ... often had the effect of obscuring or rendering invisible to them the constraints they faced and under which their decisions were actually carried out. Women are indeed bombarded with messages of choice, but seeing structure is difficult when ideas and practices around mothering as well as professional work are taken for granted. (Stone, 2007, p 114)

Stone (2007) concluded that women are aware of the constraints they face but in the light of powerful cultural beliefs, and in the absence of alternative discourses, it is hard to connect with just how constrained they are. Moreover, successful professional women tend, according to Stone, to have a strong sense of personal agency, and this informs their perception of having choice. As a worker, pressure comes from the 'setting of goals, targets and standards, and measuring human achievement against these, [which] is an integral feature of late modern society' (Gatrell, 2008, p 12). It also comes from employers and women's own sense of what is needed to do the job. Stone's main conclusion was that for most of the professional women in her sample who ultimately quit, 'work, not family considerations were paramount and deciding factors' (Stone, 2007, p 19). Women grapple with many, complex push and pull factors when considering how to combine work with motherhood. These include their own desires to be good mothers and good workers, workplaces that do not flex well enough around their family responsibilities, and tension between affordable, available childcare and work and family demands (Gatrell, 2005, 2008; Stone, 2007; Thomson et al, 2011).

Debates in the media are also often couched in terms of every individual having the choice to be the kind of mother they want to be: to work or not to work, or to work part-time. Williams (2000) suggested that the facile media depiction of choices obscures understanding of the complexity of women's motivations and ability to influence outcomes. An example of one of many 'facile' examples comes from the *Daily Telegraph* report on the day after the announcement of the UK Coalition Government's policy of offering shared parental leave: 'Once yesterday's speech is forgotten, parents will no doubt continue to choose the work-life balance that best suits their circumstances' (Kirby, 2012).

Contemporary cultural scripts of motherhood

I now focus on the cultural scripts of motherhood, defined to mean 'collective stories of discernible groups in wider society, which provide the contours of the available, and importantly, acceptable cultural scripts' (Miller, 2005, p 11). Furedi (2002) characterised contemporary parenting culture as shifting towards parental determinism. That is, parents, particularly mothers, being held directly and principally responsible for the welfare, health and success of their children. This cultural shift is illuminated by Smith's observation that the verb 'to parent', deployed to describe the behaviour of mothers and fathers, entered into common usage only in the early to mid-1970s (Smith, 2010, p 360). The primary responsibility for parenting continues to be gendered, so the verb 'to parent' is usually a surrogate for 'to mother' (Gatrell, 2005, 2008; Miller, 2005; Faircloth, 2014). Furedi argued that the rise of parental determinism is paralleled by a growing cultural consciousness of perceived risk to our children, which a parent is expected to manage. These cultural shifts mean that whereas good parenting was traditionally associated with nurturing, stimulating and socialising children, 'today it is associated with monitoring their activities' (Furedi, 2002, p 5). Faircloth (2014) made explicit the link between risk consciousness and the rise of 'intensive parenting'. This is a term originally coined by Hays to describe an ideology of motherhood, in Euro-American settings, that involves spending 'a tremendous amount of time, energy and money in raising their children' (Hays, 1996, p x). As with all ideologies, it is not embraced by all mothers or to the same degree by all who are influenced by it. However, many scholars of motherhood have anatomised this trend. Of particular relevance to working mothers is Christopher's (2012) definition of 'extensive responsibility', which describes the time and mental energy mothers spend on intervening to influence and improve the daily lives and life chances for their children, even when they are outsourcing responsibility to others. Also, Thomson et al's research on first-time mothers offers the term 'intensification of responsibility' to describe 'the inflation of parental expectations and the proliferation of interventions aimed at improving children' (Thomson et al, 2011, p 277). They, like Baraitser (2009) and Lareau (2011), observed that this trend is an expression of the desire to equip one's child for life's competition for educational success and good jobs. Facilitating one's child's progress has also become an outlet for competition between women who are more home-centred and those who work longer hours out of the home. While these social factors apply to most mothers, they are exacerbated by 'middle class anxiety expressing an increased perception of insecurity' (Thomson et al, 2011, p 277).

The rise of parental determinism is illustrated in the increasingly directive advice given by parenting experts and mothers who publish (Lee et al, 2014). Baraitser (2009) conceptualised modern motherhood as being played out in public, in mothers' desires to mould an individual who stands out from other children. Motherhood as a more public act also encompasses the use of social media such as Mumsnet (which claims to have 50 million monthly page views), Facebook and Instagram. Social media can also be argued to facilitate comparison and competition. In this way, social expectations about how one *should* mother seem greater for mothers today than for those who had children in the more private family environments of the 1980s and 1990s.

The effect of these cultural scripts about motherhood is to establish strong public notions about the right and wrong way to mother, which has an obvious link to feelings of maternal guilt. Good mothering also becomes linked to the physical presence of the mother investing hours in her child/children's development, which is challenging to a mother with a demanding career. These ideas are particularly pertinent to intergenerational research, with its focus on personal biographies (Bjerrum Nielsen and Rudberg, 1994; Lawler, 2000; Thomson et al, 2011) and the way these intersect with cultural and psychosocial expectations of mothering.

Complexity of drivers of decisions about working hours

falling hours to Labour market X

US quantitative research has suggested that college-educated women are unique among those surveyed in supplying a falling amount of hours to the labour market. Vere's (2007) research found that college-educated women born in 1978/9 were supplying fewer hours to the labour market than their predecessors born in 1972/3. He ruled out demand-driven factors because women's cumulative labour income to age 27 had risen, and increased hours spent in education accounted for only one sixth of the decline in hours given to the labour market. He also ruled out increasing fertility. Therefore, Vere suggested that this fall could be attributable to these women being less willing to supply more hours to the labour market 'at any given market wage' (2007, pp 826–7). What Vere's research leaves unexplored is the reason for this decline in hours.

Much research literature argues that motivations behind choices made about working hours post childbirth are emotionally complex, as well as being practical responses to concerns about economic factors, such as what level of income a family unit requires. Moreover, so-called practical constraints are also suggested to have emotional influences. Economic need is argued by Duncan (2006) to be, in part, a cultural constraint, because ostensibly economically based decisions tend to be intertwined with other factors such as women's experience of intense and perhaps unexpected maternal feelings when they give birth that lead to a desire to be more home-based. Conversely, Wolf points out that there is an economic imperative, albeit a culturally constructed one, to work full-time to afford childcare and also entertainment, holidays and home help – 'the things that make it easier to combine going to work with a nice home and enjoyable leisure time' (Wolf, 2013, p 32). Mothers in managerial or professional employment are more likely than other women to outsource childcare to people outside the family, with around 15% of managerial/professional women in the UK employing a childminder, nanny or au pair and around 35% using nurseries (Wolf, 2013, p 77). This suggests a self-perpetuating circle in which the demands of a career bring with it the costs of buying support in the domestic sphere that, in turn, fuels a need for the income a demanding career can bring.

Another economic factor that may influence full-time or close to full-time commitment to work among this cohort is divorce, either because of an increased imperative to earn or because financial security brings with it more freedom to make the choice to divorce. McRae's longitudinal study of women working 10 years after the birth of their first child in 1988 found that 26% of those working continuously full-time had experienced marital disruption compared to 8% of those working continuously part-time (McRae, 2003, p 324–6). On the other hand, research using the Millennium Cohort Study looking at whether couples with young children are more likely to split up when the mother is the main or equal earner, found no link between this and destabilised relationships (Kanji and Schober, 2014). However, my research does suggest a link between the length of working hours of the 'daughter mothers' and awareness of financial insecurity caused by divorced parents.

Having a career history of the mother being the main breadwinner also clearly influences work choices. Evidence from the Millennium Cohort Study suggested that mothers who were the main earners were most likely to persist in full-time employment and that these main earners made up 25% of all mothers who worked full-time continuously in the first five years of their child's life. Those in full-time work were also much more likely to have jobs classified as SOC 1 and 2 (Kanji, 2011). It may therefore be interpreted that for these women, work is experienced as a necessity rather than, or as well as, a choice.

Unrelated to motherhood, as argued in Chapter Three, the millennial generation may simply be more motivated to have more time for leisure outside of work than older generational cohorts (for a review, see Twenge, 2010).

Leisure

Choosing a career with motherhood in mind

Turning to my research, the three who had chosen their careers with children in mind were only found among the 'daughter mothers'. Kelly, an educational psychologist, had planned her career path around the idea of having children prior to going to college. The attraction of the job was that it was common practice to work part-time, the hours were predictable and it could still be a fulfilling career while also satisfying her professional view that children below primary school age thrive better being with their mother. Kelly's mother, who works in a similar field, had told her all these things. Kelly's planning for the time she had children also extended to moving house to be close to her parents, so that her mother could take care of her granddaughter when Kelly returned to work. Kelly worked full-time until she had her first child, and was on maternity leave at the time of our interview. Kelly said of her job:

"For a woman it's a great job because I mean I know people who work full-time and pick their kids up from school and get paid a full-time salary; there aren't many people who can do that. You can take time off, holiday times are much slower, and generally there are a lot of services, mine in particular, that allow you to work from home, so it's really great."

Two others who had chosen their career with having children in mind had switched careers after they married. Hannah had left behind her career in the performing arts to become a teacher, like her mother, with whom she had discussed this choice. Paula switched into dentistry. She had considered medicine but had been deterred by her own observations and those of her doctor husband. She said: "If you want children it's not particularly conducive, and we've both seen friends, both medics, married together, really struggling to juggle everything." Paula worked 29 hours a week and commented that predictable, sessional hours and the fact that there was no after-hours working (except for professional training), made dentistry "a great job for women". All three of these 'daughter mothers' cut their hours to accommodate their caring responsibilities. Therefore, it is interesting that all three also expressed misgivings and irritation that their husbands' careers took priority. During our interview, Kelly connected with her irritation about the career compromise she had made in comparison to her husband, who did the same job:

"I'm main-grade senior and he's a deputy principal! And we trained at the same time! And I'm loads better than him. The person he took over from was a man; he was interviewed by a man. Once you get to that high position they are all men ... Must be a bit of sexism, must be. And he's not going to take time off for having babies. They always know that we are, we would. Yeah. God. It's still out there isn't it?"

The views of those who had chosen their career with children in mind and, in particular, their use of the phrase "a great job for women", corroborates the deeply embedded idea that women should take the primary responsibility for their children (Hays, 1996; Williams, 2003; Miller, 2005).

'The best of both worlds'

The narratives of the daughters who were child-free made it clear that the majority imagined that they would substantially reduce their working hours once they had children. In other words, they envisaged shaping their careers around having children. The daughters who thought they would work part-time were strongly motivated by the same dominant idea that this would give them a balance between 'the best of both worlds'. The idea of 'balance' represents a shift from the 'having it all' rhetoric of their mothers' generation. Rottenberg (2014, p 147) argued that envisioning progressive middle-class motherhood as 'balancing' has helped create a new gender norm in which women are expected to find satisfaction by combining their responsibilities for both work and the domestic sphere. This represents progress in the sense that women are no longer being asked to choose one sphere of their life over the other. However, Rottenberg pointed out that 'balance' is just as hard to achieve as 'having it all' because women have still not been liberated from their primary responsibility for domestic life and are now also saddled with the idea that they should be making better choices to ensure they are living a happy life. This idea is encapsulated in my research by the phrase 'the best of both worlds'. The view that mothers should work part-time was based on an idea almost all of these daughters expressed, as exemplified by Ursula (who was introduced in the opening of this chapter). She said: "I sort of feel like what's the point of having kids if you are never going to see them." In other words, if you work full-time, you will never see your children. This seems to be an example of generalised thinking about binary choices that are rooted in strong cultural narratives associating mothers with the role of primary parent (Miller, 2005; Breitenbach, 2006). Jessica, an undergraduate, showed that some are aware of getting conflicting messages from society:

> "It's a bit 'rock and a hard place'. On the one hand, as a mother, your duty is to your child; you don't want to be an absent mother or let your child be brought up by nannies. But on the other hand you don't want to be frustrated by the limitations of your life if there's nothing external to your family. I think those are the contrasting pictures that are filtered through film or books."

Many of the daughters in this study espoused the desire to significantly cut their working hours, despite their investment in a career and their acknowledgement that their work forms a key part of their identity. Kelly, who is planning to return to work part-time after her maternity leave, said:

who on nus?

> "We're all having children later, so I've spent 15 years building my career, so to drop it all is a nightmare ... I wouldn't be me ... This is my identity isn't it? I couldn't just be a mum ... Otherwise what are we training our women to do? Train for years and then just give up ... Thinking about it, women are in an impossible position aren't they?"

This commitment to working part-time persisted even though some of the daughters had noticed the career problems experienced by women with children in their workplace. As a result, these daughters also knew that there are many drawbacks to working part-time, from the point of view of "being left behind", having to make a "career compromise", losing out on promotions and finding it hard to cope with the demands of the workplace when mothers are expected by most to achieve what they did before they cut their hours – but for less money. For example, Natalie, a lawyer, said:

> "You do get career compromise because you are going to take a year off and therefore you have lost out on a whole year's worth of progress. People will have changed, networks, systems. So yeah, you're going to compromise by virtue of the fact that you are having time out."

Zara, working in marketing, demonstrated how these views are reconciled:

> "Working part-time gives you the best of both worlds. You get to have a career although it might not be as successful as you want it to be because of the perceptions about people who work part-time. But you still get a career, respect and human civilisation ... and you also get to bond with your child and have a balance."

The daughters interviewed also said that some of their friends were planning to switch their highflying careers into less demanding roles when they had children. Xenia, an undergraduate, said: "I think because a lot of people who are choosing jobs that could be problematic with having children would be quite happy to only do these jobs for a few years. When they have a child at 30 they will re-evaluate everything."

The 'best of both worlds' idea is aligned with the dominant social discourse that part-time work is the most appropriate choice for a mother of preschool age children. As discussed in Chapter Three, the British Social Attitudes survey showed that only 11% of all ages surveyed supported working options that did not describe the mother as the primary carer (Scott and Clery, 2013).

The daughters in my research who imagined they would work full-time fell into two groups. Those who thought of full-time work as a positive choice tended to be those who imagined, or had started, working for themselves or knew of models within their profession that offered autonomy or flexibility. The other group simply felt that they will have little choice but to work full-time for economic reasons. I observe that, across all the interviews, there was far less discussion of working full-time after childbirth. It is also significant that those who imagined themselves working full-time felt that their careers would be negatively impacted anyway, whether they have children or not, because of the *possibility* of them becoming pregnant. Fiona, working in finance, gave this example: "I think if you are getting married ... you might be sidestepped by a guy because they would think, well, the guy isn't going to have his career impacted in the same way."

What is more remarkable is that so many of the daughters should alight on the idea that part-time work is the best option, given that they had already invested heavily in a career path. Moreover, most believed that their experience of growing up with a mother who worked full-time or close to full-time hours in a demanding career had not affected them negatively. However, their aspirations to work part-time were influenced by the daughters' lack of knowledge about flexible working options. This led many to think that they had a binary choice between full-time and part-time work. The accepted definition of part-time work is a working pattern that reduces the amount of contracted hours in which employees perform their roles. Flexible working also describes flexi-time (varying start and finish times), compressed hours, regular working from home, working in term time only, working an agreed number of days per year and job-sharing, where two or more people perform one role (Tipping et al, 2012). These participants did not have access to the arguments of scholars such as Gambles et al (2006) that the traditional perception of part-time work as being the best way to combine work with motherhood is a myth, as demonstrated by the experiences of part-time working mothers for whom work spills over into life. Nor did the daughters express any *depth* of knowledge of the

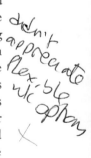

didn't appreciate flexible wk option

penalties in terms of career rewards and satisfaction that come with part-time work – as described by many researchers (Gatrell, 2007, 2008; Connolly and Gregory, 2008; Durbin et al, 2010b). It was also apparent that there was little knowledge of what flexible working meant or could mean beyond vague views about working school hours or working from home and a few mentions of job sharing.

The 'daughter mothers' did have knowledge of more flexible ways of working and it is clear that being able to work flexibly or with autonomy correlated with positive feelings about combining work with motherhood. Amy, for example, was working full-time hours compressed over four days in her role in the health service. She found her job very satisfying because of the content and social value of the role and also because, as she reported, her employers cared about her output rather than the time she spent at work. She contrasted this with her sister's experience as a corporate lawyer, who felt her firm had grudgingly allowed her to reduce the number of days she worked and then made it clear to her that, because of her reduced availability to them, they would be happy for her to leave.

It can also be argued that mothers collude in this downgrading of their status at work by feeling that they are doing neither job well enough (see, for example, Stone, 2007; Fagan et al, 2008). Women also routinely report that they work longer than their contracted hours but are neither financially rewarded nor positively recognised for this (see, for example, Durbin et al, 2010a). Also, many of the mothers and 'daughter mothers' in my study described themselves as working part-time when they did not work many fewer than 40 hours per week – the standard definition of full-time work – in their place of work and often worked additional hours at home. It is telling that there is no official definition of what constitutes full-time or part-time hours in the UK (CIPD, 2015).

Contemporary motherhood culture

The nine 'daughter mothers' showed me why the 'best of both worlds' discourse is hard to resist. They too equated being a good mother with cutting the hours they were prepared to commit to work and only one of them worked standard full-time hours. Most of their accounts were focused not on work, but on the way they wanted to mother. I noted the frequent use of the phrase *being with* their child, or its alternative, *not leaving* them. This echoes the work of Baraitser (2009, p 80) who argued that the constant interruption of mothers' lives by the immediate demands of a child may leave the mother feeling that she only dwells in the moment. The notion of 'being with' the child extended far beyond physical presence to being emotionally available to help and guide them. When asked to consider what lies behind these views, the 'daughter mothers' talked about how they wanted to mother and also recounted many conversations with other women at NCT coffee groups, at antenatal groups, at yoga classes, online and in all the places women meet. Baraitser (2009) described these public spaces where mothers mass as locations in which a mother has to learn what is, and is not, acceptable behaviour for her and her child. This influence applied from the moment they became pregnant and became stronger as they built their networks around other mothers-to-be and, subsequently, mothers. The 'daughter mothers' in my research often reported "feeling under emotional pressure" about the decisions they were taking. Many felt that pressure turned into judgement, especially around childcare, from women who worked fewer hours. This goes to the heart of the concerns of working mothers about how their children are looked after when they are not there. Sophie, a full-time working 'daughter mother' with one child who, speaking dramatically to make her point, paraphrased conversations with other mothers as follows:

"Are you back at work full-time?"
"Yeah she's at nursery from 8 in the morning to 1 minute past 6 in the evening."
"There are criminals that spend less time locked up than she is, poor child."

Many of the mothers and daughters also commented that there are still few positive examples of professional working women in films or on TV. Belle, a 'daughter mother' of two, said that, on TV, "'Mum' is never seen doing anything self-developmental or getting a job or anything." She also pointed out that "the policewomen in TV drama are all portrayed as neglecting their children for their job." These stereotypes about it being negative to be a mother and a worker are clearly still perceived to be held in the popular consciousness, and this arguably gives people, other women in particular, permission to criticise working mothers. As Lily, 'daughter mother' of three and working part-time, said:

"I think some people have said some outrageous things to me ... 'And how *are* your kids doing? It must be really hard.' ... but you never feel as a working mother you can say, 'You've not worked for eight years and its made you really dull.' So the moral high ground is very much against the working mother."

Conversations like this had left Lily feeling that some women, while generous in many other ways, are ungenerous and unsupportive of the way in which others decide to combine motherhood with work, because "motherhood creates anxieties for people". Lily said: "I find the yacking about motherhood ... people talking at length about breastfeeding, immunisations, about the food you give your babies, about childbirth, about everything ... can be very oppressive and not very helpful for women. So I think I didn't find motherhood a great place of sisterhood."

Most recent mothers thought that social media was amplifying pressure to mother in a certain way. While social media can be a useful source of advice and information, it is also where the mothers witness what Belle, 'daughter mother' of two, termed "humble bragging" about the achievements and activities of other people's children. This could make the 'daughter mothers' feel inadequate as mothers. Belle was a primarily stay-at-home mother who had an internet business. She commented about Pinterest:

> "The [Pinterest] pins that come my way very much emphasise perfect parenting ... I suppose people select, or create, a brand image for themselves that they put forward in social situations and on Facebook and the like and you don't see the rough steps around the edges ... that stuff is edited out for public consumption."

Amy also commented on the increased pressures from social media:

> "I don't think that it's easy and with social media [sighs] ... all your choices are more painted out there in bold technicolour but also all the guilt is given to you that way as well: 'You should be doing it this way,' 'You should be doing it that way,' and 'If you want your baby to be intelligent you should be doing x, y and z.'"

The evidence from the daughters' generation accords with the growing trend towards parental determinism described by Furedi (2002) and framed by Thomson et al (2011, p 277) as the 'intensification of responsibility', amplified by middle-class anxiety and insecurity about the way they mother. This is not to argue that mothers should not work part-time. The issue I wish to highlight is the strength of social pressure that makes this a difficult choice to resist. A further important point is the lack of availability of well thought through options in the workplace that work for the employer as well as allowing for the flexibility and autonomy at work that many parents with careers want.

Conclusions

My research shows that of the 22 child-free daughters, all but four anticipate having children and have ideas about how they aspire to shape their careers around this. Tanya, who has recently started work, underlines that motherhood and work is "talked about a lot. It doesn't feel like an issue that has been dealt with."

A key finding is that almost all of the daughters believe, and back up the belief, that having a mother who worked long hours out of the home in a career that she found satisfying is consistent with their feeling well loved and well mothered. Despite this, a clear majority do *not* want to emulate their mothers, and instead embrace a dominant idea that part-time work offers 'the best of both worlds'. While there are many possible explanations for wanting to cut back the hours one gives to work, the accounts of the daughters make a clear connection between the way they want to mother and their desire to substantially cut back working hours. The dominant cultural scripts influencing this view are the measurement of good parenting by time spent at home versus time spent at work. Another influencing factor is that the daughters who are child-free at the time of interview have no depth of knowledge of ways of working other than part-time or full-time. The dominance of the notion of the 'best of both worlds' coexists with the strong identification with work of this generation of daughters who have invested in their careers since being in education. Moreover, it coexists with, albeit imperfect, knowledge of the negative impact having children has upon co-workers and friends. These ideas do not sit comfortably together and therefore still necessitate the kind of 'emotion management' that Hochschild (1983, p 44) memorably described.

The daughters who are anticipating motherhood and, even more so, 'daughter mothers' are strongly influenced by the contemporary culture of motherhood with its growing emphasis on 'balance' (Rottenberg, 2014) 'parental determinism' (Furedi, 2002) and the 'intensification of responsibility' (Thomson et al, 2011, p 277). Other key aspects of contemporary motherhood culture are increasing public scrutiny (Baraitser, 2009) and the experience and expectation of many that the primary responsibility for childcare was and will be theirs and not

[handwritten marginal note: but what leisure + what social & desirable home anymore Use eg my os. ?]

their partners. This is the case even though most women do not realise just how constrained their choices are (Hochschild and Machung, 1990; Stone, 2007; Thomson et al, 2011). As 'daughter mother' Kelly observes: "We're a bit confused really. I don't know if we really know what the Holy Grail is really for working women, with motherhood." All of these factors put pressure on individual mothers to be actively guiding and monitoring their children. This is very difficult to do while also working in a demanding job. For many of the 'daughter mothers', striving for success in a career seems to be combined with, or even outweighed by, the idea of being a success as a mum. This idea is put eloquently by Hannah, mother of two under-fives and working part-time as a teacher:

> "In the nursery ... they [other mums] are all very on it, about, you know, nurseries or what different primary schools can offer and blah, blah, blah. So there's definitely an element of the way they talk about mothering as being a bit like a job. And how you succeed at it. How you succeed at being a mother."

In the light of much research that demonstrates that part-time work presents strong barriers both to career satisfaction and to progress, I contend that the 'best of both worlds' trope is likely to compromise the progress of gender equality in careers. This reinforces the need for organisations to identify and offer more genuinely flexible ways of working in senior roles that work for the organisation too. It would also help to publicise these different options at an early career stage given that young women appear to be shaping their career aspirations in the anticipation of having children. For individuals, I also advocate challenging the idea of measuring good mothering by 'balanced' hours spent at work and at home.

Three key points made in this chapter are:

- The vast majority of the daughters without children have views anticipating how they might manage working motherhood. This shapes their relationship with work.
- A clear majority of the daughters anticipate (or are) working part-time to achieve what they think of as 'the best of both worlds'.
- For a significant majority of the daughters, knowing they feel well-mothered by women working full-time or close to full-time hours seems not to be strong enough to withstand the contemporary

cultural concept that being a successful mother means working part-time.

Chapter Seven expands upon generational differences in attitudes towards working motherhood, and examines the influence the mothers' and grandmothers' generations have had upon their daughters' views about combining work and motherhood.

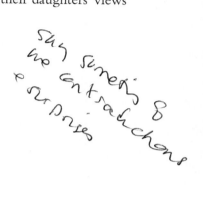

Working motherhood across generations

Chapter themes

The findings of my research corroborate existing research evidence that if a daughter observes her mother combining work with motherhood, it is more likely that she will do the same (see, for example, Moen et al, 1997; McGinn et al, 2015). This chapter examines more closely the influence the mothers and grandmothers have had upon their daughters' views about the hours they intend to work *when* they become mothers or, in the case of the 'daughter mothers', the hours they are working now. The 'grandmothers' who participated in this research were often 10 years older than the mothers of the daughters who did not (yet) have children. Their different experiences of the times in which they had their first child affected what they verbally transmitted to their daughters. Moreover, the arrival of a new generation substantially changed the way mothers talked to their daughters about combining work with motherhood. The views of the 'daughter mothers' and grandmothers are therefore contrasted with the mothers and their daughters who were child-free at the time of interview.

Wendy is the director of her own STEM business and her daughter Willow is working as a junior doctor in a hospital and does not have children at the time of interview. Wendy is the first of her family to go to university and says that, as a result, her family see her as "a bit of an oddity". She also comments that not being economically independent led to her mother being "bullied" by her father. Being "at odds" with the experience of her mother, coupled with considerable difficulties she experienced at work when she became pregnant, hardened her sense of motivation to continue to work: "I'd already started a career and I wanted to continue it. I was very clear." This awareness of being motivated to have a different experience to her stay-at-home mother is a theme that applies both to the mothers and the grandmothers.

Wendy tells me that she has conveyed to her daughter that "being happy at work is very important." She is proud of her daughter's choice to be a doctor and they talk about the day-to-day issues

Willow experiences at work. Wendy expresses worry about how "her epic shifts" affect Willow's mood and health and says: "I can see she pushes herself and it's good to push yourself out of your comfort zone but I think you need to do it knowingly. Not because of external pressures but because it's something you want to do." As a result of her concerns, Wendy has talked to her daughter about combining work with motherhood even though Willow does not (yet) have children.

> "I think it's very difficult for doctors, because they do so much training for so many years ... I think she called it her 'middle period' when she'd be expected to work extremely hard and working part-time in a hospital environment didn't seem to be an option; she says it's not an option ... Whereas I have a friend who is a GP and I know she combines that with her children very successfully. She works a couple long days, they get paid very well ... I've talked to her about that as a role model. So we have talked about what are the options, yeah."

Wendy's concerns about the effect of her working hours on her daughter are both understandable and typical of many of the mothers' generation. She also draws on the experience of her professional friends (and her own experience as an employer). This is also a recurrent theme in this study.

Willow is typical of many of the daughters in that she talks at length about her thoughts on how she may reconcile her career with family life without making reference to conversations with her mother. Willow is articulate about the gender issues in medicine that mean it will be hard for her to choose a specialty that comes with little flexibility. She is torn between her ambition to do well, her preference for the medical specialties that come with shift work and long hours, and her desire to have children and be there for them. Willow says:

> "Only the women talk about it; we talk about it in a kind of ... [sighs] fatalistic way, kind of like, 'Oh well if I want to have children I may as well be a GP' ... because it's flexible. I kind of always imagined having children around the age of 30 ... but if I'm in training for the next five, six, seven years and having all these crazy shifts ... where does it fit in? It doesn't. I deserve to have a career that I find interesting and that I can follow my own path and ... [pauses] reach my potential, I guess, and then on the other side I quite like

the idea of working three or four days a week, or maybe every morning and having the afternoons off. I can see in my head, you know, children coming home from school and me being able to be there at two or three o'clock in the afternoon."

The only reference Willow makes to her parents in this context is that their acrimonious divorce probably lies behind her desire for a "settled" family life.

Turning now to the narratives of a grandmother and 'daughter mother'. Sophie works full-time in a marketing role in education and has one child under the age of five. Both Sophie and her mother, Stella, say that Sophie regularly rings her mum for advice and also for emotional support. Sophie's view is that her mother set her a positive example in being a financially independent working mother and that she would like to do the same for her daughter. She is already thinking about how useful it would be to her daughter to live in another culture given the globalisation of work. Sophie is typical of many of the daughters in thinking that her mother transmitted a general sense of the value and feasibility of combining work with motherhood and is now being emotionally supportive of Sophie's difficulties with her life load.

Stella, a retired academic who was a lone mother for most of her children's upbringing, says she encouraged both of her daughters to work hard and stick at a job to keep their independence. However, she also worries that what she has transmitted to her daughter Sophie is that she should do everything, even at a cost to her own wellbeing: "The only trouble is, I think she's learned this thing of you actually drive yourself into the ground trying to do everything. That's unfortunate ... She's just driving herself into the ground at work, working all hours. She's really doing the same thing that I did."

She also underlines a theme that came up in many interviews: that her daughter's generation is under more pressure to 'get parenting right'.

"Now I think the balance is different because everyone works but there's that much more pressure on everyone these days ... There are so many experts on everything that you read all the books and you do all the right things and it doesn't necessarily work. I think that can contribute to a sense of incompetence or that you're not doing it right. Whereas we just muddled through much more."

Stella and Sophie have discussed Sophie's problems with her life load. Sophie is the only one of the 'daughter mothers' who works extra long, full-time hours. Shortly after our interview Sophie resigned. She is ambitious and still plans to work full-time, but in a way that gives her more control. Stella also points out the limit of her influence, because her other daughter who has children does not work. Their accounts illustrate that the mother has influence but that this is only part of the picture. Personal biographies, agency and circumstances also carry much weight in decision-making about work.

Historical, biographical and generational time

Temporal issues are embedded in many aspects of working motherhood, from the zeitgeist of the times in which decisions are being made, to the ways mothers experience maternal time and views about time spent at work and at home. This study sees intergenerational relationships through the interaction of both historical time, which exposes the cultural location of generations at a specific point in time, and biographical time, which focuses on the smaller stories of the interactions of generations within family chains (Kehily and Thomson, 2011). This is a psychosocial approach that emphasises the interconnectedness of big and small histories.

This way of analysing intergenerational relationships has its foundations in Mannheim's (1952) argument that a shared social location means it is likely that values and attitudes are shared. These values and attitudes are not static and each successive generation influences the next. As Newman posited, generational consciousness is shaped both by its social location and 'through the marking of differences between the generations that came before' (Newman, 2014, p 466). Studying mothers and daughters has particular power in helping us understand how different generations experience change because 'families express the coexistence of the past and the present, with the past constantly being reworked by contemporary demands' (Thomson, 2008, pp 20–21). Biographical differences can exist alongside the transmission of similar values and attitudes. Bjerrum Nielsen and Rudberg's (1994) theory offered a compelling perspective on how continuity of values is passed on intergenerationally between mothers and daughters while simultaneously accommodating social and cultural change. They drew a distinction between gender identity (I am a woman and therefore I act in a particular way) and gender subjectivity (I am me and therefore I act in a particular way). Both of these aspects of identity are consciously and unconsciously influenced by our mothers and also influenced by the possibilities offered by society at the time.

In relation to maternal transmission of attitudes towards working motherhood, the generations of my study stand in stark contrast to one another. The mothers and grandmothers were committed to work. Some of *their* mothers had worked long hours too, but the majority either did not work after they had children or worked in part-time roles that were not managerial or professional. The generation of daughters in my study, as reported in Chapter Six, include a majority who either aspire to, or are, taking a different path to their mothers by substantially cutting their working hours. As other researchers have found, mother and daughter relationships involve both identification and repudiation (Lawler, 2000). These different responses can be an act of rebellion on the part of the daughters, or they may be more appropriately explained as the daughters' indifference to the way that their mothers combined work and motherhood. McRobbie (2007) argued that postfeminist young women often perceive no gender inequality and expect to be treated as genderless workers. It follows, then, that they may believe their mother's experience of work is irrelevant to them. Moreover, the same child may respond to maternal influence in different ways at different times. When a daughter becomes a mother, this impacts upon, rearticulates or creates new family narratives (Thomson et al, 2011). This is a time when mothers and daughters re-evaluate their relationship from both sides, both unconsciously and through conversation, when they compare experiences, and when the new mother seeks advice.

Maternal time

Having a child causes mothers to relive their relationship to their own mothers. This idea is well expressed from a psychosocial perspective by Stone, who stated that 'the mother is a relational subject but doubly so: she inhabits two sets of relations transposed upon one another' (2012, p 147). Stone explained that new mothers are prompted to reproduce their pasts because as infants they have schematised 'ways of *being with* the mother' (2012, p 133, emphasis added). However, as Stone acknowledges, daughters do not just reproduce the way they were mothered because, as Baraitser (2008) pointed out, she is more than just a daughter. Baraitser described maternal subjectivity as a fundamentally changed or transformed state (2008, p 52) rather than a repetition of the way one was mothered. This time of being entwined with the other and the all-consuming nature of being with young children, described from Baraitser's own experience as 'desperate days'

(2009, p 19), are also the moments in which decisions are being made about work. Careers are associated with linear progression over time and the way in which maternity disrupts this is brought to life by the theories of Baraitser (2008). She argued that the constant disruption of the mother's life by the immediate demands of the child may leave the mother feeling she only dwells in the moment (2008, p 80) and that her concerns about the future are focused not on herself but on the future of her child (2008, p 43).

Work and time

It is not surprising that women think literally about the allocation of hours between work and home because hours worked is the unit most workplaces use to allocate roles and assess productivity. Long hours are often judged by organisations to be evidence of the commitment of individuals to their jobs. Williams (2000) coined the term 'ideal worker' to describe these expectations. Professional and senior managerial workers today spend a lot of time at work. Men and women in professional jobs spend on average 43.2 hours at work every week and those in senior managerial roles 46.2 hours (ONS, 2011a). Moreover, today's working mothers have to contend with work within a globalised economy. This leads employers to expect adaptability of hours around a global clock (Kelliher and Anderson, 2010). Technological developments have also caused a blurring of time spent at working, at home and in the workplace, and contributed to feelings of being in a time-bind (Hochschild, 2003).

Women who work part-time are far from immune to these pressures. Durbin et al's (2010a) study of women managers and senior professionals argued that the emphasis from organisations on hours worked contributes to women's acceptance of being rewarded on the basis of their input of contracted hours, not the hours actually worked or their outputs. Beyond the workplace, working mothers tend to give more of their time than their male partners to their caring responsibilities and domestic chores (Crompton and Lyonette, 2008). For single mothers the burden is obviously more acute because they have no partner with whom to share the life load and because single mothers in professional and managerial jobs tend to work longer hours than partnered mothers (Williams, 2010). Researchers of the generations of daughters in my study have claimed that these acute time pressures make the experience of working mothers stressful and mentally and physically tiring. A *Daily Telegraph* article drew on government Health and Safety Executive (HSE) figures to point out that women aged between 35 and 44 (when many tend to have children) are 67% more likely to suffer workplace stress than men of the same age (Bingham, 2015; HSE, 2015). Blair-Loy's (2003) and Stone's (2007) influential studies also drew a line between negative work and family events, caused by pressures on time, and changes being made in career trajectories.

Daughters before children: the mothers' influence over their daughter's work/family aspirations

Chapter Four showed that most of the mothers encouraged their daughters to work. Fewer mothers reported that they actively talked to their daughters about combining work with motherhood. One explanation is that the mothers of daughters who did not have children expected continuity between their experience of working and that of their daughters, so gave the issue little thought. It is now expected that mothers also work (Adkins, 2002). Other mothers were perhaps avoiding conversations that tapped into maternal guilt, as previously discussed in Chapter Two. Some explicitly said that they did not want to "poke their nose in" and feel like they were putting pressure on their daughters to deliver them a grandchild. Other mothers considered it inappropriate to discuss their daughters' career choices through the prism of a future intention to have children, because so many unknown variables may come into play, such as daughters changing their mind about their priorities over time or not being able to have children. These themes are well exemplified by mother Valerie, a senior marketing manager, whose daughter had been working for a few years:

> "I would probably not recommend making career choices around having a family because you never know what's around the next corner. There are careers that will give you an easier or a harder life when you are having children ... I also think that if you make a choice other than the one you really want to, for example, to become a GP when you really want to be a surgeon, then that will eventually catch up with you and make you feel unfulfilled ... You could make all your decisions around having a child and then find you can't get pregnant and that surely would make you feel worse. You can't suppress yourself forever."

By contrast, many daughters (such as Rachel, quoted at the start of Chapter One) did report that their mothers had given them verbal encouragement regarding the combination of work with motherhood. Undergraduate Jessica said:

> "My mum has taught me to be ambitious, to know what I want from work and life, and know that I can get it. I guess it's encouraged me to know I could be successful if I wanted to in whatever career I wanted to, but then equally to think that I can do that and be a successful mother. To have both."

Conversations of this nature are, unsurprisingly, played back as a positive influence by those daughters who felt positive about growing up with a working mother. Just as argued in Chapter Two, this research makes a contribution in finding that mothers who identify as feminists are more likely to actively talk to their daughters about the desirability and feasibility of combining motherhood with work. Often these conversations were also about 'not making life harder' by taking on a disproportionate amount of the work involved in caring for families in relation to their partners. What was said was often extended to apply to all women and therefore was a political, feminist statement rather than just a private observation. An example came from Xenia, the undergraduate daughter of Xanthe, a director in the arts. They both identified as feminists – the mother more strongly than the daughter. Xenia says:

> "She's definitely said to me, 'Be careful as a woman you don't get forced to do all the childcare or all the cleaning,' and there's definitely an impetus behind what she's saying, 'You for you but you for women as well,' which I think she feels really strongly, maybe more than I feel or my peers feel."

These comments reflect the identification of the mothers' generation with the aims of liberal feminism in encouraging equality of access to the most senior positions in work and contesting the assumption that women should be primarily responsible for the domestic sphere. The mothers' generation thought that these issues were still unresolved, as argued by academics such as Epstein and Kalleberg (2004) and Gerson (2011). By contrast, many of their daughters felt more comfortable with the idea that caring for children would be their role, as was argued in Chapter Six.

Another significant factor is this generation of mothers' awareness of a sea change in expectations and opportunities for their working lives in comparison to that of their mothers. They reflected often on whether they personally had actively rejected or just not wanted their *own* mothers experience of being largely home-based. By far the majority of the sample, working class and middle class, had mothers who were mainly or entirely home based. The mothers with a working-class background also had access through education to the kinds of jobs that had not been possible for their mothers. This heightened awareness crystallised the motivation of many to work. Gayle, a director in a consultancy company, talked about her "extraordinary, strong" mother having had a difficult childhood that gave her a strong sense of family and meant a stay-at-home role suited her. However, Gayle was grateful that she had instead had access to a career, because looking after children full-time would have felt unsatisfying to her and would have involved all the housework tasks she dislikes in life. The generational discontinuity also caused some to articulate that they felt that their actions impacted on society's view of working women, so they were representing women of their generation, not just themselves. This accords with Mannheim's (1952) depiction of active generations. This strength of feeling perhaps accounts for some of the discontinuity of attitudes between the daughters and mothers, in that many daughters aspired to combining motherhood with part-time work.

A number of mothers also discussed specific strategies for combining motherhood with work by drawing on the experience of their professional female friends or because of their professional responsibility for managing staff and negotiating maternity arrangements. Significantly, some of the (few) daughters who expressed aspirations about flexible working were the daughters of women who had professional reasons to have thought about, and talked about, work-life balance in a contemporary context. Rachel's mother Rose is one such example:

> "I don't believe in compressed hours. I think that's an excuse for working less and being paid more ... We're very, very strong on flexible working. We've got every shape and form of parenting. It's always a negotiation and it depends upon what works and we expect them to be flexible about reviewing that. I think it works pretty well."

Jessica, the undergraduate daughter of a business owner, also talked about her mother's approach to working (long hours) in a flexible way: "I don't think I would ever stop work. I mean, I haven't really thought it through but my idea would be to do something similar to my mum ... do flexible hours."

Tanya, one of the three daughters who reacted against the hours her mother had worked when she was a child, is an example of a daughter who had emulated her mother's choice of career field and whose mother, Tara, talked to Tanya about the possibilities of working in a different, more flexible way than had been possible for her. Tanya saw herself working longer hours and work being more central to her identity than did the other two of the 31 daughters who, as reported in Chapter Three, wanted to combine work and motherhood in a different way than they had experienced in childhood. These two daughters were Yasmin, who wanted to work part-time, and Olivia, who didn't want to work at all.

Analysis of the accounts of the daughters who wanted to work part-time, or were working reduced hours, also revealed that these daughters tended to have mothers who displayed an 'idealistic' attitude to combining work with motherhood – whether their mothers directly discussed combining work with motherhood or not. A typical example was provided by Isabelle, who reflected on what her mother, Imogen, who had reached the highest level in her career, had communicated to her:

> "I have seen Mum really struggle with work and not being with her children. She often talks about work and motherhood and how she felt about it and I think she has a lot more guilt than my dad. But I think if Dad had been more equal with Mum she wouldn't have felt like the c★★p one in going off to work. That's probably why we always moaned at her for going to work because she'd always be like, 'Your daddy is doing very important things. I'm just going to work,' because she's very self-effacing."

Isabelle also reported how pleased her mother had been to hear public reassurance that it was possible to do both motherhood and work well.

> "[Mum and I] went to a women's dinner at college ... and [a famous author] was talking about career and motherhood and Mum cried and I was like, oh nooo! But I think it's because [the author] was saying, 'You can be a mum and have a career that you love and integrate both into your life.'"

Isabelle's conclusion was that she intended to combine work and motherhood herself, but that she did not want to work as many hours as her mother had. Interestingly, the daughters of mothers with 'pragmatic' attitudes did not show a particular tendency towards working either full-time, flexibly or part-time. This may be because there was no clear idea governing the 'pragmatic' mothers' notion of the way they should 'do' motherhood.

These findings build on the work on Moen et al (1997) and McGinn et al (2015) in showing that attitudes about work and gender roles are transmitted intergenerationally. What my research adds is that position in the workforce plays a role. The mothers who had a professional interest in employment policies and who had experience of autonomous working environments passed on the advantages of both to their daughters. By contrast, some mothers communicated ambivalent feelings about combining work and motherhood to their daughters, whether they said anything or not. However, it was also evident that far from all the daughters wanted to emulate their mothers' way of combining work and motherhood. This aligns with Thomson et al's observation that 'Women respond differently: some daughters of working mothers are keen to reproduce something like the model provided by their mothers, while others embrace the possibility of being at home full time' (Thomson et al, 2011, p 174).

'Daughter mothers': the grandmothers' influence over their work/family choices

The grandmothers' influence was most evident during and shortly after their daughters' maternity leave. Some grandmothers and their daughters commented that they had become closer after the arrival of the third generation. The 'daughter mothers' were obviously in the moment of combining work and family life, and reported discussions with their mothers (the grandmothers) about how they combined work with motherhood. This corroborates the findings of several that new mothers tend to reconnect with their own mothers (Baraitser, 2008; Thomson et al, 2011; Stone, 2012). It seems that when the daughters announced their pregnancy, this was a relevant moment for this intergenerational conversation to occur and absolved the mothers from the feeling they were putting on pressure, as discussed above. Another important difference was the generational situation of the grandmothers. Many were working in education, meaning that their working hours fitted more easily around their children. Professional and managerial employment accounted for only 12% of women in the workforce in 1971 (Institute for Employment Studies, 1995). Also, their own work experience was more likely than that of the younger generation of mothers to feature extended maternity breaks (often three years or more) or varied career paths, as was common in the early 1970s (Walker et al, 2001). Therefore, the decisions of some the 'daughter mothers' to cut their working hours closely matches the experience of their own mothers. It also reflects the increasing availability of flexible working arrangements (Gardiner and Tomlinson, 2009) that attracted some of the 'daughter mothers'.

The grandmothers offered valuable practical and emotional support when their daughters were struggling with their life load. Several retired grandmothers had been asked to help out regularly in caring for their grandchildren, for one or two days a week, and several who were still in work stayed for weeks at a time to help. As already reported, educational psychologist Kelly moved house to be close to her mother so her mother could be her primary source of childcare. Grandmother Cheryl, head of an NHS body, described her daughter and grandchild as "the owners" of her time outside work.

A slim majority of the grandmothers initiated conversations with their daughters about the desirability of combining work with motherhood. Their views were often underpinned by their own biographies and their liberal feminist opposition to the social barriers to taking women's careers seriously after childbirth.

Several 'daughter mothers' drew comparisons between *how* they worked and how their mothers had worked and, in doing so, demonstrated that they had been influenced by their mother's approach. Paula, a dentist and mother of three, explained:

> "It's a very structured day so I know I'm going to be there 8.30 am to 5 pm and I don't have to do anything in the evenings ... It's probably in between my mum's job, in that she had the longer holidays, she had time off in school holidays, but had the downside of doing work in the evenings once we were in bed."

Grandmother Anita had been obliged to leave her position as a senior civil servant when she became pregnant and had an extended maternity break. She then retrained and became a teacher, a career from which she was very reluctant to retire. She pointed out that, despite her extended career break, she has worked for exactly the same number of years as her husband.

> "I've tried to show them [her two daughters] that you can be a working woman and a mother. I have set them an example and been quite a good role model to them and

I've never glossed over the fact that ... it will be tough ... When they both said they were pregnant and going back to work and we talked about how ... and why I didn't go back to work and what it was like not going back to work."

What her daughter Amy had taken from her mother's example was combining motherhood with working compressed hours – an approach she feels happy with. As she said: "I wouldn't have swapped more money for less time with my mum."

The most direct verbal influence came from a few of the grandmothers who encouraged their daughters to substantially cut back their working hours and *not* emulate how they had worked. They took this view because they were worried about their daughters' life load, and were trying to support their daughters' mental and physical health. These were often the grandmothers with an 'idealistic' attitude who had felt guilt about their own working arrangements when their children were young. The conversation recorded here shows mother and daughter 'swapping stories' about the difficulties of managing work and childcare and ends with grandmother Harriet's advice about putting work on a back burner while the demands of her daughter's children are so great:

Harriet (mother): "I think Hannah is quite anxious not to have ... precarious arrangements like I used to have ... when your children are ill. I mean everything just kind of falls apart then."

Hannah (daughter): "It happens a lot ... we do swap stories don't we Mum ... because I'm always complaining and she always says, 'Yep, it was horrible for me too!' ... I suppose her advice has always been ... do the minimum amount of work you need to stay in your job."

Harriet (mother): "Yes that's true. Get by. In this situation you cannot be a perfectionist."

The interviews produced clear evidence that the way the 'daughter mothers' decided to work after motherhood was influenced by their mothers. Their mothers were more involved and present in their daughters' lives when they were pregnant and had recently given birth. Their influence has been transmitted by a mixture of unconscious modelling and, in the moment of becoming grandmothers, verbal advice.

However, the accounts of the 'daughter mothers' make clear that other influences carry more weight. The 'daughter mothers' renegotiated their relationship with their employers as individuals and were operating in a different social and legislative climate from their mothers. Their contracts with work were dictated by what their employers would allow. Their economic circumstances dictated choices and childcare arrangements. Their relationships with partners, their partners' involvement with parenting responsibilities and their relationship with childcarers shaped more of their everyday experiences (Hochschild and Machung, 1990; Gatrell, 2008, 2013; Thomson et al, 2011, Lyonette and Crompton, 2015; Young, 2017). As discussed in Chapter Six, the influence of peers who are mothers and the beliefs inherent in the contemporary cultural context are also highly influential in shaping women's ideas about the way they want to mother and shape motherhood around work. The advice of the grandmothers that their daughters should cut back on work arguably just reinforced what the 'daughter mothers' thought they wanted to do.

Gains and losses of contemporary motherhood

The grandmothers reflected on their personal histories over time and the differences between their daughters' and their own experiences of combining motherhood with work. There were many ways in which the grandmothers thought that now is a better time to be a working mother. Chief among these were considered to be better entitlement to maternity leave, easier access to childcare of a higher standard and the sea change in the attitudes of fathers, many of whom want to be more involved in the everyday care of their children. As Barbara, mother of Belle, commented with laughter: "Well, the difference between your father and your husband is pretty phenomenal isn't it?"

However, many more references were made in the interviews to the ways in which the grandmothers perceived working motherhood to be harder. Many commented on the high cost of housing and childcare that took a greater proportion of their daughters' income than it had theirs. Several of the grandmothers had lived close enough to their parents to involve them in childcare, but this option was rarely open to their daughters because of increasing geographical mobility (Brannen, 2003). The grandmothers' concern was that the punitive costs of running a family might force their daughters into giving up on careers they had invested in and enjoyed. Anita, a teacher, said:

"I think that the amount of money people pay for childcare now is just horrendous ... and a lot of people are prevented I think from going back to the high-powered jobs they had before they had children because they can't afford the cost of childcare. My daughter lives in London ... every month she says, 'When I look at my bank balance there is a massive sum of money going on childcare so I can go to work and the money I've got left in my hand is quite small, but I do want to be doing the job. I don't want to be at home.'"

The grandmothers also voiced two main concerns about the culture of 'intensification of responsibility' (Thomson et al, 2011, p 277). First, they were concerned that the child becomes too much the focus of the mother, as described by Barbara, who started her career in media and then worked in a portfolio of jobs while her children were under school age, partly to be more available to them and partly because of her involvement in her husband's work. Barbara is the mother of Belle, who is a stay-at-home mother with an internet business she runs from home:

"I find it deeply troubling. I always managed to have a life as well as being a mother. It was important to me and I think it was good for the children. I think both my girls are excellent mothers, but I think they are almost too focused on it. And I'm not convinced it's good for the child. I think the child becomes too important ... I don't think it's a comfortable place for the mothers and I'm not entirely convinced it's a comfortable place for the children in the end."

Second, almost all of the grandmothers expressed a view that their daughters are under more public scrutiny and given more advice by 'experts' than they had experienced as parents. The grandmothers thought that this could be unhealthy because it encouraged competition which put their daughters and their grandchildren under pressure. Examples of this came from Stella, quoted at the start of this chapter, and Donna, a retired teacher whose observations applied both to her daughter and to her professional experience of parents:

"I think you are more judged now. In the past ... it wasn't so judgemental, whereas now women have been out in the workplace and they are used to things like targets and deadlines and then ... they turn that on their children and the next thing is, 'They are at that level or this level,' and they are always monitoring."

These findings corroborate those of Thomson et al (2011) who also found that the grandmothers' generation thought that there were more demands upon their daughters to combine work with being expert parents. The same themes were also discussed by many of the mothers of daughters who did not have children. Several picked up on the phrase 'professionalisation of motherhood', which has been used in the media. Valerie, a senior marketing manager, said: "There are rule books and there are handbooks and there's a right way to do it." Tara, MD of a media company, said:

> "If you are a middle-class mother then perhaps you are under more pressure to do it all right ... I wonder whether, because of social media, we are more competitive in every aspect of our lives ... being a parent it's like your job to get them into the right schools and everything. When I grew up you just went to the school that was near."

Conclusions

This research builds on the findings of others in showing that the time at which the mothers' generation become grandmothers is the time at which they are most likely to verbally transmit their views about combining work with motherhood to their daughters (Miller, 2005; Thomson et al 2011). According to psychosocial researchers, this is also the time in their biographies that daughters are most receptive to their mothers' influence, unconsciously or consciously (Baraitser, 2008; Stone, 2012). Some of the mothers verbally encouraged continuing commitment to work after becoming mothers. This is explained by their personal experience of working motherhood and the liberal feminist view that it is important that women work. In terms of specific influence over hours worked, it was clear that stronger influence was exerted by mothers who were concerned about the negative effects, of trying to do too much, on the health and wellbeing of their daughters. These mothers discouraged their daughters from committing to work while their children were preschool age. This aligns with the dominant social attitude and also with the experience of the grandmothers' generation, six of whom worked in education with long school holidays and two of whom took maternity breaks of several years. However, many other factors shaped the way in which the 'daughter mothers'

transitioned back into work after motherhood, including their partners' career plans and income, what employers would allow and what the 'daughter mothers' asked for (influenced by the contemporary culture of motherhood). Arguably, the grandmothers' influence over their daughters' decision to cut back on their working hours was stronger because it acted in the same direction as peer influence driven by the prevailing culture of motherhood.

Fewer conversations around managing work and motherhood took place between the mothers and the daughters who were not yet mothers, for reasons such as the mothers not wanting to be thought to be 'putting pressure' on their daughters to have children. However, more conversations about the desirability of combining work with motherhood took place than one would perhaps expect, due to the heightened awareness of this generation of the opportunities and satisfaction that comes from a continuing commitment to work. Some mothers took one step further and discussed ways of combining work with motherhood. This is explained by their experience as employers, senior managers or what they had learned in conversations with professional friends.

This chapter, in conjunction with Chapter Six, seeks to explain the key generational differences that lie behind the finding that the majority of daughters of mothers who worked relatively long hours through their childhoods are inclined themselves to work part-time. One key difference in the biographies of the different generations of working mothers in this study is more intense pressures on the time spent working for the daughters' generation. This is attributable to the increasingly global market and the seeping of work into the home facilitated by the internet and technology. On the other hand, the generations of mothers and grandmothers had far fewer opportunities to work flexibly or to cut their hours at the time their children were young (McRae, 2003). Recent work in the United States by Damaske and French (2016) tracked the working hours of women belonging to the baby boomer generation born between 1957 and 1964 and found 60% – an unexpectedly high proportion – of them followed the same full-time working pathway that is traditionally associated with men. It is worth pointing out that in the 1980s and 1990s many scholars wrote about the costs to women in managerial and professional jobs in similar terms to current academic discussion (Hoschchild, 1990; Faludi, 1992; Beatty 1996): that is, pressure on relationships, mothers experiencing work–life conflict because of their life loads, expectations that mothers have primary responsibility for their children, and mothers feeling that they are being negatively judged by other mothers, and society in general, about the time they spend at work. Moreover, childcare was not regulated by the UK government until the National Childcare Strategy was launched in 1998. As a consequence childcare was often more ad hoc, less professional, and therefore more unpredictable and stressful. Combining motherhood with commitment to work has always been challenging in terms of the management of time and 'emotion management' (Hochschild, 1983, p 44). Different generations can be argued to have faced different challenges, but with very similar implications and outcomes.

What does seem fundamentally different is the shift in the cultural expectations of motherhood since the late 1970s, when the first of the mothers in this study had their children. One key change is the movement of parenting from the private into the public domain (Edwards et al, 2012; Fink and Gabb, 2014). The second and linked change is the shift towards parental determinism and the 'intensification of responsibility' (Furedi, 2002; Thomson et al, 2011, p 277). Markers of these changes include the intervention of government policy and 'experts' into parenting and childcare. The Labour government in the 1990s saw children as a social asset for the state, and this led to a plethora of policy interventions, including the championing of parenting advice and skills (Edwards et al, 2012). Other markers include the growing public scrutiny of how one is 'expected' to mother, which is facilitated by the media and, especially, the internet. As argued in Chapter Six, ways of parenting are now seen as important in determining children's life chances. Middle-class mothers are increasingly expected to monitor their children to keep them safe from 'risk' and to cultivate soft and hard skills needed for them to succeed in life's competition (Furedi, 2002; Baraitser, 2009; Lareau, 2011; Christopher, 2012). These social shifts are highly significant for the generation of daughters and 'daughter mothers' and their views about working hours. Ways of 'doing' parenting typify contemporary discussions about motherhood and clearly require a substantial investment of time. All of these factors conspire to make contemporary mothers feel it is both socially uncomfortable and high risk not to substantially cut their working hours, at a time at which their attention is anchored to the demands they experience in the present. This suggests that the contemporary culture of motherhood is the primary explanatory factor of the generational shift for women working in professional managerial careers to measure good motherhood in terms of hours spent, and aspire to working part-time to achieve the 'best of both worlds'.

Three key points made in this chapter are:

- Most of the mothers and grandmothers communicated that their daughters should continue to work after motherhood. This was influenced by liberal feminist views and their position as a generation who pioneered working motherhood.
- The strongest evidence is that mothers give verbal advice to their daughters about combining work with motherhood after their daughters become pregnant. However, liberal feminist views and professional experience of today's workplace prompts conversations about commitment to work and hours of work in *anticipation* of their daughters having children.
- The most clear and direct advice from the mothers and grandmothers came in response to difficulties experienced by their daughters and reinforced the idea of cutting back at work. However, examining intergenerational differences in working hours, sources of work–life conflict and motherhood culture suggests that shifts in motherhood culture are the strongest actors in determining attitudes to work.

Chapter Eight considers the role of partners and fathers across the generations in facilitating commitment to a career in a way that minimises work–life conflict.

Partners in parenting

Chapter themes

This chapter reveals the crucial role of partners in influencing both the positive and negative feelings mothers have about combining work with motherhood. This chapter also explores the continuities, discontinuities and contradictions arising from intergenerational differences in aspirations and differing experiences of negotiating shared parenthood.

Beth is a few years into her career in media and is about to marry her partner. He works fewer hours than she does. She describes their approach to domestic work as "relentlessly equal". Her account of her expectations and future aspirations for combining motherhood with work paints a vivid picture of the emotional complexity of career women's feelings on this subject. This complexity derives from the clash between persistent social gender norms and changes in the times – described by Bjerrum Nielsen and Rudberg as 'gendered subjectivity' (1994, p 92). Beth says: "I don't understand how an educated woman can have no ambition for work, because essentially that's what you do with most of your life ... I've put a lot of effort into work and I don't want to throw it all away."

However, she also says she wants to work part-time even though her partner has said he would be happy to be primary carer and that his job lends itself more to part-time work than hers: "I'm quite affronted by the fact that he says he'll be quite happy to be a house husband.... I feel that would be stealing my role."

Beth acknowledges that this is a contradiction, but feels strongly that she wants to be the main carer. Beth draws a comparison with her parents' traditional arrangement where her mother shouldered all of the domestic load. She is happy to reject the inequality of her parents' approach to domestic work but wants to replicate her mother's model of being the primary parent. Her mother, Bridget, worked fewer hours in the same career as her husband, until her children reached their teenage years. Nevertheless, she did work four, often long, days a week throughout their childhood, relying on childcare. She sometimes felt that her life load was unfair but never questioned that she would be the primary carer. Bridget says she took her approach from her mother: "It was her role to facilitate my father working."

By contrast, lawyer Christina, (another member of the generation of mothers) was always the main breadwinner, but moved home to be near her husband's job. This meant she had to commute. Therefore, her husband did most of the day-to-day parenting and cooking. Other domestic chores were outsourced. Christina has a 'pragmatic' attitude to working motherhood, in that she does not feel a generalised sense of guilt about working and does not feel that her career has negatively affected her daughter. A key theme of this chapter is how important involved fathers are in enabling this attitude. However, Christina also reports that the way her and her husband split their responsibilities came at a cost to their relationship: "It's not very good for your relationship because you tend not to talk about things. You get into grooves as to who does what, when you are so tired and so busy, and you just lose track of each other, looking back on it."

She also describes feeling exhausted for years because of the commuting she had to do on top of managing work and family life. This illustrates some of the difficulties that can arise between dual career partners when negotiating or managing work and family life.

Christina's daughter, Chloe, an academic, aspires to egalitarian parenting. She even imagines splitting maternity leave fifty-fifty with her partner. Chloe feels that she would be following the pattern set by her parents. She says: "I think there's a very strong sense of teamwork from my parents and different abilities being used in different ways.... If one parent is physically more absent because they work long hours then it's important to have one parent based at home."

Growing up, Chloe was happy for this to be her father, and she also feels that her mother was an involved parent when she was present. She does not say that her parents' arrangement came at a cost, because she did not experience problems with the way her parents parented her. This confirms points made in Chapter Two about the mothers absorbing compromises so that their children did not experience them.

Negotiating shared parenthood

The management of responsibilities between parents is a complex mix of practical and emotional considerations, as Thomson et al, point out: 'The micro-politics through which domestic labour and childcare are shared, delegated and entrusted to others is important moral terrain in the contemporary politics of motherhood' (Thomson et al, 2011, p 194).

Hochschild's study of *The second shift* (Hochschild and Machung, 1990) – defined as the extra domestic workload on top of paid work – was based on interviews and observation of both men and women among 50 working couples living in California in the 1980s. This is contemporary with the time at which many of the generation of mothers in my research had children. Hochschild found that working women were absorbing most of the 'second shift' and that the implications of this for their emotional state of mind was based on their 'gender strategy' (1990, p 198) – that is, how they chose to view and manage their own role and how well their strategies meshed with that of their partners, whose views were often slower to change from the traditional model of male breadwinner and female carer. Hochschild argued that compromises and resultant strains were most evident in upper middle-class households facing the demands of two high-pressure careers. Those women who cut back on work, despite their egalitarian aspirations, and those who experienced marital conflict because of these competing demands, often 'settled for containing their differences without, alas, resolving them' (Hochschild, 1983, p 216). This had a cost in terms of the 'emotion management' (1983, p 44) required both to maintain marital harmony and women's sense of gender identity. Hochschild went on to observe that 'sharing the second shift improved a marriage *regardless* of what ideas either had about men and women's roles' (1983, p 221).

Clearly things have changed since Hochschild's research and there is now a trend towards more equality in the home. The time fathers spent caring for infants increased sevenfold between 1975 and 1997, from 15 minutes to 2 hours in the working day (Burgess, 2011). Eräranta and Moisander (2011) coined the term 'involved fathers' to describe those who express that they want to spend more time with their children. Nearly half of the fathers interviewed by Ellison et al (2009) said they would like to spend more time with their children and less time at work. Dermott and Miller reviewed cross-national academic research on fatherhood and found evidence of 'irrevocable change across discourse, practice and policy as well as ongoing momentum for further change' (Dermott and Miller, 2015, p 190). In essence, their review shows that many fathers want to be more engaged in co-parenting, that varying efforts have been made to signal this change by policy makers and that this reflects a change in social views of masculinity.

However, Miller (2011) questioned these findings on the basis of her longitudinal interviews with 17 new fathers. Many fathers stated their commitment to being involved fathers before the birth and yet, one year after the birth, Miller found that these intentions had often not translated into practice. The vast majority had 'fallen back' into gender normative roles and continued to prioritise their professional lives and roles as breadwinners over their caring responsibilities. Miller attributed this to issues such as men's typically superior earning power and the poor availability of flexible work. In the UK, the right to request flexible working was extended to all workers only in 2014 and shared parental leave was introduced in 2015. Shared parental leave gives parents the right to split statutory parental pay and parental leave. Research taking place since the introduction of these initiatives shows that men have been slow to take up this opportunity, perhaps because they do not feel supported to do this by employers or peers. A Fawcett Society (2016b) survey of more than 2,000 fathers of children under the age of 18 found that the most common length of leave taken by men was six to 11 days (43%) and a further 18% took less than five days leave. However, only 35% of employed fathers said they felt unsupported by their workplace. This suggests that peers and partners may also be reinforcing traditional gender behaviour.

Turning to the division of household chores, this, too, tends to fall to mothers. Kodz et al (2003) used British Household Panel Survey data to show that fewer than 20% of women working long hours reported that their partner was mainly responsible for each of four domestic chores investigated – cleaning, washing, ironing and grocery shopping. Jacobs and Gerson's (2004) seminal study compared data from the US and Europe and showed that, even though men are increasingly spending more time caring for their children and doing household chores, working women still shoulder a greater amount of the responsibility for caring or organising care for their children and doing domestic chores than their male partners. Recent research from the UK Office of National Statistics (ONS) found that women do more than twice as much unpaid work as men when it comes to cooking, childcare and cleaning (ONS, 2016a). Crompton (2006) argued that feelings of dissatisfaction about the sharing of caring are linked to work-life conflict. Crompton supported her argument with the finding that the lowest level of work-life conflict is experienced by Norwegian parents, who tend to share childcare and domestic chores. Crompton concluded that 'making men more like women – that is, individuals who routinely engage in both caring and market work – is a necessary condition of achieving a true "balance" between work and family life for men and women in dual earning societies' (2006, p 217).

Finally, it seems that Hochschild's comment that 'a gender strategy of resisting the emotional and social work of the second shift is built into the very clockwork of male-dominated careers' resonates still

(Hochschild and Machung, 1990, p 19). Male executives are rarely asked how they balance work with family life. Yet that question is commonly addressed to professional working mothers (González Durántez, 2013; Spohr, 2015). The cultural script that is implicit here is the notion that it is the mother's, not the father's, responsibility to ensure her child is well cared for.

Partners sharing parenting responsibilities

In order to unpick the perceptions of the mothers in my research, about the role of their partners, it is useful to borrow Hochschild's model of describing fathers as 'traditional', 'transitional' or 'egalitarian'. 'Traditional' fathers leave the responsibility for childcare to the mothers, 'egalitarian' fathers share the parenting responsibilities and 'transitional' fathers lie somewhere in between. Of the 13 mothers in my research sample who were not living with the fathers of their daughters, most said that the fathers were involved in their daughters' lives and one shared care equally with her former husband. Only three daughters had no active relationship with their fathers and these fathers are recorded here as 'absent' partners (see Figure 8.1). Some of those who were divorced reported receiving some domestic support from their current partners, but that has not been recorded here. Two of the divorced mothers were now in same-sex relationships, but that had no bearing on the classifications used here because in both cases the daughters researched had been born to their mothers' former husbands, with whom the daughters were still in close touch. The accounts of the mothers and daughters led to the characterisation of the fathers as shown in Figure 8.1.

Figure 8.1: Partner is what type of father?

	Partner is what type of father?			
	Traditional	Transitional	Egalitarian	Absent
Mothers (n = 30)	11	7	9	3
'Daughter mothers' (n = 9)	4	2	3	

The presence of a range of parenting strategies endorses the view of Crompton (2006) and Thomson et al (2011) that there is no inevitable correlation between a mother's commitment to working and traditional gender relations. Using NVivo, the types of fathers were mapped against the comments made by mothers and daughters about positive and negative effects of working. Triangulating the comments of mothers and daughters makes these accounts as robust as possible, given that fathers and partners were not interviewed. For both of the generations of mothers and 'daughter mothers', there was a clear link between those mothers who were happier about their work–life choices and their experience of egalitarian parenting, and those who were less happy having partners with traditional or transitional models of parenting.

Looking first at the generation of mothers in this study, traditional models of fatherhood predominated. This is only partly accounted for by the grandmothers in the sample who started work in the 1970s when it was common for women to work in roles that had fewer, more predictable hours than their partners (McRae, 2003). This meant that the majority of the 'second shift' of childcare and domestic chores fell to the mother (Hochschild and Machung, 1990). The grandmothers and the mothers with 'traditional' partners said their partners believed that it was, and should be, the primary responsibility of the mother to take care of the children. This point is illustrated by grandmother and teacher, Anita, who said: "He was not very domestically minded." In the online questionnaire completed prior to the interviews, only 14% of the mothers' generation disagreed that their partner was only happy for them to work if it fitted into family life. The implication for most was exemplified by teacher and grandmother Karen, who said of her partner that, "he was very supportive of me working in principle, but he was not in any way active or responsible for anything [domestically]."

The effect of this 'traditional' attitude had been to add to the difficulties of the 'emotion management' (Hochschild, 1983, p 44) involved in how well the mothers felt they managed their caring responsibilities and how well the views and behaviour of their partners meshed with their own expectations. Hochschild described this as the mothers' 'gender strategy' (Hochschild and Machung, 1990, p 198). Many mothers reported annoyance with their partner's assumption that they would always be the one planning family life, and that it was taken for granted that their male partners could go out after work until late without prior notice. Sometimes the effects of this on the relationship were perceived to be severe, as expressed by Alison, a divorced mother of two and marketing director, in these terms: "Neither of us could understand the perspective of the other. It was not a very happy period." The comments made by the 'daughter mothers' with partners with 'traditional' attitudes were very similar to those of the mothers' generation. An example of the link between mothers who felt more negatively about their work–life balance and traditional parenting came from Hannah. She commented that her husband embraced the example of his father's traditional approach to being absolved from family responsibilities and said he would have preferred her not to go back to work if they could have afforded it. Hannah expressed resentment about how little help she got, even though she was at work three days a week: "He doesn't see the problems that might arise and he doesn't think, 'Oh, everyone looks a bit mental, I'll cook some dinner.'" She referred to the "silent warfare" that ensued in their relationship. Others with partners exhibiting 'traditional' attitudes also described "resentment creeping in" and "feeling trapped and knackered".

The examples of 'transitional' parenting fell into two main camps. Some mothers reported that their own attitude to holding on to responsibility for their children was a barrier to their partner becoming more involved, as illustrated both by Beth, at the start of this chapter, and by Eve, a doctor: "He's been a very involved parent ... I think I could have empowered him a lot more and he would have done a lot more if I hadn't said, 'Leave it. Fine, I'll do it.'"

Many described their partners' support for them working as enthusiastic but also reported that they had to negotiate almost every day about who was doing what in terms of domestic responsibilities. That was said to be stressful. The mothers often said they got lots of help with practical tasks but the worry and the planning was their province, as illustrated by Xanthe, a public sector director: "He does a lot of the day-to-day domestic tasks. It's just not shared head space." 'Daughter mother' Lily made the point that her partner was very helpful practically but that the "emotional work", which she felt was important, was all done by her. By "emotional work" she meant paying attention to the children's friendship groups and wellbeing. This was a key reason behind her decision to work part-time. Several others also argued that while their partners took on many practical tasks, it was they who were expected to be in charge of childcare unless something exceptional was negotiated. On the whole, in this sample, 'transitional' fathers provided much support that facilitated the management of dual careers and childcare. However, the reported level of negotiation involved and the emotional cost to the relationship adds support to those who have commented on the resilience of the cultural notion that the woman is the primary parent and domestic worker (Breitenbach, 2006; Doucet, 2006; Lyonette and Crompton, 2015).

By contrast, 12 of the relationships in this sample were 'egalitarian', and in some families the father took on more of the second shift than the mother, as illustrated by lawyer Christina: "To be fair, he did pretty well everything in terms of domestic shopping and cooking ... it was really a hugely supportive partnership." In other relationships the childcare was shared according to the partners' availability and playing to their personal strengths:

> "He's always been able to finish fairly promptly so on the three days I was working from the office he could do a lot more picking them up. I would tend to work longer days on those days. [I valued] the willingness and enthusiasm for sharing ... There was just a complete expectation that we would share it." (Jan, MD in the private sector)

> "The joke in the family is that I do policy and he does implementation. He's always been much, much better at playing with them." (Martha, CEO in the public sector)

Egalitarian parenting strategies included a 'tag team' approach to being the one in charge of parenting. Sometimes, but not always, this had meant that the couple were running on separate tracks, which was reported to have negatively affected the closeness of the relationship. In addition, while there were reports of talking about taking it in turns to prioritise each career, there was little evidence of that happening. On the other hand, in two cases, the 'transitional' partners of the 'daughter mothers' were reported to be more egalitarian in attitude than they were able to be in practice, due to the attitudes of their employers. Amy, 'daughter mother' of two, said:

> "They're all right and they allow him to do a long day on Monday and a short day on a Wednesday so he gets to pick the children up one day a week, but when he's needed to take time off if they've been poorly they've asked him, 'Why can't your wife do it?'"

The existence of barriers, put up by employers, to involved parenting by fathers is supported by Gatrell et al's (2014) study. The same study also emphasised that, contrary to the perceptions of fathers, mothers also experience difficulties accessing flexible arrangements. It is noteworthy that this research shows more evidence of egalitarian parenting in practice than suggested by Miller's (2011) argument about 'falling back into gender'. I theorise that it is probable that changing social attitudes are starting to translate into changing behaviour, particularly in the types of families studied here, where both parents value work and identify with their work roles as well as their roles as parents.

An obvious benefit of egalitarian parenting was that there was much less sense of compromise or stress in the stories told by the mothers, in relation to either their partners or their children. This builds upon the view of Thomson et al (2011) that the emotional ramifications of shared parenting need to be accounted for when looking at the distribution of household labour. A linked point is that many of those with 'pragmatic' feelings about motherhood had much more support from their partners, with whom they practised egalitarian parenting. Those with a 'pragmatic' attitude reported fewer fundamental concerns about the effect on their children of their careers. The evidence of this link is an original contribution made by this research. There was only one case in this research where the father was the full-time parent while the mother worked. Paradoxically, the daughter in this case described this as 'unnatural', and she was one of the examples in this study of a daughter feeling that her mother's career had caused her unhappiness.

Overall, most of the mothers and 'daughter mothers' reported that childcare arrangements were organised almost entirely by them. Moreover, when mothers were asked in the online questionnaire about their level of agreement with the statement that 'women are expected to do too much', 84% of the mothers and 'daughter mothers' either agreed or agreed strongly. This perhaps accounts for the disparity in the accounts given by men and women in other research studies, about their level of involvement in caring for children and the household. A survey of over 2,000 parents living with their partners found that 31% of fathers said they shared primary responsibility for their children, whereas only 14% of the mothers reported the responsibility was shared (EHRC, 2009). Given that most of the couples, in my study, had established careers before the birth of their children, normative gendered parenting roles are evident in that it was almost always the mothers who adapted their careers to be more flexible or predictable to work around parenthood. Indeed, some mothers expressed irritation that their children also seemed to feel that their father's career was the more important. Wendy, director of her own STEM company, described her daughter phoning her at work asking her to do something for her school: "I said, 'Why can't you ask your dad?' and she said, 'He's at work,' and I said, 'Yes I'm at work too.' Willow had somehow picked up that my work was not real work."

The daughters' tendency to underestimate the importance to the household of their mother's work was also evidenced by answers given in the online questionnaire about whether the daughter's mother or father was the main breadwinner or whether they were roughly equal earners when the children were at preschool stage, at primary school and at secondary school. Comparing the answers of mothers and daughters to this same question, and removing the five long-term lone mothers from the analysis, showed that the daughters were only right about their mother's contribution 40% of the time. This makes it more remarkable that the daughters felt strongly about having egalitarian partnerships themselves.

The daughters' generation: expectations of partners

Almost 80% of the daughters who did not have children expected to have (or were hoping for) shared parenting arrangements with their partner (whether their parents had shared responsibilities or not). Nevertheless, many daughters still felt they wanted to work part-time because, even though they said that they wanted their partners to be fully involved, emotionally, they wanted the role of primary parent to be theirs. Beth's interview, discussed at the start of this chapter, illustrates this point. The online questionnaire, completed before the interviews, asked whether they were happy that it had mainly been/ would mainly be their responsibility to look after their child/children. The answers are shown in Figure 8.2.

Figure 8.2: Responsibility for children (n = 52)

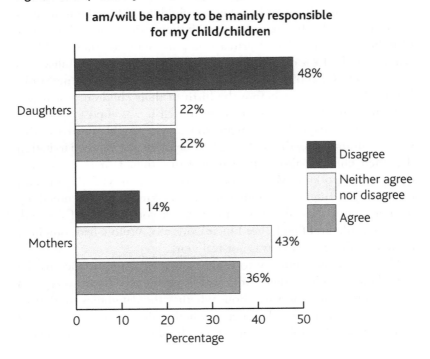

I am/will be happy to be mainly responsible for my child/children

Percentage

In comparison to the mothers' generation, a bigger proportion of the daughters disagreed that the responsibility to look after children should be mainly theirs. Conversely, the grandmothers almost all agreed or strongly agreed that they had been happy to take the lead role. These differences reflect changing social attitudes over time (Scott and Clery, 2013). Some of the daughters were in relationships and their partners were taking equal responsibilities for the domestic chores, and others were adamant that they would not tolerate a relationship that was not equal. This is consistent with the characterisation of well-educated middle-class girls as highly agential by researchers such as O'Brien and Fassinger (1993) and Walkerdine et al (2001). Even though five of the daughters felt comfortable that the role of looking after their children would be mainly theirs, what they said in the interviews made it clear that they were also expecting a lot of help from their partners. Beth's account given at the start of this chapter illustrates this point. Ursula, who was working and single at the time of interview, also expressed this rather contradictory attitude:

> "Would I like my partner to be actively involved with our kids? Yeah. I'd definitely like an equal relationship ... But I think I want to be in control of the cleaning ... I would want to be the prime carer ... even if they were the better parent. If it were completely equal ... I'd still want to be 1% better at taking care of them and making their life better."

This is an important finding because, on the one hand, women are arguing for more egalitarian parenting arrangements and, on the other, they are wanting to keep the main role for themselves. This is representative of enduring gendered attitudes to caring for children but also seems somewhat unfair to fathers.

Some daughters who had observed the way their parents worked together in an egalitarian way had a more detailed view of how the responsibilities might be shared. Undergraduate Jessica talked about playing to the strengths of each parent:

> "I would definitely be looking for support in terms of active, hands-on parenting. I would hope I would never have a partner who would solely delegate child-rearing to me. I would like a partnership in that sense, equal division of these things. As my parents have done, you play to your strengths a bit. If one person tends to be better [at something] then that becomes their role."

On the other hand, a few daughters said they would be willing to accept that their career would be sidelined while their children were young, as illustrated by Fiona, working in finance: "I wouldn't mind [giving up work] as long as I felt it wasn't assumed it would be me because it's my role in life, and it was my choice." Fiona also said that, if she did give up work, she intended to return to work later.

It needs to be remembered that these comments show the hopes expressed by those 22 daughters in this study who do not (yet) have children. Their behaviour if and when they do have children will not necessarily follow their prior attitudes. However, the strength of feeling that they wanted egalitarian relationships may be facilitating a shift in the role of fathers, towards being actively and regularly involved in bringing up their children, that is being reported elsewhere (ESRC, 2013; Gatrell et al, 2014, 2015). Baxter and Smart (2011) found that the more hours mothers work, the more involved the fathers tend to be. This is particularly interesting given that almost all of the daughters' generation in this study are (or intend to be) working in professional and managerial careers. Conversely, some argue that the egalitarian aspirations of this generation of daughters may be frustrated. Research by Ely et al (2014) among male and female Harvard MBAs found that 42% of women aged 26–31 expect to take primary responsibility when they have children. Tellingly, 66% of men in the same age group expect their partners to take primary responsibility. This mismatch suggests that many women's aspirations for shared parenting will be disappointed. Ely et al's (2014) research also explored the issue of inequities between male and female levels of job satisfaction and career attainment. They found that while ambition and time taken out of the workforce to look after children were factors, the key explanation lay in how couples distributed career and family responsibilities. Traditional arrangements prevailed in which women took the main responsibility for childcare while most often also working themselves. The women who had egalitarian expectations often had their hopes dashed, and this frustration appears to be linked with higher levels of dissatisfaction expressed about their career progression, in contrast with those women who had expected to be primary carers. Conversely, my research also shows that many women hold contradictory views, and that this sends mixed messages to partners.

Conclusions

In the words of Tina Miller, 'for the most part it remains the mother who is left holding the baby' (2011, p 1107). Much research shows that taking the role of primary parent impacts career progression and how career women feel about combining work and family life, long after the baby stage (see, for example, Hochschild, 1983; Crompton, 2006; Gatrell, 2005, 2008). My research findings also show that most of the mothers took on an unequal amount of domestic responsibility. This has persisted across generations, as exemplified by the fact that over half of the daughters had or were planning to adopt a male breadwinner, female part-time model that they perceived as 'the best of both worlds'. The power of the 'best of both worlds' discourse is more surprising when one considers the evidence of my research that a majority of these daughters with careers felt more strongly than their mothers that they did not want to be primarily responsible for their children. The fact that the daughters underestimated the importance of their mothers work to the household may help explain this and certainly illustrates the strength of traditional gendered associations with men as the main breadwinners and women as the primary carers. Also, as this research and many other studies attest, motivations and experiences involved in negotiating shared parenting are practically and emotionally complex and full of contradictions (see, for example, Thomson et al, 2011; Miller, 2012).

Of the 25 partnered mothers in this study, 12, almost half, exhibited egalitarian relationships that persisted and adapted over years. Those who had partners who were willing and able to take an 'egalitarian' approach to caring for their children reported more positive feelings about their experience of combining work with motherhood. These findings add weight to the arguments of others that organisations and policy should help facilitate and shift social attitudes by supporting men who want to be more involved fathers (Miller, 2011; Gatrell et al, 2014, 2015; Lyonette and Crompton, 2015). This research also suggests that mothers who want egalitarian partners in parenting should think about how they make room for their partners to be more involved.

Returning to Hochschild's notion of 'emotional management' (1983, p 44), there was evidence of negative emotions creeping into relationships because of perceptions about an unfair distribution of domestic labour among most partnerships, even some of those where the partners had more egalitarian attitudes. These negative emotions tended to simmer in the background rather than being talked about. I draw on Morgan's (1996) understanding of families as being fluid and adaptable to point out that while the needs and desires of both parents change over time and are contingent upon the weight of the domestic life load at any given moment, there is little evidence of individual families renegotiating how well their needs are being met in terms of what both partners want from work and family life. Rather, the focus of discussion is on who is doing what on a daily basis. I therefore suggest that partners in parenting should periodically review how well their strategies are working for them.

Three key points made in this chapter are:

- Mothers, across generations, who have experience of egalitarian approaches to sharing parenting responsibilities tend to feel more positive about their experiences of managing work and family life.
- Contradictions are evident in that 80% of the daughters who do not (yet) have children said in the online questionnaire that they expect or hope to take an egalitarian approach to parenting and yet in the interviews, when attitudes were explored in depth, more than 50% said they planned to adopt the prevalent male full-time, female part-time model.
- 22% of the daughters want to be primary parent – even as many say they want lots of help from their partners. This sends a mixed message to fathers and suggests that couples have work to do in unpicking and discussing their motivations.

Chapter Nine summarises the conclusions of this research and develops ideas for implications for organisations, public policy and families.

NINE

Making working motherhood work

Generations and gender equality in careers

The progress of women to top leadership positions has stalled over the last decade (CMI, 2016). Academics widely acknowledge that work and parenting values are passed on intergenerationally and that women are encouraged to believe that they can occupy the top jobs in society by seeing other women thrive in their careers (Eagly and Carli, 2007; Carter and Silva, 2010; Tutchell and Edmonds, 2015). Who better, then, to be a role model of career success, combined with motherhood, than your own mother? This landscape informs the aim of this research, to explore to what extent having a mother with a successful career leads her daughter to want to follow in her mother's footsteps. What follows from this question is whether the daughters of mothers who have been committed to their careers think that this has benefited or compromised them. This is asked partly because of the tensions women experience between their roles as mothers and workers, and partly because the generation of mothers in this study consistently worked full-time or close to full-time hours because, prior to the millennium, employees in career roles had little or no opportunity to work part-time or flexibly.

The intergenerational perspective taken in my research intertwines the accounts of relationships between mothers and daughters with social changes in the expansion of opportunities for women in the workplace. The 61 daughters and mothers who participated in this study revealed both the continuities and changes over time in the satisfactions, responsibilities and challenges of combining family life with careers. Consequently, in this chapter I make recommendations for individuals within families. However, individual strategies lack resilience if they are not supported by changes to Acker's (2012, p 215) 'gendered substructure' in organisations, backed up and facilitated by policy changes in parental leave, childcare provision, and the symbolic and material benefits of tackling the gender pay gap. Therefore, recommendations focusing on structural, systemic changes are also made.

Headline key findings

- Almost all the adult daughters feel positive about having a mother who worked long hours in a career she found satisfying.
- Despite feeling well mothered, the majority of daughters have substantially cut their working hours since they became mothers, or are anticipating doing so. The daughters describe this as having "the best of both worlds".
- This is *not* a reaction to their mothers' full-time working hours.
- Powerful cultural scripts foregrounding women's individual responsibility for their children's progress and wellbeing outweigh many daughters' aspirations for success in a career. Many feel conflicted about how it is possible to continue to work in a demanding career role and be good mothers.
- Mothers have been the primary influence over their daughters' aspirations at the early stages of their careers.
- Both mothers and daughters seem reticent about expressing ambition – or thinking of getting to positions of power as a desirable or probable outcome – even though some mothers have reached the top levels of their careers. Daughters directly expressing ambition have been encouraged in this more by their fathers.

Key findings

Well-mothered daughters

Almost all the daughters interviewed felt well mothered which shows that good (enough) mothering is compatible with working long hours outside the home. Much recent research, including my own, presents a convincing challenge to the idea that having a mother who works long hours in a career role has a negative effect on children (Cunningham, 2001; Backett-Milburn et al, 2011; Mendolia, 2014; McGinn et al, 2015; Milkie et al, 2015). My research also shows that very few of these mothers with careers modelled work as being stressful or negative in other ways, because almost all enjoyed and derived satisfaction from their work, most of the time. On the other hand, the mothers worked hard to absorb the inevitable day-to-day strains between their responsibilities. This resulted in many mothers having little or no room in their lives for a social life, for other interests, and in the case of some, no room for their partners or for building new romantic relationships.

Many of the mothers felt a generalised sense of guilt about working. However, many others took a more 'pragmatic' attitude to managing their feelings about combining motherhood with work. The accounts of these mothers also corroborate the findings of Laney et al (2014) and Bataille (2014) whose work on the mothering and professional identities of women questions the binary positioning of these in much work-life scholarship as twin identities in conflict. Bataille's (2014) work is particularly relevant to my findings. She takes a psychosocial approach and typifies the construction of sense of self as a narrative pathway through various transitions in the woman's life course. She argues that professionals who are also mothers conceptualise their *identity* as integrated, while the *roles* they prioritise change. I theorise that when one's sense of self does not feel under threat, this facilitates more positive (or at least fewer negative) feelings about the competing claims on one's time that come with being a working mother. In my research, I found a correlation between mothers demonstrating a 'pragmatic' attitude and progressing to positions of influence in a career. This attitude was enabled for many by supportive partners with an egalitarian approach to parenting and, in some cases, by the ability to work flexibly or autonomously.

The daughters articulated that their mother's work had benefited them in terms of access to interesting worlds, communicating the value and enjoyment to be had in work, and the benefits that came from their mothers' earnings. An important contribution of this research is the insight offered by the daughters into how their mothers (and fathers) had minimised any ill effects of their working hours. Five clear themes emerged: mothers being there for the events where parents (especially mothers) were expected to be, daughters being able to predict their mother's routine, their mothers being emotionally present and available when at home and reachable at work, daughters (as much as possible) being cared for at home after school, and daughters being encouraged to be independent. It seemed to be much more important to the daughters that their mothers were *not* absent from significant public events than it was to have their mothers present in a more everyday way. These findings suggest that the continuing lack of representation of women in the most senior positions in the workplace cannot be accounted for by a backlash of daughters reacting against their upbringing by mothers who were also committed to their careers.

Mothers as career mentors

Most of the daughters think that their mothers have been the primary influence over their choice to embark upon a career path themselves. Indeed, a third of the daughters have followed their mothers into the same or very similar careers. The mothers' influence is apparent in indirect ways, such as encouraging the educational achievement that has led to a career path, and modelling the value of an enjoyable and satisfying career. They have also influenced their daughters' career decisions in direct ways, such as facilitating work experience that could open the door to a career or in talking about what their work involves. In this way, the mothers have acted as career role models, even more than they realise.

The mothers have also acted as career mentors to their daughters since they left home, in that the mothers often talk and give advice about situations experienced by their daughters at work. This advice is often based on the mothers' experiences as employers and senior leaders in today's workplace. However, the mothers' influence over their daughters' longer-term ambitions for their careers seems much weaker than over their initial career choices. Although many of the daughters describe their mothers' careers as "successful", they have not really internalised what this means. My research found that the mothers tend not to talk to their daughters about their career successes or the values that motivate ambitious women. I call this 'quiet ambition'. Consequently, many mothers have left their daughters with a sense that their career success was mainly a by-product of hard work and producing quality work. Therefore, acknowledging their mothers' career successes has not resulted in the daughters' generation thinking that getting to positions of power is a desirable or probable outcome. Conversely, this research corroborates that encouragement from fathers has a positive impact on women's ambition (Nielsen, 2012; Tutchell and Edmonds, 2015).

The 'best of both worlds'

Despite the daughters' view that they were well mothered by a mother who worked long hours, over half of the daughters have *substantially* cut their working hours since they became mothers – or they intend to when they become mothers. This is an issue for gender equality at work because much research has demonstrated that there are career penalties for women in high-status roles who change their contract with their organisation to work part-time or flexibly (Drew and Murtagh, 2005; Connolly and Gregory, 2008; Durbin et al, 2010a, 2010b; Gatrell et al, 2014). The daughters' motivations for wanting to substantially cut their working hours seem to be a response to powerful 'cultural scripts' (Miller, 2005, p 11) that have inflated the expectations of the responsibility of middle-class mothers. Global markets and technological change affect demands on the time workers need to give to the organisation they work in, and make the boundary between work and home more permeable. There is a social expectation that the generation of daughters in this research will work (Adkins, 2002) while also experiencing stronger public pressure than previous generations about the right and wrong way to mother (Ribbens-McCarthy et al, 2000; Baraitser, 2009; Lee et al, 2014). Many of the daughters in this study feel that striving for success in a career seems to be combined with, or even superseded by, the idea of striving to be a success as a mother. They are far from impervious to the demands upon them and many think that they will experience more difficulties than men in combining a career with children. The modern culture of motherhood is variously described as 'parental determinism' (Furedi, 2002, p 45), 'concerted cultivation' (Lareau, 2011, p 1) and the 'intensification of responsibility' (Thomson et al, 2011, p 277). The language commonly used by women in this research is wanting "the best of both worlds" – meaning good motherhood is being equated with finding an (elusive) optimum balance between hours spent at home versus hours spent in the workplace.

Some of the daughters' mothers are reinforcing this view. This is suggested by the family link between mothers who felt a sense of generalised guilt and the daughters seeking the 'best of both worlds'. The daughters often picked up on their mothers' feelings, whether anything was said or not.

Direct advice about combining work and family life is given by many mothers in response to the effect of intense pressures on their daughters, either due to their working environments or, in the case of the 'daughter mothers', because they are struggling to manage work and having young children. This advice reinforces the idea of shaping careers to reduce working hours or make them more predictable. The grandmothers are particularly influential over the 'daughter mothers' due to the renewal of involved mother–daughter relationships prompted by the arrival of the next generation.

This social pressure combined with maternal advice makes working part-time hard to resist despite the negative effects this has upon career progress and satisfaction. This has implications both for organisations and individuals to reconcile the needs of both parties.

Individualisation and feminisms

As signalled by Beck and Beck-Gernsheim (2002) the generational perspective of this research highlights just how much the responsibility and pressure is becoming more intensive and extensive for individual women, particularly mothers and those anticipating combining work with motherhood. Mothers, including those in dual income households and working in high-skill roles, mainly continue to be positioned as having the responsibility for the emotional and physical wellbeing of their children (Gatrell 2005, 2008; Breitenbach, 2006; Crompton, 2006; Thomson et al, 2011). Conversely, even though men are becoming more involved in the domestic sphere, the idea that a demanding career conflicts with men's domestic role seldom arises. At work, the passing of generational time clearly illuminates the persistent inhibition of women's upward progress in organisations. Overt sexism is still alive (Bates, 2014; TUC, 2016). More covert sexism is prevalent and embedded in working practices that are dominated by masculine workplace culture (Eagly and Carli, 2007; Kelan, 2009; Cahusac and Kanji, 2014). Yet, despite this, only 9% of a nationally representative sample identify as feminists (Fawcett Society, 2016a). Feminism has been repudiated by many largely because of its perceived anti-male cultural legacy and because the need for it is associated with the past (Tasker and Negra, 2007; McRobbie, 2013). The same 2016 Fawcett Society survey shows that 65% believe in equality for men and women. However, this belief does not necessarily equate to understanding the sources and scope of gendered inequality. Workplace bias is often hidden, even to women (Glick and Fiske, 1997; Bohnet, 2016). Gendered inequalities have become 'unspeakable' in workplaces as the issues are met with animosity, fatigue or incomprehension (Gill et al, 2017, p 226). Postfeminist sensibilities have subsumed the well-defined sociopolitical aims associated with second wave feminism (Gill, 2007; McRobbie, 2009). A large body of work, including my study, shows that individual women believe it is possible to make any choice about how they will combine motherhood with work, without appreciating the extent to which their choices are constrained (Gatrell, 2005, 2008; Duncan, 2006; Stone, 2007; Thomson et al, 2011). Feminist scholars have anatomised the contemporary context of gendered inequality or, as McRobbie (2009) deftly sums it up, 'the illusion of equality'. The drift from liberalism to neoliberalism put the onus on individual middle-class, professional career women to take responsibility for the right decisions for their families while simultaneously depicting this as 'choice'. The landscape of power has birthed a 'corporate' feminism that supports the expectation (and socioeconomic need) for women to work while downplaying structural or cultural constraints (McRobbie, 2013; Gill et al, 2017; Lewis and Simpson, 2017). Or, as Wolf describes it, the rise of an elite of professional women has resulted in increasing

this important

inequalities between women, which she calls 'the end of sisterhood' (Wolf, 2013, p 5).

The women who participated in this study identified as feminists in a far higher proportion than the national averages discussed above: 57% of the daughters, 44% of the 'daughter mothers' and 65% of the mothers identified as feminists, as shown in Figure 9.1. As expected, identification with feminism drops off from the mothers' generation and the largest proportion of those who actively disagreed that they were feminists were found among the daughters. However, intergenerational transmission of attitudes is clear because the majority of mothers who agreed strongly that they were feminists had daughters who also identified as feminists. A few daughters identified as feminists when their mothers did not, usually because of particular political interests or personal experience of inequalities.

Figure 9.1: "I am a feminist" – combined agreed/strongly agreed (n=52)

Differences are evident within generations in that those claiming feminist identities were found more commonly among those who worked in the public sector – particularly those who worked with children or young adults – than with those working in corporate roles.

Moreover, the large minority of daughters who did not identify as feminist offered explanations that accord with the feminist scholarship discussed above. This could be argued to corroborate McRobbie (2013) and Rottenberg's (2014) critique of the feminism claimed by middle-class professional women as privileging their own personal, professional gains. However, this would poorly represent the women of this study. Looking more deeply at our discussion of their feminism in the joint interviews, many were actively involved in challenging inequalities, not only in their professional workplace but also in a broader social space. This was summed up by company CEO Jan, in conversation with her daughter, university student Jessica:

Jan (mother): "I want a workplace for Jessica that will help her achieve what she wants to achieve. But what I think I'm more preoccupied with is a broader social justice for gender, which I think is incredibly important."

Jessica (daughter): "[My definition of feminism is] not just to kind of agree with it; it's more than just thinking, 'Something's not right,' you have to actively want that to change. So in that sense maybe some people would say they're feminist who maybe don't fulfil those criteria. But that's not me."

The nature of feminist activism is different for different generations. The more professionally powerful among the mothers' generation can engage in *changing* structures as well as influencing their daughters. The daughters' generation can *challenge* the inequalities they observe or experience, although working women with young children have such heavy life loads that their ability to look outwards is curtailed. Those expressing an active commitment to challenging inequalities were many, albeit in the minority, but are noteworthy in the light of the societal turn towards individualisation and choice discourses that have, in many ways, elided antifeminism with third wave and postfeminism, and risk undermining the gains made by women. Gendered inequalities clearly need to be challenged and it is encouraging that the belief in equal moral personhood (Stansell, 2010) inherent in second wave feminism is being intergenerationally transmitted and picked up by some representatives of this younger generation of women. The fact that gains can be reversed has been perceived by the millions of women who marched against the Trump presidency in January 2017, in the United States and around the globe. The next section discusses specific ways in which individuals and social and corporate policy can address gendered inequalities.

Implications for families

Implications for families: daughters

A key finding is that even though, in the eyes of most of the daughters, their own mothers have demonstrated that it is possible to combine enjoyable, satisfying and largely full-time work with being a hands on, encouraging and emotionally involved parent, this awareness seems not to be strong enough to withstand the cultural concept that being a successful mother means working fewer hours in order to be physically present for much of the time. In other words, that part-time work offers 'the best of both worlds'. The intergenerational perspective offered by this research shows that this is an understandable response based upon the growing public pressures on individual mothers and on the intensification of the demands placed on them at work. It is not the recommendation of this research that women return to trying to combine full-time work out of the home with motherhood. Compromises discussed by the generation of mothers in this study are clearly not desirable and technological change has increased slippage between work and home. However, part-time work has been comprehensively shown to offer the worst of both worlds for most. This suggests a pressing need for flexible work arrangements to be better designed for women in senior roles. This will be discussed in a later section.

On an individual level, it would seem useful to connect young women with their views of their own childhood and also to share the research finding that the adult daughters of successful career women did not feel ill affected in any profound or prolonged way, and indeed saw advantages in growing up with a mother with a demanding career. The benefit of this will be to challenge feelings of generalised guilt about combining commitment to a career with motherhood and to encourage women to be sceptical about some aspects of the contemporary culture of motherhood. I advocate a return to the idea of the concept of the 'good enough mother' (Winnicott, 1953). The daughters in this study pointed out five practical steps that could help mothers to ensure that work works for their children. This research also suggests that it is more important for mothers to be to be more available after school when their children hit adolescence. This corroborates the research of Milkie et al (2015). Being around more during early adolescence is likely to coincide with periods at work when women are managing more than doing and have more career capital to negotiate around this. In addition, the research finding that lone mothers with only one child experience particular problems in working relatively long hours prompts a suggestion that lone mothers team up with other parents to support each other, particularly after school.

The research also suggests that it is helpful for daughters to be encouraged by their mothers to achieve their ambitions. This is not to argue that getting to the top should be the aim of all women. Rather, my argument is that ambition should not be restricted by socialised gender-biased expectations, and particularly the ambivalence women feel about expressing or enacting ambition – whatever those ambitions may be. This idea will be developed in the next section.

Implications for families: mothers

When the mothers in this study were asked 'What is the one thing I think would make the most positive difference to the lives of working mothers?' their answers were equally split between more opportunities for flexible working, more affordable childcare and partners sharing more of the parenting. All of these issues are clearly important, as are other interventions that are less top-of-mind for career women. Given that women continue to be underrepresented in positions of power, I argue that it would be helpful to the daughters' generation if their mothers encouraged their daughters' ambition by talking more about what they have been able to achieve at work – not least because women tend to have broader criteria for success than men (Bostock, 2014; Hewlett and Marshall, 2014). Mothers with careers are in a strong position to talk about the point of ambition in a way that their daughters will find motivating, for example, encouraging their daughters to appreciate how continued enjoyment of work is affected by being recognised for achievement and how progressing vertically through the organisation provides the status and seniority that puts individuals in a stronger position to effect change. Mothers with careers, because of their experience accumulated over time, are also in a good position to advise about impediments to career progress that affect women more than men due to workplace culture, implicit bias and the impact of motherhood (Armstrong, 2016). Mothers who have achieved career success can also congruently challenge, privately and publicly, the still evident social stereotyping of women in the workplace as diligent and hard-working rather than talented and effective (Meyer et al, 2015). Mothers with careers are often (or have been) employers or senior leaders in today's workplace, so can use their positions of power to challenge barriers to achieving gender parity and other aspects of equality in careers

Of course, what might get in the way of these recommendations is that every conversation needs a willing audience and not all adult daughters expressed interest in hearing about their mothers' jobs. A career is, however, a long game, and there are moments when many daughters seem particularly receptive to the advice of their mothers. The time when daughters start to reconcile work and motherhood is such a moment. Another is when the pressures of work become hard to handle. A third is when the daughters are thinking about promotion or switching career fields or roles.

Mothers who were advanced in their careers had the perspective to appreciate that social expectations about being a good mother and a good worker simultaneously are set impossibly high. Moreover, many mothers did not see commitment to their career as a threat to their identity as a mother. As several of the mothers in this study pointed out, the dichotomy often drawn between work and family life is a false distinction because, to quote one of the mothers who participated in this study, "life is so much lived at work as well". It is arguably unhelpful to feel that these aspects of life are in competition, because this means that life is lived in a state of anxiety about gains and losses. The findings of this research (and other studies) challenge the need for mothers to feel (and potentially transmit) generalised guilt because of a belief that by working they are prejudicing outcomes for their children. Recent research also finds that so-called 'helicopter parenting', (parents, usually mothers, hovering over their children) has links with negative outcomes on self-efficacy that indirectly negatively affects mental health and physical wellbeing (Reed et al, 2016). With this evidence in mind, and given that many mother–daughter relationships are emotionally supportive, this prompts the thought that it may be helpful for mothers to make visible to their daughters their practical strategies and ways in which they have managed their feelings about combining a career with motherhood. In addition, mothers talking about their personal experience could also help change beliefs about what constitutes good mothering by challenging the cultural scripts that are becoming more draconian.

Implications for families: partners

Led by my sample, my findings have been focused on fathers. However, the implications of these findings are relevant to all partnerships in parenting. Thinking about Hochschild's (1983, p 44) idea about 'emotion management', there was in this study evidence of negative emotions simmering beneath the surface in relationships because of perceptions about an unfair distribution of domestic labour. This was evident among most partnerships, even some of those where the partner had more egalitarian attitudes. One observation arising from my findings is that women who argue for joint parenting will also need to be prepared to make more room for fathers to be fully involved. Those who want to be involved fathers need to be prepared and encouraged to make adjustments to their working practices and/or to switch roles to become primary parent. Partners who are parents often do not seem to engage in sufficiently re-evaluating whether both parties are getting what they want and need from work and family life, as events unfold. On a family level, implications are that it would be helpful to broaden the practical day-to-day negotiations about who is doing what to include periodic reviews of aspirations for work and life in order to arrive at strategies for fulfilling this, given that demands and opportunities presented by careers change from year to year. Indeed, as some of my participants noted, this could be far less emotionally bruising to relationships than the alternative of day-to-day negotiations.

Implications for organisations and social policy

Flexible working

One explanation of the dominance of the daughters' part-time narrative in my research is that most of the daughters are uninformed about alternative ways of working. Most conceptualise their choices as being between full-time and part-time work. An implication is that it would be helpful for a broader debate to be had within companies (and perhaps also within families) about potential options, in advance of parenthood and involving both men and women. Recognising and acting upon the fact that many career women are anxious about how to manage career and motherhood, even in advance of becoming pregnant, might help women experience more of the choice that many, unaware of the constraints they face, currently believe that they have.

However, organisations continue to grapple with ways of offering flexibility and autonomy in senior career roles, especially for women in the mid-career stage that often coincides with having children (Kellliher and Anderson, 2010; Young, 2017). This suggests that more progressive solutions are needed to achieve the flexibility and predictability parents want and to match this with the needs of an organisation.

The lack of gender parity at all levels of organisations has social and economic costs that are increasingly well recorded and accepted. When women cut their hours, or are switched into support roles – which make less of a contribution to the earnings or output of an organisation – this has a cost in terms of the loss of potential income, and the loss of the investment an organisation has made in training professional and managerial employees. Studies from management consultancies have attempted to quantify this cost. McKinsey Global Institute (2016) argue that bridging the gender gap in the UK has the potential to add £150 billion to GDP by 2025. They calculate that 38% of this figure will be delivered by increasing female participation in the labour force, 35% through women working in more productive sectors (for example in STEM roles) and 27% through an increase in women's working hours by an average of 25–30 minutes a day. PwC's (2016) report on women returners shows that 500,000 professional women are currently taking extended career breaks and that when women return to work after childbirth 65% of them work below their potential. PwC suggests that improving initiatives to get professional women back into high-quality work roles will increase annual earnings in business by £4,000 per woman.

In this context it is surprising that negotiating ways of working after childbirth is seen as an issue for the individual. Young's (2017) research into the experiences of women in managerial and professional careers pioneering flexible working, shows that both organisations and individual women believe that the responsibility for finding ways to reduce or compress hours, and to make that arrangement work, tends to rest with the employee. Moreover, when the arrangements do not work well women tend to blame themselves or the 'nature of the job'. Young's compelling argument is that high-skill roles need to be redesigned collectively, led by organisations, who have the capabilities and the insight into what the business requires (something that is often overlooked in discussions about flexible roles). Redesigning the role is a more sustainable solution that can adapt to changes in personnel, the ebb and flow of business needs, and the pressure points experienced by a parent over time (Young, 2017, p 151). Most research on flexible working is done with women. This is indicative of the fact that men tend to face censure for seeking flexible working to facilitate their desire to be involved fathers (Williams et al, 2013; Gatrell et al, 2014). Making a success of flexible working also means actively encouraging fathers to participate – and not penalising their career progress when they do.

Inclusive workplaces

Another imperative to create a more sustainable inclusive workplace is to acknowledge that there is a growing body of evidence to suggest that women's definitions of career success, and their approaches to an organisational career, require different ways of encouraging their talent. For example, roles could be redesigned in a way that allows for a team, rather than an individual to take responsibility for outcomes. A simple policy could be timing management meetings to avoid the end-of-day rush to meet family responsibilities. Moreover, it would be beneficial to challenge current norms concerning the age at which individuals are expected to progress upwards in organisations. This is obviously a particular issue for women, given the age at which it is most common to have children. Setting a longer timeframe for the achievement of career milestones will be consistent with the increasing length of women's careers, given their retirement age will be 66 by 2020. There is also a clear need for men and women to collaborate in changing workplace culture to be more inclusive and to make the most of the different skills and approaches and ambitions that men and women bring. Ideas to implement in order to change workplace culture are suggested by Maheas (2016) and Armstrong (2016). These ideas are based upon building understanding, respect and stronger relationships between male and female colleagues in order to improve working lives, outputs, access to sponsorship and women's progress to the top of careers. Overall, my point is that the intertwined nature of caring responsibilities and work needs to be acknowledged and reflected upon by organisations so that it becomes part of an organisation's mandated policy to address the implications of domestic responsibilities in order to transform gendered inequalities. It is not enough for gender equality to be positioned as a matter for individual action.

Childcare

The availability and cost of childcare is a problem that is more acute for working parents in the UK than in other European countries, and more acute in London than in the rest of the UK (Ben-Galim and Thompson, 2013; Family and Childcare Trust, 2016). In the UK, the cost of childcare for two children under the age of five is estimated to account for a huge 28% of median household income (Fawcett Society, 2016c). The Institute for Fiscal Studies (IFS) suggests that there is a lack of clarity in government about the aims, objectives and rationale for state intervention in the provision of nursery care (IFS, 2015).

A potential strategy would be to incentivise workplaces to provide more in-house care by contributing to start-up costs or facilitating the availability of suitable sites. Less than 10% of employers currently offer on-site nursery provision and much of this is biased to the public sector (Department of Education, 2013). In terms of parental leave, more progressive policy solutions are suggested that mimic policies in Sweden and Iceland of allocating a substantial period of leave to fathers as a non-transferrable right. This would assist in reframing childcare as an issue for both parents. The gender equality lobby group the Fawcett Society recommends that men who take time off to look after children should be entitled to the same pay and amount of leave as women (Fawcett Society, 2016b). Moreover, offering greater rights to paid parental leave for fathers will help challenge the persistent association between motherhood and being primarily responsible for children, from which gender inequalities persist.

A reframing of the debate about childcare from a women's issue to an issue for both parents is likely to help men become the more involved parents many now want to be (Ben-Galim and Thompson, 2013). This has been argued for many years but perhaps the growing evidence that many men do aspire to egalitarian parenting makes it more plausible that change will come. A possible action is to continue to change the language used in workplaces to challenge gender stereotyping of childcare as a women's issue. Indeed, some, such as The Ms. Foundation in the US, are arguing that the achievement of the aims of feminism means those organising politically or in lobby groups under this umbrella need to widen their campaign to achieve gender equality for all genders. There is certainly good reason to make the achievement of gender equality in the workplace and at home an issue for equal personhood, not just for women in professional and managerial careers, at the heart of feminist thinking, as it was in the 1970s and 1980s.

Summary of recommendations

The main recommendations informed by this research are:

- Disseminate the finding that daughters are not ill affected by their mothers working mainly or close to full-time hours and therefore generalised guilty maternal feelings derived from working are misplaced.
- Communicate the five steps identified by daughters that made their mothers' work, work for them.

- It would be of benefit for mothers with careers to openly challenge the contemporary cultural scripts propelling young mothers into substantially cutting their working hours.
- Mothers with careers are well placed to encourage career ambition by talking about achieving success at work in a way that motivates women and encompasses motherhood, rather than framing it as happening in spite of motherhood.
- More successful ways of making career roles work flexibly are more likely to be achieved by organisations and individuals working together to redesign jobs.
- Organisations should consider discussing potential options for flexible working in advance of, and unrelated to, parenthood with both men and women.
- Organisations' definitions of successful career milestones need to stretch in time to take account of childbearing years.
- Organisations would benefit from mandating initiatives designed to challenge biases within workplace culture to be more inclusive for women and to benefit men too.
- It would benefit 'emotion management' (Hochschild, 1983, p 44) in families to deliberately plan the sharing of caring in the context of relatively short-term career aims and opportunities, rather than working it out on a day-to-day basis.
- Public policy on childcare needs to be reframed to be an issue for both parents and a social issue.
- Good, affordable, convenient childcare is a key enabler of female careers across the social spectrum.
- We should take up again the second wave feminist emphasis on policy being informed by equal moral personhood to challenge the widening socioeconomic gulf where the gains of the few are at the expense of the many.

Concluding remarks

The debate between women about whether relatively long hours spent working in high-level careers is damaging to their children has been raging for generations and will be hard to challenge. Therefore it seems important to reiterate that the vast majority of the daughters judged that they did not need a constant maternal presence to feel well loved and well mothered. All the career women interviewed for this research worked thoughtfully, as eloquently described by this 'daughter mother' participant:

"I think work has probably become more important to me since having children because before it didn't have any meaning in relation to anything else ... Before I just did it in a much more unthinking way. Now I work very thoughtfully because I think it gives me different things. A sense of myself that's separate from my children and my life as a mother."

The following expressive words, spoken by one of the older generation of mothers, represent an important theme running through this book, about the importance of their children to these mothers who also had absorbing and satisfying careers. For them, their careers are the stuff of their everyday lives and their children are "extraordinary":

"Feeding her one afternoon, listening to some music we had often played, I had the saddest feeling of coming to the end of a magical 'other time' and returning to my long established reality of work. To this day (and two other daughters later) the fact of having had and raised them seems slightly marvellous and extraordinary. Whereas the stuff of my daily work seems an absolute given, as much as knowing my own name."

Improving the way in which work is reconciled with caring for children, in social policy, in workplaces and in families, is critical to ensuring that there are opportunities for women to occupy the highest occupational levels and thus advance the achievement of wider gender equality for both men and women in their family and working lives. This is likely to be beneficial both to the life satisfaction of individuals and to the economy. The voices of those arguing that being a 'good mother' means 'being there' by working substantially reduced hours seem to be louder than those expressing other points of view. It is hoped that the evidence of this research encourages mothers, and those who are anticipating motherhood, to question assumptions that part-time work inevitably 'gives you the best of both worlds' and assert with confidence that being committed to a career can be consistent with being committed to your family and being thought of by your children as a good enough mother.

Appendix 1:
Study design and method

Research questions

The research questions for my doctoral research, upon which this book is based, were:

- What impact did growing up with a mother with a career who worked mainly full-time have on the daughters' thinking about combining motherhood with work compared to other influences?
- Did observing their mothers work long hours result in the daughters wanting to work fewer hours?
- To what extent did being mothered by women with successful careers encourage their daughters to aspire to high-level positions themselves?

Methods

Prior to the interviews, participants were asked to complete one of three online questionnaires that were tailored to the generations of daughters, mothers and 'daughter mothers'. The questionnaires recorded biographical detail on maternity leave, relationship status, work history and childcare arrangements made for preschool, primary and secondary school years. It recorded attitudes towards work, gender roles and working motherhood, replicating questions from the Women and Employment Survey and the British Social Attitudes Survey (see Crompton, 2006; Scott et al, 2008). The daughters were asked to rate sources of influence over their choice of career and the mothers to record how much they had enjoyed work at different periods of their lives. The 60 questionnaires were invaluable in providing a common context for each interview and the topic guide was tailored to seek explanations for the answers given. Both mothers and daughters were also asked questions that mirrored each other and invited neither a positive nor negative response. The questions asked them to 'make some notes on any events or feelings that stand out for you in relation to being/having a working mother and tell me how old you/your daughter was at each of these times'. 'Daughter mothers', and their mothers, were also asked to include comments relating to becoming a mother/grandmother. This pre-task was used to compare and contrast the memories and emotions of mothers and daughters.

The primary research method used in this study was qualitative, narrative biographical interviews with both mothers and daughters. The interviews were conducted separately and then both mother and daughter, with their express permission, were brought together for a joint interview. This method was chosen because intergenerational research is particularly complex. Intergenerational research needs to illuminate change in the social context as well as individuals and relationships in change (Brannen, 2003; Thomson et al, 2011). Participants' views are affected by how the present shapes their telling of the past and the interpretive contexts available according to their position in the generational hierarchy. Participants need to be given the time and space to reflect both upon similarities and upon differences between the generations, and upon their own past, present and imagined future. As Thomson et al put it: 'the qualitative paradigm demands that we take seriously the process through which meanings are made and remade through changing configurations of agents and resources' (Thomson et al, 2011, p vi.). The selection of individual in-depth and joint interviews was influenced by the idea of 'configuration', derived from the work of Norbert Elias (1978). Elias suggested that one's sense of personal identity is closely connected to the 'we' and 'they' relationships within one's group (1978, p 128). I was able to access several social positions among the interview participants: their personal points of view, their commentary upon their relationships with each other, and their joint points of view that emerged from a conversation between the mother and daughter, and myself, the interviewer. The interviews were semi-structured in order to ensure that the same broad topic areas were covered with each of the participants while also facilitating reflective conversations led by the individual participants. The interviews were also tailored specifically to cover issues raised in the pre-tasks and more generally to reflect the different life stages of the generations of daughters, mothers and 'daughter mothers'.

Analysis

My approach to the analysis drew on the thinking of Miles and Huberman (1994) that the process of analysis starts with the approach to data collection and continues through the coding of the data and the thinking that takes place during the process of writing. The aspect of the research analysis specifically concerned with the coding of the data on NVivo 10 was informed by, rather than applied, Grounded

Theory (Strauss and Corbin, 1998), meaning that the research data was primarily analysed inductively in order to allow themes to emerge from the data and avoid bias as much as possible. In addition, a deductive approach was employed in adding some top-level codes informed by the literature review of the social and psychological phenomena that may or may not be found to be actors in the narrative accounts of the participants in this study and to establish a clear link between the research objectives and the findings.

NVivo 10 has limited analytical tools and the process of entering data can become mechanistic and get in the way of analytical thinking (Welsh, 2002). I circumvented these potential problems by manual coding (meaning writing memos on my observations as the fieldwork took place) and by printing out and visualising on paper connections between the codes and characteristics of the participants. This process stimulated recoding as deeper patterns emerged and informed ideas during the writing up of the research.

Ethical approval

Ethical approval for this research was granted by the C-REC (Ethical Review Committee) at the University of Sussex.

Appendix 2:
Table of participants

Pair	Mother	Daughter(s)
1. Alison and Ashley	Marketing director	Recent graduate (looking for work at time of interview)
2. Bridget and Beth	Doctor	Media
3. Christina and Chloe	Lawyer	Academic
4. Deborah and Diana	Retail business owner	Final year university
5. Eve and Emily	Doctor	Recent graduate (looking for work at time of interview)
6. Faith, Fiona and Florence (twins)	Lawyer	One in finance, one in marketing
7. Gayle and Gina	Director of a private sector consultancy	Recent graduate (looking for work at time of interview)
8. Harriet and Hannah	Education (retired)	Teacher Two children under the age of three
9. Imogen and Isabelle	Lawyer	Official in education
10. Jan and Jessica	Managing director of a private sector company	Final year university
11. Karen and Kelly	Teacher	Educational psychologist One child under the age of one.
12. Leah and Lily	Therapist	Academic Three children, youngest under the age of five.
13. Martha and Megan	CEO, public sector	Marketing
14. Naomi and Natalie	Lawyer	Lawyer
15. Orla and Olivia	Senior management in finance	Final year university
16. Patricia and Paula	Teacher	Dentist Three children under the age of five
17. Rose and Rachel	CEO, public sector	Final year university

18. Stella and Sophie	Academic	Senior manager in education One child under the age of five
19. Tara and Tanya	MD of a media company	Media
20. Una and Ursula	Academic	Health service
21. Valerie and Verity	Senior marketing manager	Academic
22. Wendy and Willow	MD of STEM company	Doctor
23. Xanthe and Xenia	Director, public sector	Final year university
24. Yvette and Yasmin	Company owner, public sector	Final year university
25. Zadie and Zara	Lawyer	Marketing
26. Anita and Amy	Civil service, education (retired)	Health service Two children, one under the age of five
27. Barbara and Belle	Media then portfolio career	Retail management, mainly full-time mother Two children under the age of five
28. Cheryl and Cara	Director of NHS body	Retail One child under the age of five
29. Donna and Denise	Teacher	Director of a marketing consultancy Two children, one aged five
30. Eiona and Elly	CEO in corporate sector	Own business in retail

Biographical details were all correct at the time of interview and have been kept vague because giving specific detail, even of occupations, for mother and daughter risks recognition and therefore would breach confidentiality. Within the legal profession, a judge, an in-house barrister, a partner in a Magic Circle law firm and solicitors were interviewed. Within the medical profession, hospital consultants, junior doctors, GPs, NHS managers and dentists were interviewed. Careers in the commercial sector were in journalism, TV production, retail, brand management, marketing, market research and advertising. Several of the interviewees had founded and run their own businesses employing many other people. Four participants worked in financial roles. From education, school teachers, school inspectors, educational psychologists, academics and researchers were represented. Other public sector careers in the sample included chief executives or directors of local authorities, museums and arts funding organisations. All names are pseudonyms.

References

Acker, J. (2012) 'Gendered organisations and intersectionality', *Equality, diversity and inclusion: An international journal*, 31 (3): 214–224.

Adkins, L. (2002) *Revisions: Gender and sexuality in late modernity*, Buckingham: Open University Press.

Apter, T. E. (1990) *Altered loves: Mothers and daughters during adolescence*, New York: Ballantine Books.

Apter, T. E. (2001) *The myth of maturity*, London: W. W. Norton.

Armstrong, J. (2016) *Collaborating with men: Changing workplace culture to be more inclusive for women* [online]. Available from: www. murrayedwards.cam.ac.uk/sites/default/files/Collaborating with Men - FINAL Report.pdf [accessed 20/10/2016].

Aughinbaugh, A. and Gittleman, M. (2004) 'Maternal employment and adolescent risky behavior', *Journal of Health Economics*, 23(4): 815–38.

Backett-Milburn, K., Harden, J., Maclean, A. and Cunningham-Burley, S. (2011) *Work and family lives: The changing experience of young families* [online]. Available from: www.timescapes.leeds.ac.uk/assets/ files/Final-Reports/final-report-project-5.pdf [accessed 8/2/2015].

Bailey, L. (1999) 'Refracted selves? A study of changes in self-identity in the transition to motherhood', *Sociology*, 33(2): 335–52.

Baker, C. and Cracknell R. (2014) *Women in public life, the professions and the boardroom*, London: House of Commons Library

Baraitser, L. (2008) *Maternal encounters: The ethics of interruption*, London: Routledge.

Baraitser, L. (2009) 'Mothers who make things public', *Feminist Review*, 93: 8–26.

Barnett, R. C., Gareis, K. C. and Brennan, R. T. (2008) 'Wives' shift work schedules and husbands' and wives' well-being in dual earner couples with children', *Journal of Family Issues*, 29: 396–422.

Barsh, J. and Lee, Y. (2012) *Unlocking the potential full potential of women at work* [online]. Available from: https://online.wsj.com/public/ resources/documents/womenreportnew.pdf [accessed 21/1/2016].

Bataille, C. (2014) *Identity in transition: Women's narrative identity work on the path to professional and mother*, DPhil thesis, McGill University, Montreal.

Bates, L. (2014) *Everyday sexism*, London: Simon and Schuster.

Battersby, C. (1998) *The Phenomenal Woman: Feminist Metaphysics and the Patterns of Identity*, London/New York: Routledge.

Baxter, J. and Smart D. (2011) *Fathering in Australia among couple families with young children* [online]. Available from: http://ssrn.com/abstract=1776522 [accessed 8/5/2015].

Beatty, C. A. (1996) 'The stress of managerial and professional women: is the price too high?' *Journal of Organizational Behaviour*, 17(3): 223–51.

Beck, U. (1992) *Risk society: Towards a new modernity*, London: Sage.

Beck, U. and Beck-Gernsheim, E. (2002) *Individualization*, London: Sage.

Becker, J. C. and Wright, S. C. (2011) 'Yet another dark side of chivalry: benevolent sexism undermines and hostile sexism motivates collective action for social change', *Journal of Personality and Social Psychology*, 101(1): 62–77.

Bem, S. L. (1981) *Bem sex-role inventory*, Palo Alto, CA: Consulting Psychologists Press.

Ben-Galim, D. and Thompson, S. (2013) *Who's breadwinninng? Working mothers and the new face of family support* [online]. Available from www.ippr.org [accessed 8/5/2015].

Benjamin, J. (1995) *Like subjects, love objects: Essays on recognition and sexual difference*, New Haven, CN: Yale University Press.

Bianchi, S. M. (2000) 'Maternal employment and time with children: dramatic change or surprising continuity?' *Demography*, 37(4) 401–14.

Bimrose, J., Watson, M., McMahon, M., Haasler, S., Tomassini, M. and Suzanne, P. (2014) 'The problem with women? Challenges posed by gender for career guidance practice', *International Journal for Educational and Vocational Guidance*, 14(1): 77–88.

Bingham, J. (2015) 'Do-it-all' generation of women suffering work stress epidemic [online]. Available from: www.telegraph.co.uk/women/womens-life/11983974/Do-it-all-generation-of-women-suffering-work-stress-epidemic.html [accessed 30/102016].

Bjerrum Nielsen, H. (2017) *Feeling gender: A generational and psychosocial approach*. London: Palgrave Macmillan.

Bjerrum Nielsen, H. and Rudberg, M. (1994) *Psychological gender and modernity*, Oslo: Scandinavian University Press.

Blair-Loy, M. (2003) *Competing devotions: Career and family among women executives*, Cambridge, MA: Harvard University Press.

Blos, P. (1979) *The adolescent passage: Developmental issues*, New York: International Universities Press.

BoardWatch (2016) Tracking appointments of women directors to FTSE 100 and FTSE 250 companies [online]. Available from: www.boardsforum.co.uk/boardwatch.html [accessed 3/3/2016].

Bohnet, I. (2016) *What works: Gender equality by design*, Cambridge, MA: Belnap Press.

Bostock, J. (2014) *The meaning of success: Insights from women at Cambridge*, Cambridge: Cambridge University Press.

Brannen, J. (2003) 'Towards a typology of intergenerational relationships', *Sociological Research Online*, 8(2) [online]. Available from: www.socresonline.org.uk/8/2/brannen.html [accessed 8/12/2015].

Brannen, J., Moss, P and Mooney, A. (2004) *Working and caring over the twentieth century: Change and continuity in four-generation families*, Basingstoke: Palgrave Macmillan.

Breitenbach, E. (2006) *Gender statistics: An evaluation*, Manchester: Equal Opportunities Commission.

Broadbridge, A. M., Maxwell, G. A. and Ogden, S. M. (2007) 'Experiences, perceptions and expectations of retail employment for Generation Y', *Career Development International*, 12(6) 523–44.

Burgess, A. (2011) *Family man: British fathers' journey to the centre of the kitchen* [online]. Available from: http://bit.ly/1rdtry8 [accessed 17/7/2014].

Burke, R. J. and Mattis, M. C. (2005) *Supporting women's career advancement*, Cheltenham: Edward Elgar.

Butler, J. (1990) *Gender trouble: Feminism and the subversion of identity*, London: Routledge.

Cahusac, E. and Kanji, S. (2014) 'Giving up: how gendered organizational cultures push mothers out', *Gender, Work and Organization*, 21(1): 57–70.

Callender, C. (1997) *Maternity rights and benefits in Britain 1996*, London: The Stationery Office.

Carter, N. M. and Silva, C. (2010) *Mentoring: Necessary but insufficient for advancement* [online]. Available from: www.catalyst.org/system/files/Mentoring_Necessary_But_Insufficient_for_Advancement_Final_120610.pdf [accessed 3/3/2016].

Catalyst (2016) 'Working parents' [online]. Available from: www.catalyst.org/knowledge/working-parents [accessed 3/5/2016].

CFWD (2014) *Sex and Power 2014: Who runs Britain* [online]. Available from: www.cfwd.org.uk/uploads/Sex_and_PowerV4%20FINAL.pdf2014.pdf [accessed 18/1/2016].

CFWD (2015) *Sex and Power 2015: Who runs Britain* [online]. Available from: www.cfwd.org.uk/uploads/Sex and Power.pdf [accessed 18/1/2016].

Chambers Student (2014) '2014 Gender in the law survey' [online]. Available from: www.chambersstudent.co.uk/where-to-start/newsletter/2014-gender-in-the-law-survey [accessed 18/1/2016].

Chodorow, N. (1978) *Reproduction of mothering: Psychoanalysis and the sociology of gender*, Berkeley, CA: University of California Press.

Christopher, K. (2012) 'Extensive mothering: employed mothers' constructions of the good mother', *Gender & Society*, 26(1): 73–96.

CIPD (2015) 'Part-time workers' [online]. Available from: www.cipd.co.uk/hr-inform/employment-law/employees-and-workers/part-time-workers/indepth.aspx [accessed 4/8/2016].

CMI (2016) 'A broken pipeline' [online]. Available from: www.managers.org.uk/campaigns/gender-salary-survey [accessed 8/2/2017].

Coffman, J. and Neuenfeldt, B. (2014) 'Everyday moments of truth' [online]. Available from: www.bain.com/publications/articles/everyday-moments-of-truth.aspx [accessed 1/3/2015].

Connolly, S. and Gregory, M. (2008) 'Moving down: women's part-time work and occupational change in Britain 1991–2001', *The Economic Journal*, 118(526): 52–76.

Cosslett, R. (2013) 'The myth of female elites and the XX factor' [online]. Available from: www.theguardian.com/commentisfree/2013/apr/26/myth-female-elites-xx-factor [accessed 27/9/2013].

Crompton, R. (2006) *Employment and the family*, Cambridge: Cambridge University Press.

Crompton, R. and Harris, F. (1998) 'Explaining women's employment patterns: "Orientations to work" revisited', *The British Journal of Sociology*, 49(1): 118–36.

Crompton, R. and Le Feuvre, N. (2000) 'Gender, family and employment in comparative perspective', *Journal of European Social Policy*, 10: 334–48.

Crompton, R. and Lyonette, C. (2008) 'Mother's employment, work-life conflict, careers and class', in J. Scott, S. Dex and H. Joshi (eds) *Women and employment*, Cheltenham: Edward Elgar, pp 283–308.

Cunningham, M. (2001) 'Parental influences on the gendered division of housework', *American Sociological Review*, 66(2): 184–203.

Damaske, S. and French, A. (2016) 'Women's work pathways across the life course', *Demography*, 53(2): 365–91.

Davidson, M. J. and Burke, R. J. (2011) *Women in management worldwide*, Farnham: Ashgate Publishing.

Davis, S. N. (2007) 'Gender ideology construction from adolescence to young adulthood', *Social Science Research*, 36(3): 1021–41.

Department of Education (2013) *Childcare and early years providers survey 2013* [online]. Available from: https://www.gov.uk/government/statistics/childcare-and-early-years-providers-survey-2013 [accessed 16/6/2015].

Dermott, E. and Miller, T. (2015) 'More than the sum of its parts? Contemporary fatherhood policy, practice and discourse', *Families, Relationships and Societies*, 4(2): 183–95.

Dex, S., Ward, K. and Joshi, H. (2006) *Changes in women's occupations and occupational mobility over 25 years*, London: Centre for Longitudinal Studies, Institute of Education.

Doucet, A. (2006) *Do men mother? Fathering, care, and domestic responsibility*, Toronto: University of Toronto Press.

Drew, E. and Murtagh, E. M. (2005) 'Work/life balance: senior management champions or laggards?' *Women in Management Review*, 20(4): 262–78.

Duncan, S. (2006) 'Mother's work–life balance: individual preferences or cultural construction?' in D. Perrons and C. Fagan (eds) *Gender divisions and working time in the new economy*, Cheltenham: Edward Elgar, pp 127–47.

Durbin, S., Fleetwood, S. and Tomlinson, J. (2010a) 'Female part-time managers' *Equality, Diversity and Inclusion: An International Journal*, 29(3): 255–70.

Durbin, S., Fleetwood, S., Wilton, N. and Purcell, K. (2010b) 'The impact of partnership and family-building on the early careers of female graduates in the UK', *Equality, Diversity and Inclusion: An International Journal*, 29(3): 271–88.

Eagly, A. and Carli, L. (2007) *Through the labyrinth: The truth about how women become leaders*, Boston, MA: Harvard Business School Press.

Eagly, A. H. and Karau, S. J. (2002) 'Role congruity theory of prejudice toward female leaders', *Psychological Review*, 109: 573–98.

Edwards, R., Gillies, V. and Ribbens McCarthy, J. (2012) 'The politics of concepts: family and its (putative) replacements', *British Journal of Sociology*, 63(4): 730–46.

EHRC (2009) *Working better: Fathers, family and work* [online]. Available from: www.equalityhumanrights.com/sites/default/files/documents/research/41_wb_fathers_family_and_work.pdf [accessed 17/7/2014].

Eichenbaum, L. and Orbach, S. (1983) *Understanding women*, Harmondsworth: Penguin.

Elias, N. (1978) *What is sociology?* New York: Columbia University Press.

Ellison, L., Barker, A. and Kulasuriya, T. (2009) *Work and care: A study of modern parents* [online]. Available from: www.equalityhumanrights.com/sites/default/files/documents/research/15._work_and_care_modern_parents_15_report.pdf [accessed 17/7/2014].

Ely, R. J., Stone, P and Ammerman, C. (2014) 'Rethink what you "know" about high-achieving women' [online]. Available from: https://hbr.org/2014/12/rethink-what-you-know-about-high-achieving-women [accessed 6/12/2014].

Epstein, C. F. and Kalleberg, A. L. (2004) *Fighting for time: Shifting boundaries of work and social life*, New York: Russell Sage Foundation.

Eräranta, K. and Moisander, J. (2011) 'Psychological regimes of truth and father identity: challenges for work/life integration', *Organization Studies*, 32(4) 509–26.

ESRC (2013) 'Modern fatherhood' [online]. Available from: www. modernfatherhood.org [accessed 17/7/2014].

Fagan, C. McDowell, L., Perrons, D., Ray, K. and Ward, K. (2008) 'Class differences in mothers' work schedules and assessments of their "work-life balance" in dual earner couples in Britain', in J. Scott (ed) *Women and Employment*, Cheltenham: Edward Elgar, pp 199–212.

Faircloth, C. (2014) 'Intensive parenting and the expansion of parenting', in E. Lee, J. Bristow, C. Faircloth and J. Macvarish (eds). *Parenting culture studies*, Basingstoke: Palgrave Macmillan, pp 25–50.

Faludi, S. (1992) *Backlash: The undeclared war against women*, London: Random House.

Family and Childcare Trust (2016) '2016 childcare survey' [online]. Available from: https://www.familyandchildcaretrust.org/childcare-survey-2016-0 [accessed 18/1/2017].

Fawcett Society (2016a) *Gender issues poll* [online]. Available from: http://survation.com/wp-content/uploads/2016/01/Fawcett-Tables-MF-s5611.pdf [accessed 28/1/2016].

Fawcett Society (2016b) *Sex equality: State of the nation* [online]. Available from: www.fawcettsociety.org.uk/wp-content/uploads/2016/01/Sex-equality-state-of-the-nation-230116.pdf [accessed 30/1/2016].

Fawcett Society (2016c) *Parents, work and care: Striking the balance* [online]. Available from: www.fawcettsociety.org.uk/wp-content/uploads/2016/03/Parents-Work-and-Care-2016.pdf [accessed 7/11/2016].

Fels, A. (2004) 'Do women lack ambition?', *Harvard Business Review*, 82(4): 50–60.

Finch, J. (2007) 'Displaying families', *Sociology*, 41(1): 65–81.

Fink, J. and Gabb, J. (2014) 'Configuring generations: cross–displinary perspectives', *Families, Relationships and Societies*, 3(3): 459–63.

Furedi, F. (2002) *Paranoid parenting: Why ignoring the experts may be best for your child*, Chicago: Chicago Review Press.

Gagnon, J. D. (2016) 'Born to fight': The university experiences of the daughters of single mothers who are first-generation students in the United Kingdom, DPhil thesis, University of Sussex.

Galinsky, E. (1999) *Ask the children: What America's children really think about working parents*, New York: William Morrow.

Gambles, R., Lewis, S. and Rapoport, R. (2006) *The myth of work-life balance: The challenge of our time for men, women and societies*, Chichester: John Wiley.

Gardiner, J. and Tomlinson, J. (2009) 'Organisational approaches to flexible working', *Equal Opportunities International*, 28(8): 671–86.

Gareis, K. C. and Barnett, R. C. (2002) 'Under what conditions do long work hours affect psychological distress', *Journal of Health and Social Behaviour*, 45: 115–31.

Garey, A. I. (1999) *Weaving work and motherhood*, Philadelphia, PA: Temple University Press.

Gatrell, C. (2005) *Hard labour: The sociology of parenthood, family life and career*, Maidenhead: Open University Press.

Gatrell, C. (2007) 'A fractional commitment: part-time working and the maternal body', *International Journal of Human Resource Management*, 18(3): 462–75.

Gatrell, C. (2008) *Embodying women's work*, Maidenhead: Open University Press.

Gatrell, C. (2013) 'Maternal body work: how women managers and professionals negotiate pregnancy and new motherhood at work', *Human Relations*, 66(5): 621–44.

Gatrell, C., Burnett, S. B., Cooper, C. L. and Sparrow, P. (2014) 'Parents, perceptions and belonging: exploring flexible working among UK fathers and mothers', *British Journal of Management*, 25(3): 473–87.

Gatrell, C., Burnett, S. B., Cooper, C. L. and Sparrow, P. (2015) 'The price of love: the prioritisation of childcare and income earning among UK fathers', *Families, Relationships and Societies*, 4(2): 225–88.

General Medical Council (2012) *The state of medical education and practice in the UK* [online]. Available from: www.gmc-uk.org/The_state_of_medical_education_and_practice_in_the_UK_2012_0912.pdf_49843330.pdf [accessed 2/04/12].

Gerson, K. (2011) *The unfinished revolution*, Oxford: Oxford University Press.

Gibson-Beverly, G. and Schwartz, J. P. (2008) 'Attachment, entitlement, and the impostor phenomenon in female graduate students', *Journal of College Counseling*, 11(2): 119–32.

Giddens, A. (1991) *Modernity and self-identity*, Cambridge: Polity Press.

Gill, R. (2007) 'Postfeminist media culture: elements of a sensibility', *European Journal of Cultural Studies*, 10(2): 147–66.

Gill, R. and Orgad, S. (2015) 'The confidence cult(ure) ', *Australian Feminist Studies*, 30(86): 324–44.

Gill, R., Kelan, E and Scharff, C. (2017) 'A postfeminist sensibility at work', *Gender, Work and Organisation*, 24(3): 226–244.

Gillies, V. (2003) *Family and intimate relationships: A review of the sociological research* [online]. Available from: www1.lsbu.ac.uk/ahs/downloads/families/familieswp2.pdf [accessed 2/2/2017].

Gilligan, C. (1982) *In a different voice: Psychological theory and women's development*, Cambridge, MA: Harvard University Press.

Gilligan, C. (2011) *Joining the resistance*, Cambridge, MA: Polity Press.

Glick, P. and Fiske, S. T. (1997) 'Hostile and benevolent sexism: measuring ambivalent sexist attitudes towards women', *Psychology of Women Quarterly*, 21(1): 119–35.

Golombok, S. (2015) *Modern families: Parents and children in new family forms*, Cambridge: Cambridge University Press.

González Durántez, M. (2013) 'Why I'm calling on brilliant British women to go back to school', *The Telegraph* [online]. Available from: www.telegraph.co.uk/women/womens-life/10360903/Miriam-Clegg-Why-Im-calling-on-brilliant-British-women-to-go-back-to-school.html [accessed 9/10/2013].

Gottfredson, L. (1981) 'Circumscription and compromise: A developmental theory of occupational aspirations', *Journal of Counseling Psychology*, 28(6): 545–79.

GOV.UK (2013) 'School workforce in England: November 2012' [online]. Available from: www.gov.uk/government/statistics/school-workforce-in-england-november-2012 [accessed 18/1/2016].

Greer, G. (1970) *The female eunuch*, London: MacGibbon & Kee.

Gurley-Brown, H. (1982) *Having it all: Love, success, sex, money even if you're starting with nothing*, New York,: Simon and Schuster.

Hadfield, L., Rudoe, N. and Sanderson-Mann, J. (2007) 'Motherhood, choice and the British media', *Gender and Education*, 19(2): 255–63.

Harris, A. (2003) *Future girl: Young women in the twenty-first century*, New York: Routledge.

Hay Group (2014) *Women in Whitehall: Culture, leadership, talent* [online]. Available from: www.gov.uk/government/uploads/system/uploads/attachment_data/file/351195/Rpt-GMA-Cabinet_Office-Talented_Women-Final_Report___9.5.14_.pdf [accessed 3/4/2016].

Hays, S. (1996) *The cultural contradictions of motherhood*, New Haven, CT: Yale University Press.

Hewlett, S. A. (2003) 'Executive women and the myth of having it all', *Harvard Business Review*, 84(12): 49–59.

Hewlett, S. A. and Marshall, M. (2014) *Women want five things* [online]. Available from: www.talentinnovation.org/publication. cfm?publication=1451 [accessed 3/2/2015].

Himmelweit, S. and Sigala, M. (2004) 'Choice and the relationship between identities and behaviour for mothers with pre-school children', *Journal of Social Policy*, 33(3): 455–78.

Hochschild, A. (1983) *Managed heart: Commercialization of human feeling*, Berkeley, CA: California University Press.

Hochschild, A. and Machung, A. (1990) *The second shift: Working parents and the revolution at home*, London: Piatkus.

Hochschild, A. (2003) *The time bind: When work becomes home and home becomes work*, 2nd edition, Toledo, OH: Owls Books.

Horner, M. (1972) 'Towards an understanding of achievement-related conflicts in women', *Journal of Social Issues*, 28(2): 157–74.

HSE (2015) 'Work related stress, anxiety and depression statistics in GB 2014–5' [online]. Available from: www.hse.gov.uk/statistics/causdis/stress/index.htm [accessed 30/10/2016].

Institute for Employment Studies (1995) 'Women in the labour market: Two decades of change and continuity' Available from: www.employment-studies.co.uk/system/files/resources/files/294.pdf [accessed 26/4/2013].

Institute for Fiscal Studies (2015) *Green budget* [online]. Available from: www.ifs.org.uk/budgets/gb2014/gb2014_ch8.pdf [accessed 12/6/2015].

Jacobs, J. A. and Gerson, K. (2004) *The time divide: Work, family, and gender inequality*, Cambridge, MA: Harvard University Press.

James, L. (2015) 'Women's work orientations: a study of young women without dependent children', *Families, Relationships and Societies*, 4(3): 401–16.

Joshi, A., Dencker, J. C., Franz, G. and Martocchio, J. J. (2010) 'Unpacking generational identities in organizations', *Academy of Management Review*, 35(3): 392–414.

Kanji, S. (2011) 'What keeps mothers in full-time employment?', *European Sociological Review*, 27(4): 509–25.

Kanji, S. and Schober, P. (2014) 'Are couples with young children more likely to split up when the mother is the main or an equal earner?', *Sociology*, 48(1): 38–58.

Kay, K. and Shipman, C. (2014) *The Confidence Code*, New York: HarperCollins.

Kehily, M. J. and Thomson, R. (2011) 'Figuring families: generation, situation and narrative', *Sociological Research Online*, 16(4) article 16.

Kelan, E. K. (2009) *Performing gender at work*, Basingstoke: Palgrave Macmillan.

Kelan, E. K. (2012) *Rising stars*, Basingstoke: Palgrave Macmillan.

Kelan, E. K. (2015) *Linchpin: Men, middle managers and gender inclusive leadership* [online]. Available from: www.som.cranfield.ac.uk/som/dinamic-content/research/Linchpin.pdf [accessed 2/2/2015].

Kelan, E. K. and Mah, A. (2014) 'Gendered identification: between idealization and admiration', *British Journal of Management*, 25(1): 91–101.

Kelliher, C. and Anderson, D. (2010) 'Doing more with less? Flexible working practices and the intensification of work', *Human Relations*, 63(1): 83–106.

Kirby, J. (2012) 'Clegg's not going to give her a helping hand', *The Telegraph* [online]. Available from: www.telegraph.co.uk/women/womens-life/9675110/Nick-Clegg-is-not-going-to-give-working-mothers-a-helping-hand.html [accessed 24/11/2012].

Kodz, J., Davis, S., Lain, D., Strebler, M., Rick, J., Bates, P., Cummings, J. and Meager, N. (2003) *Working long hours: A review of the evidence*, London: Institute for Employment Studies.

KPMG and 30% Club (2016) *The Think Future study* [online]. Available from: https://30percentclub.org/assets/uploads/UK/Research/Think_Future_Study_Final.pdf [accessed 9/7/2016].

Kray, L., Thomson, L. and Galinsky, A. (2001) 'Battle of the sexes', *Journal of Personality and Social Psychology*, 80(6): 942–58

Laney, E. K., Carruthers, L., Lewis Hall, M. E. and Anderson, T. (2014) 'Expanding the self: motherhood and identity development in faculty women', *Journal of Family Issues*, 35(9): 1227–51.

Lanning, T. (2013) *Great expectations: Exploring the promises of gender equality*, London: IPPR.

Lareau, A. (2011) *Unequal childhoods: Class, race and family life*, Berkeley, CA: University of California Press.

Law Society (2011) *Trends in the solicitor profession: Annual statistical report*, London: Law Society.

Lawler, S. (2000) *Mothering the self: Mothers, daughters and identity*, London: Routledge.

Lee, E., Bristow, J., Faircloth, C. and Macvarish, J. (2014) *Parenting culture studies*, Basingstoke: Palgrave Macmillan.

Lewis, J. (2010) *Work–family balance, gender and policy*, Cheltenham: Edward Elgar.

Lewis, P. (2014) 'Postfeminism, femininities and organization studies: exploring a new agenda', *Organization Studies*, 35(12): 1845–66.

Lewis, P. and Simpson, R. (2017) 'Hakim revisited: preference, choice and the postfeminist gender regime', *Gender, Work & Organization*, 24(2): 115–33.

Lorber, J. (2010) *Gender inequality: Feminist theories and politics* (4th edn), Oxford: Oxford University Press.

Lyonette, C. and Crompton, R. (2015) 'Sharing the load? Partners' relative earnings and the division of domestic labour', *Work, Employment and Society*, 29 (1): 23–40.

Lyonette, C., Crompton, R. and Wall, K. (2007) 'Gender, occupational class and work–life conflict', *Community, Work & Family*, 10(3): 283–308.

Maheas, M.-C. (2016) *Gender balance, when men step up*, Paris: Eyrolles.

Mainiero, L. A. and Sullivan, S. E. (2005) 'Kaleidoscope careers: an alternate explanation for the opt-out revolution', *The Academy of Management Executive (1993–2005)*, 19(1): 106–123.

McKinsey (2012) *Women Matter* [online]. Available from: www. mckinsey.com/business-functions/organization/our-insights/women-matter [accessed 18/1/2016].

McKinsey & Company and Lean In (2016) *Women in the workplace 2016* [online]. Available from: https://womenintheworkplace.com [accessed 19/10/2016]

McKinsey Global Institute (2016) *The power of partity: Advancing women's equality in the United Kingdom* [online]. Available from: www.mckinsey. com/global-themes/women-matter/the-power-of-parity-advancing-womens-equality-in-the-united-kingdom [accessed 9/11/2016]

Mannheim, K. (1952) *Essays on the sociology of knowledge*, London: Routledge & Kegan Paul.

Mason, M. A., Wolfinger, N. H., Goulden, M. (2013) *Do babies matter? Gender and family in the ivory tower*, New Brunswick, NJ: Rutgers University Press.

McGinn, K., Ruiz, M. and Lingo, E. (2015) 'Mum's the word! Cross-national effects of maternal employment on gender inequalities at work and at home', Harvard Business School Working Paper, No. 15-094.

McMunn, A. (2011) 'Maternal employment and child socio-emotional behaviour in the UK', *Journal of Epidemiology and Community Health*, 66(7): e19.

McRae, S. (2003) 'Constraints and choices in mothers' employment careers', *British Journal of Sociology*, 54(3): 317–38.

McRobbie, A. (2007) 'Top girls? Young women and the post-feminist sexual contract', *Cultural Studies*, 21(4): 718–37.

McRobbie, A. (2009) *The aftermath of feminism: Gender, culture and social change*, London: Sage.

McRobbie, A. (2013) 'Feminism, the family and the new "mediated" maternalism', *New Formations*, 80–81: 119–37.

Merton, R.K. (1968) *Social theory and social structure*, New York, NY: The Free Press.

Mendolia, S. (2014) *Maternal working hours and the well-being of adolescent children* [online]. Available from: http://ftpiza.org/dp8391.pdf [accessed 25/1/2015].

Meyer, M., Cimpian, A. and Leslie, S.-J. (2015) 'Women are underrepresented in fields where success is believed to require brilliance', *Frontiers in Psychology* [online]. Available from: www.princeton.edu/~sjleslie/Frontiers2015.pdf [accessed 7/7/2015].

Miles, M. B. and Huberman, A. M. (1994) *Qualitative data analysis: An expanded sourcebook* (2nd edn), Thousand Oaks, CA: Sage.

Milkie, M. A., Nomaguchi, K. M. and Denny, K. E. (2015) 'Does the amount of time mothers spend with children or adolescents matter?', *Journal of Marriage and Family*, 77(2): 355–72.

Miller, T. (2005) *Making sense of motherhood: A narrative approach*, Cambridge: Cambridge University Press.

Miller, T. (2011) 'Falling back into gender? Men's narratives and practices around first-time fatherhood', *Sociology*, 45(6): 1094–109.

Miller, T. (2012) 'Balancing caring and paid work in the UK: narrating "choices" as first-time parents', *International Review of Sociology*, 22(1): 39–52.

Moen, P. (2005) 'Beyond the career mystique: "time in", "time out", and "second acts"', *Sociological Forum*, 20(2): 189–208.

Moen, P., Erickson, M. A. and Dempster-McClain, D. (1997) 'Their mother's daughters? The intergenerational transmission of gender attitudes in a world of changing roles', *Journal of Marriage and Family*, 59(2): 281–93.

Morgan, D. (1996) *Family connections*, Cambridge: Polity Press.

Morris, C. (2013) *Intimacy scripts*, DPhil thesis, University of Sussex.

Newman, J. (2014) 'Telling the time: researching generation politics', *Families, Relationships and Societies*, 3(3): 465–68.

Nielsen, L. (2012) *Father-daughter relationships: Contemporary research and issues*, New York: Routledge.

Oakley, B. (2014) *Podium: What shapes a sporting champion*, London: Bloomsbury Sport.

O'Brien, K. M. and Fassinger, R. E. (1993) 'A causal model of the career orientation and career choice of adolescent women', *Journal of Counseling Psychology*, 40(4): 456–69.

Olivetti, C., Patacchini, E. and Zenou, Y. (2013) 'Mothers, friends and gender identity' [online]. Available from: www.nber.org/papers/w19610 [accessed 26/1/2015].

(2010) *Standard Occupational Classification*, Cardiff: Palgrave Macmillan.

ONS (2011a) 'Hours worked in the labour market, 2011' [online]. Available from: www.ons.gov.uk/ons/dcp171776_247259.pdf [accessed 3/9/2014].

ONS (2011b) *Labour market: Social trends 41*, London: ONS.

ONS (2013a) 'Graduates in the UK labour market: 2013', www.ons.gov.uk/employmentandlabourmarket/peopleinwork/employmentandemployeetypes/articles/graduatesintheuklabourmarket/2013-11-19.

ONS (2013b) 'Women in the labour market: 2013', www.ons.gov.uk/employmentandlabourmarket/peopleinwork/employmentandemployeetypes/articles/womeninthelabourmarket/2013-09-25.

ONS (2016a) 'Women shoulder the responsibility of "unpaid work" [online]. Available from: http://visual.ons.gov.uk/the-value-of-your-unpaid-work/ [accessed 11/11/2016].

ONS (2016b) 'Childbearing for women born in different years, england and wales: 2015' [online]. Available from: www.ons.gov.uk/peoplepopulationandcommunity/birthsdeathsandmarriages/conceptionandfertilityrates/bulletins/childbearingforwomenbornindifferentyearsenglandandwales/2015 [accessed 11/11/2016].

ONS ASHE (2012) Table 14.6a [online]. Available from: www.equalityhumanrights.com/sites/default/files/briefing-paper-6-gender-pay-gaps-2012.pdf [accessed 10/4/2014].

Opportunity Now (2014) *Project 28-40: The report* [online]. Available from: http://opportunitynow.bitc.org.uk/sites/default/files/kcfinder/files/Diversity/28-40/Project 28-40 The Report.pdf [accessed 10/4/2014].

Orrange, R. M. (2002) 'Aspiring law and business professionals' orientations to work and family life', *Journal of Family Issues*, 23(2): 287–317.

Parker, R. (1995) *Torn in two: The experience of maternal ambivalence*, London: Virago Press.

Peacock, L. (2013) 'Graduates face toughest job market since depths of recession', *The Telegraph* [online]. Available from: www.telegraph. co.uk/finance/jobs/9798981/Graduates-face-toughest-job-market-since-depths-of-recession.html [accessed 16/4/2014].

Pew Research Center (2015a) 'For most highly educated women, motherhood doesn't start until the 30s' [online]. Available from: www.pewresearch.org/fact-tank/2015/01/15/for-most-highly-educated-women-motherhood-doesnt-start-until-the-30s/ [accessed 10/7/2016].

Pew Research Center (2015b) 'Working mother statistics' [online]. Available from: www.statisticbrain.com/working-mother-statistics/ [accessed 3/7/2016].

Pew Social Trends (2014) 'Public views on staying at home vs. working' [online] Available from: www.pewsocialtrends.org/2014/04/08/chapter-4-public-views-on-staying-at-home-vs-working/ [accessed 16/9/2015].

Phipps, A. (2014) *The politics of the body: Gender in a neoliberal and neoconservative age*, Cambridge: Polity Press.

Procter, I. and Padfield, M. (1998) *Young adult women, work and family: Living a contradiction*, London: Mansell.

PwC (2016) *Women returners: The £1 billion career break penalty for professional women* [online]. Available from: www.pwc.co.uk/economic-services/women-returners/pwc-research-women-returners-nov-2016.pdf [accessed 12/11/2016].

Ragins, B. and Cotton, J. (1999) 'Mentor functions and outcomes', *Journal of Applied Psychology*, 84(4): 529–50.

Reed, K., Duncan, J. M., Lucier-Greer, M., Fixelle, C. and Ferraro, A. J. (2016) 'Helicopter parenting and emerging adult self-efficacy: implications for mental and physical health', *Journal of Child and Family Studies*, 25(10): 3136–49.

Ribbens-McCarthy, J. (1994) *Mothers and their children: Towards a feminist sociology of childrearing*. London: Sage.

Ribbens-McCarthy, J. and Edwards, R. (2011) *Key concepts in family studies*, London: Sage.

Ribbens-McCarthy, J., Edwards, R. and Gillies, V. (2000) 'Moral tales of the child and the adult: narratives of contemporary family lives under changing circumstances', *Sociology*, 34(4): 785–803.

Rich, A. (1986) *Of women born: Motherhood as experience and institution* (10th anniversary edn), New York: Norton.

Risman, B. (1998) *Gender vertigo*, New Haven, CT: Yale University Press.

Rottenberg, C. (2014) 'Happiness and the liberal imagination: how superwoman became balanced', *Feminist Studies*, 40(1): 144–68.

Rowbotham, S., Segal, L. and Wainwright, H. (1979) *Beyond the fragments: Feminism and the making of socialism*, London: Merlin.

Roxburgh, S. (2004) '"There just aren't enough hours in the day": the mental health consequences of time pressure', *Journal of Health and Social Behavior*, 45: 115–31.

Sandberg, S. (2013) *Lean in: Women, work and the will to lead*, London: W. H. Allen.

Schwartz, B., Ward, A., Monterosso, J., Lyubomirsky, S., White, K. and Lehman, D. R. (2002) 'Maximizing versus satisficing: happiness is a matter of choice', *Journal of personality and social psychology*, 83(5): 1178–97.

Scott, J. and Clery, E. (2013) *British Social Attitudes 30* [online]. Available from: www.bsa.natcen.ac.uk/latest-report/british-social-attitudes-30/gender-roles/attitudes-to-gender-roles-change-over-time.aspx [accessed 12/2/2015].

Scott, J. L., Dex, S. and Joshi, H. (2008) *Women and employment: Changing lives and new challenges*, Cheltenham: Edward Elgar.

Seagram, S. and Daniluk, J. C. (2002) 'It goes with the territory: the meaning and experience of maternal guilt for mothers of preadolescent children', *Women and Therapy*, 25(1): 61–88.

Sharpe, S. (1984) *Double identity: The lives of working mothers*, London: Pelican.

Simon, H. A. (1956) 'Rational choice and the structure of the environment', *Psychological Review*, 63(2): 129–38

Simpson, R. (1998) 'Presenteeism, power and organizational change: Long hours as a career barrier and the impact on the working lives of women managers', *British Journal of Management*, 9 (Special Issue): S37–S50.

Singh, V., Vinnicombe, S. and James, K. (2006) 'Constructing a professional identity: how young female managers use role models', *Women in Management Review*, 21(1): 67–81.

Sluis, S.van de., Vinkhuyzen, A. A. E., Boomsma, D. I. and Posthuma, D. (2010) 'Sex differences in adults' motivation to achieve', *Intelligence*, 38(4): 433–46.

Smart, C. (2011) 'Familes, secrets, memories', *Sociology*, 45(4): 539–53.

Smith, R. (2010) 'Total parenting', *Educational Theory*, 60(3): 357–69.

Smith, R. (2016) 'New targets to have women in 33% of top exec jobs by 2020 unveiled' [online]. Available from: www.cityam.com/253229/ftse-100-set-new-target-have-33-per-cent-executive-jobs [accessed 8/11/2016].

Spohr, M. (2015) 'How dads balance work and family' [online]. Available from: www.buzzfeed.com/mikespohr/how–dads–balance–work–and–family?utm_term=.ivj2LvbQvv - .li7rwZNEZZ [accessed 7/11/2016].

Stansell, C. (2010) The Feminist Promise: 1792 to the Present, New York, Modern Library.

Steinberg, L. (1990) 'Autonomy, conflict, and harmony in the family relationship', in S. S. Feldman and G. R. Elliott (eds) [At the threshold: the developing adolescent] Cambridge, MA: Harvard University Press, pp 255–76.

Stone, P. (2007) Opting out? Why women really quit careers and head home, Berkeley, CA: University of California Press.

Stone, A. (2012) Feminism, psychoanalysis, and maternal subjectivity, London: Routledge.

Strauss, A. L. and Corbin, J. M. (1998) Basics of qualitative research: Techniques and procedures for developing grounded theory (2nd edn), Thousand Oaks, CA: Sage.

Strauss, W. and Howe, N. (1991) Generations, New York: William Morrow.

Super, D. E. (1957) The psychology of careers. An introduction to vocational development, New York: Harper & Bros.

Sutherland, J.-A. (2010) 'Mothering, guilt and shame', Sociology Compass, 4(5): 310–21.

Tasker, Y. and Negra, D. (2007) Interrogating postfeminism: gender and the politics of popular culture. Durham, NC: Duke University Press.

Thomson, R. (2008) 'Thinking intergenerationally about motherhood', Studies in the Maternal [online]. Available from: www.mamsie.bbk.ac.uk/articles/abstract/10.16995/sim.109/ [accessed 12/2/2013].

Thomson, R. (2014) 'Generational research: between historical and sociological imaginations', International Journal of Social Research Methodology, 17(2): 147–56.

Thomson, R., Kehily, M. J., Hadfield, L. and Sharpe, S. (2011) Making modern mothers, Bristol: Policy Press.

Timewise Foundation (2017) Winners [online]. Available from: http://timewise.co.uk/campaigns/power-part-time-list-2017/ [accessed 6/5/2017].

Tipping, J., Chanfreau, J., Perry, J. and Tait, C. (2014) *The fourth work-life balance employee survey* [online]. Available from: www.gov.uk/government/uploads/system/uploads/attachment_data/file/398557/bis-14-1027-fourth-work-life-balance-employer-survey-2013.pdf [accessed 6/2/2015].

TUC (2016) Still just a bit of banter?: Sexual harrassment in the workplace 2016 [online]. Available from: www.tuc.org.uk/sites/default/files/SexualHarassmentreport2016.pdf [acessed 15/8/2016

Tutchell, E. and Edmonds, J. (2015) *Man-Made: why so few women are in positions of power*, Farnham: Gower.

Twenge, J. M. (2010) 'A review of the empirical evidence on generational differences in work attitudes', *Journal of Business and Psychology*, 25(2): 1045–62.

Twenge, J. M. and Campbell, S. M. (2008) 'Generational differences in psychological traits and their impact on the workplace', *Journal of Managerial Psychology*, 23(8): 862–77.

UCAS (2012) *End of cycle report 2012* [online]. Available from: www.ucas.com/sites/default/files/ucas-end-of-cycle-report-2012.pdf [accessed 17/9/2013]

Van Maanen, J. (1988) *Tales of the field: On writing ethnography*, Chicago, IL: University of Chicago Press.

Vere, J. P (2007) '"Having it all" no longer: fertility, female labor supply, and the new life choices of Generation X', *Demography*, 44(4): 821–8.

Vinnicombe, S. (2015) *The female FTSE board report 2015* [online]. Available from: www.som.cranfield.ac.uk/som/dinamic-content/research/ftse/FemaleFTSEReportMarch2015.pdf [accessed 18/1/2016].

Vinnicombe, S., Burke, R. J., Blake-Beard, S. and Moore, L. L. (2013) *Handbook of Research on Promoting Women's Careers*, Cheltenham: Edward Elgar.

Walker, A., Maher, J., Coulthard, M., Goddard, E. and Thomas, M. (2001) *Living in Britain, 2001* [online]. Available from: www.ons.gov.uk/ons/rel/ghs/general-household-survey/2001-edition/index.html [accessed 25/4/14].

Walkerdine, V., Lucey, H. and Melody, J. (2001) *Growing up girl: Psychosocial explorations of gender and class*, Basingstoke: Palgrave.

Weisul, J. (2015) 'Globally women gain corporate board seats – but not in the US', [online]. Available from: http://fortune.com/2015/01/13/catalyst-women-boards-countries-us/ [accessed 6/6/2016].

Welsh, E. (2002) 'Dealing with data: using NVivo in the qualitative data analysis process', *Forum Qualitative Social Research*, 3(2): art. 26.

Williams, J.C. (2000) *Unbending gender: Why family and work conflict and what to do about it*, Oxford: Oxford University Press.

Williams, J. C. (2003) 'Beyond the glass ceiling: the maternal wall as a barrier to gender equality', *Thomas Jefferson Law Review*, 1 [online]. Available from: http://repository.uchastings.edu/cgi/viewcontent.cgi?article=1805&context=faculty_scholarship [accessed 4/9/2014].

Williams, J. C. (2010) *Reshaping the work-family debate*, Cambridge, MA: Harvard University Press.

Williams, J. C. and Dempsey, R. (2014) *What works for women at work*, New York: New York University Press.

Williams, J. C., Blair-Loy, M. and Berdahl, J. L. (2013) 'Cultural schemas, social class, and the flexibility stigma', *Journal of Social Issues*, 69(2): 209–34.

Williams, Z. (2013) 'Lean in: women, work, and the will to lead by Sheryl Sandberg – review', *The Guardian* [online]. Available from: www.theguardian.com/books/2013/mar/13/lean-in-sheryl-sandberg-review [accessed 13/3/2013)

Winnicott, D. (1953) 'Transitional objects and transitional phenomena', *International Journal of Psychoanalysis*, 34: 89–97.

WISE (2014) *Women in science, technology, engineering and mathmathics* [online]. Available from: www.wisecampaign.org.uk/uploads/wise/files/WISE_UK_Statistics_2014.pdf [accessed 3/1/2016].

Wolf, A. (2006) 'Rise of professional women' [online]. Available from: www.prospectmagazine.co.uk/magazine/rise-of-professional-women-decline-female-altriusm [accessed 23/9/2013].

Wolf, A. (2013) *The XX factor: How working women are creating a new society*, London: Profile.

Women's Business Council (2013)'Maximising women's contribution to future economic growth' [online] Available from: www.womensbusinesscouncil.co.uk/wp-content/uploads/2017/02/DCMS_WBC_Full_Report_v1.0-1.pdf [accessed 10/2/2015].

Woodfield, R. (2007) *What women want from work: Gender and occupational choice in the 21st century*, Basingstoke: Palgrave Macmillan.

Young, Z. (2017) Women in the middle: Mothers' experience of transition to part-time and flexible work in professional and managerial occupations, DPhil thesis, University of Sussex.

YSC, KPMG and 30%Club (2014) *Cracking the code* [online]. Available from: https://30percentclub.org/wp-content/uploads/2015/04/Cracking-the-code.pdf [accessed 27/8/2015].

Index

A

academic attainment 75–6, 79–80, 90–1
accessibility of mother during working hours 65, 165, 173
Acker, J. 171
activities outside work and family, compromised 30, 48–9, 172
Adkins, L. 7, 18, 111
after-school period, importance of 29, 47, 51–3, 57, 58, 60, 173, 179
ambition
  clear ambition 112–13
  coded as masculine 100
  communicating value of 4–5
  and confidence 99–100, 114–15
  daughters' talk about 108–10
  encouragement in future careers 180
  key findings 172
  mothers' talk about 86, 105–8, 112–13, 180
  quiet ambition 5, 95–116, 174
  reaching for the top 97–9
Apter, T. E. 53
Armstrong, J. 184
Aughinbaugh, A. 53

B

'baby boomers' 6, 11
Bailey, L. 34, 36, 39
Baker and Cracknell 14
Baraitser, L. 123, 130, 131, 132, 141–2, 147, 152
Barnett, R. C. 63
Barsh, J. 15
Bataille, C. 173
Battersby, C. 120
Baxter, J. 168
Beck, U. 10, 33, 120, 175
Beck-Gernsheim, E. 10, 175
being fully present 51, 52, 56
'being with'/ 'not leaving' children 29, 130–1, 141
Bem, S. L. 100

Benjamin, J. 49
'best of both worlds' discourse 127–30, 132, 133, 154, 169, 172, 174–5, 187
Bianchi, S. M. 64
Bimrose, J. 37, 99, 108
Bjerrum Nielsen, H. 8–9, 18, 32, 33, 119, 123, 140, 157
Blair-Loy, M. 143
boards, women on 13, 14, 15
BoardWatch 14
boredom, fear of 36, 74, 81
Bostock, J. 63, 81, 102, 112, 115
boundaries around family life, boundaries around family life 179
Brannen, J. 16
British Household Panel Survey 64, 160
British Social Attitudes survey 7, 61, 129
Burke, R. J. 13
Butler, J. 33

C

Campbell, S. M. 11
Canada 13
capitalism 9, 176
career breaks 35, 48, 148, 183
career changes 2, 48, 118, 126, 128–9, 181
'career woman,' definition of 18–19
CFWD 14
Chambers Student 14
Chartered Management Institute 13
childcare
  in 1980s and 1990s 154
  ad hoc 50, 154
  after-school period 58
  costs 150, 184
  and feminism 144
  grandmothers as 148, 150
  and income levels 124
  mothers' responsibility for organising 31, 47, 161, 162–3, 165, 166–8, 176, 185

mothers spend greater hours on 142, 160
policy recommendations for 184–5
poor quality 43, 47
school holidays 58
and single mothers 43
childless, remaining 118
Chodorow, N. 119
choice 121–2, 133, 176
Christopher, K. 65, 123
Clery, E. 61
Coffman, J. 99
competitiveness 100, 111, 115, 123, 151, 152
compressed hours 129–30, 145, 149, 183
compromise 29, 36–7, 48–9, 63, 158, 165, 173, 179
see also 'best of both worlds' discourse
confidence
gender differences 10, 15
mothers' influence on daughters' careers 87, 89
and quiet ambition 98, 99–100, 102–3, 106, 110, 112, 114–15
Cosslett, R. 16
Cracking the code study 98–9, 102
Crompton, R. 31, 33–4, 35, 36, 38, 44, 105, 119, 120, 142, 160, 161
cultural cover ups 43
cultural scripts
contemporary fatherhood 150, 159, 168, 176
contemporary motherhood 122–3, 130–3, 150–2, 153, 154, 155, 175
flouting 67
'good mothers' 43, 61, 122–3, 181
key findings 172
motherhood and work 35, 47, 50, 51, 61–2
part-time working 70, 119, 120–1, 127–9, 174–5
women's responsibility for children 126, 127
culture, workplace 15, 97, 100–2, 105, 184
Cunningham, M. 62, 70

D

Damaske and French 153
Daniluk, J. C. 32
daughters, study focus on 17
Davidson, M. J. 13
deferred gratification 75

depression 63
see also mental health
Dermott and Miller 159
'different,' feeling 60–1, 67
digital working 52, 153
direct influence on daughters' careers 82–6, 113, 138, 174
director positions 13, 14, 15
discrimination 5, 87, 97–8
see also sexism
display 7
divorce 124–5, 161
see also lone mothers
domestic chores
daily negotiation of 163, 182
egalitarian approaches to family life 120, 158–61, 182
emotional work of 163
and feminism 144
and long working hours 64
outsourcing of 158
'second shift' 32, 159, 161, 162
women spend greater hours on 142, 158, 159, 160
women's responsibility for 31, 63, 162–3, 169
Duncan, S. 124
Durbin, S. 142

E

Edmonds, J. 15
education, access to 145
educational attainment 75–6, 79–80, 90–1
egalitarian approaches to family life 120–1, 144, 157–9, 161–70, 173, 182, 185
Eichenbaum, L. 75
Elias, N. 190
Ellison, L. 159
Ely, R. J. 168
emotion management 32, 39, 132, 154, 159, 162, 169, 182
emotional presence 51, 52, 56
emotional support for daughters 46, 103–4, 139, 148, 181
emotional support for mothers (from daughters) 53, 104
employers' attitudes 11, 130, 142, 150, 153, 160, 164, 182–5
empowerment vocabulary 9–10
enjoyment of work
career choices (daughters') 73, 80, 81, 108–10, 172, 180

daughters' aspirations for 59, 63, 68
  as key factor in success 102
  mothers' 37, 38, 54, 84, 93
Epstein, C. F. 144
equal moral personhood 178
Equality Act (2010) 14
equality policies 101
Eräranta, K. 159
evening working 107
events, important, attendance at 28, 41,
  48, 51, 56, 60, 61, 118–19, 173
everyday joy, missing out on 49
Everyday Sexism Project 92
extensive responsibility 123

F

Faircloth, C. 122
families, as sites of social practice 7
family first attitudes 38, 41
Fassinger, R. E. 167
fateful events/ serious problems 38
fathers
  ambition 113–14, 116
  attendance at school events 51
  culture of contemporary fatherhood
    150, 159, 168, 176
  daughters choosing same occupation
    as 83, 84
  father–daughter relationships 50, 90,
    96, 114
  flexible working 183
  influence on daughters' career choices
    4, 90–1, 92, 113–14, 150, 174
  in separated families 58
  shared parental leave 185
  stay-at-home fathers 60, 67, 157, 165
  see also partners
Fawcett Society 14, 160, 176, 184, 185
Fels, A. 100
feminism
  and contemporary motherhood 121,
    144, 148, 152
  feminist scholarship 8, 9–10, 12
  key findings/ recommendations
    175–9, 185
  mothers' influence on daughters
    86–9, 90
  peer influence 92–3
  postfeminism 10, 141, 176, 178
  and quiet ambition 103, 107
financial independence, aiming for 88,
  107, 124, 139
financial necessity, working out of 35,
  57, 105, 124, 125, 129

financial support for daughters 82
Finch, J. 7–8
flexible working
  difficulties in arranging 57, 60, 133,
    179
  for fathers 160
  greater availability of 70, 145–6, 148
  lack of knowledge about 129–30
  mothers' 48, 129–30, 153
  policies for 182–3
full-time work
  daughters' views of 117, 118, 129
  economic imperatives for 124
  making choices about working hours
    124–5
  other mothers' judgement of 131
  statistics on 30–1
  study subjects 17
  see also long working hours
fully present, being 51, 52, 56
Furedi, F. 6, 122, 132, 154, 175

G

Gagnon, J. D. 67
Galinsky, E. 63, 65, 66
Gambles, R. 129
Gareis, K. C. 63
Garey, A. I. 54
Gatrell, C. 63, 120, 121, 122, 130, 164
gender equality
  aiming for the top 97–9
  and the 'best of both worlds' trope
    133, 174
  expectations of future equality 12–13,
    15, 121, 141
  feminism 87, 88, 176
  history of 5, 12
  illusion of 121, 176
  inclusive workplaces 184
  normalisation of 121
  prevailing inequalities 14–16
  structural gender disadvantages 97–8
  see also egalitarian approaches to
    family life
gender identity 33–4, 119–21, 140–1
gender progress at work 11–14
gender roles 8, 61, 76–7, 97–8, 100,
  119–21, 144, 157, 160
gender strategies 159, 161, 162
gendered subjectivity 8, 32, 33, 157
generations, definition of 5–11
Gerson, K. 62, 144
Giddens, A. 18
Gill, R. 10

globalisation 142, 153, 174–5
Golombok, S. 66
good enough mothering 54, 172, 179
'good mothers'
  and 'balance' 133
  'best of both worlds' discourse
    127–30, 132, 133, 154, 169, 172,
    175, 179, 187
  better mother because of work 30,
    46, 54
  constant presence not required for 55
  construction of new definitions of 54
  cultural scripts 43, 61, 122–3, 181
'good workers' 43, 181
Gottfredson, L. 75, 82
grandmothers 18, 125, 137, 147–50,
  175
Greer, G. 88
Grounded Theory 190–1
guilt
  attitudes to working motherhood
    39–45
  daughters' 50, 58–9
  gender identity 119
  and grandmother advice 149
  and idealistic attitudes 55
  influence on daughters' career choices
    84
  and involvement of partners 158
  key findings 172–3, 181
  mothers' 29, 31–2, 146
  and pragmatic attitudes 54
  and quiet ambition 111
  and work-life conflict 63

H

Hampton-Alexander review 15
harassment and bullying 87, 101
'hard work' discourse 74, 79–80, 86,
  94, 96, 110, 174, 180–1
Harris, A. 12, 35, 38, 44, 105, 119
'having it all' 18–19, 31, 57, 127
Hays, S. 7, 122–3
helicopter parenting 181
Himmelweit, S. 34
Hochschild, A. 32, 39, 43, 63, 121,
  132, 133, 142, 153, 154, 159,
  160–1, 162, 169, 182
home, bringing work 52, 111
Horner, M. 100, 111
housework *see* domestic chores
Huberman, A. M. 190
humble bragging 132

I

ideal workers 142
idealistic attitudes
  and ambition 111
  daughters' attitudes 146
  grandmothers 149
  mothers' 39, 42–5, 47, 52, 54–6, 66
identity
  conflicting identities 173
  and domestic chores 159
  gender identity 33–4, 119–21, 140–1
  gender identity and work 33–4
  as mothers and workers 34–9, 54,
    181
  and self-efficacy 91
  women's based on relationships 33,
    119–20
  and work 75, 128, 146
ill children 40, 49
imposter syndrome 111
'in the moment' 49, 96, 130–1, 142
inclusive workplaces 184
income levels 13, 45–6, 63, 82, 106,
  110, 119, 165–6
independence, encouraging 51, 52–3,
  86, 88, 107, 173
indirect influence on daughters' careers
  79–82, 91, 97, 174
individualism 7, 10, 69, 85, 99, 121,
  175–9, 183
inequality 5, 87, 97–8, 176–7, 178,
  183
Institute for Fiscal Studies 184
intensification of responsibility 7, 123,
  132, 151, 154, 175
intensive parenting 7, 122–3, 151
intergenerational research 6–7
intergenerational transmission of values/
  attitudes 8–9, 62, 75, 76, 84, 98,
  140–1, 147, 171, 177
internet 153, 154
internships, unpaid 82, 85
intersectionality (gender/ generation)
  10

J

Jacobs, J. A. 63, 160
judgement, from others 43, 131, 151–2

K

Kalleberg, A. L. 144
Kay, K. 100
Kehily, M. J. 140

Kelan, E. K. 4, 11
key findings 172–9
Kirby, J. 122
Kodz, J. 160
Kray, L. 100

L

Laney, E. K. 34, 36, 39, 173
Lareau, A. 123
law 13, 14
Lawler, S. 75, 76, 84, 123, 141
leadership positions, women in 97–9,
    171
    see also senior levels
Lean In 82, 101
Lee, E. 123
Lee, Y. 15
leisure time, desire for more 68, 125
lone mothers
    allocation of hours 142
    childcare 50, 180
    compromise 49, 139
    financial necessity for work 57, 88,
        124–5
    idealistic attitudes 43, 66–7
    long working hours 59, 180
long working hours
    as culture 70, 109
    daughters' 67–70, 119, 138
    and daughters' independence 53
    and domestic chores 160
    drivers of decisions about 124–5
    longer than contracted 130
    as measure of 'working hard' 63
    mothers' 49, 62, 70, 142–3
    mothers' concern over daughters' 138
    negative effects of 46, 64–6
    normality of 68
    not a problem per se 63
    and senior levels 101
    switching off from 52
    time allocation 142
    'working yourself into the ground'
        139
longitudinal studies 12, 31, 53, 64, 76,
    124–5, 159–60
love 51, 54, 55, 66
Lyonette, C. 31, 62, 142

M

Machung, A. 43, 133, 161, 162
Mah, A. 4
Maheas, M.-C. 184

main earners, mothers as 118, 125, 158
Mainiero, L. A. 99, 108
male-cultured workplaces 97
male-dominated professions 69–70, 95
management studies 4, 10
Mannheim, K. 6, 87, 107, 140, 145
marriage bar 11–12
maternal time 141–2
maternity leave 30, 35, 118, 119, 147
McGinn, K. 62, 70, 77, 137, 147
McKinsey 15, 81, 101, 183
McMunn, A. 64
McRae, S. 12, 17, 31, 61, 125, 153,
    162
McRobbie, A. 9–10, 12, 121, 141, 178
media 122, 131, 154
Mendolia, S. 64, 70
mental health 63, 109, 142, 149
mentoring 3–5, 93–4, 97, 104, 115,
    173–4
Merton, R. K. 3
middle-class mothers
    aiming for 'balance' 127–30
    anxiety 132
    'best of both worlds' 174–5
    choices about work and motherhood
        31, 36, 121, 176
    cultural scripts 123
    domestic chores 159
    educational attainment 75–6, 105
    and egalitarian parenting 167
    influence on daughters' career choices
        76, 79, 80, 145
    pressure to 'get parenting right' 152,
        154
Miles, M. B. 190
Milkie, M. A. 64–5, 70, 179
millennials 11, 12, 68, 115, 125
Millennium Cohort Study 64, 125
Miller, T. 35, 62, 67, 122, 152, 159,
    164, 169
'missing out,' feelings of 49–50
mitigating effects of working 44–5,
    48–9
modesty, expected of women 109, 111,
    112, 115, 146
Moen, P. 17, 76, 77, 84, 115, 137, 147
Moisander, J. 159
Morgan, D. 7, 169–70
Morris, C. 67
mother-daughter relationships 18–19,
    49, 67, 85, 94, 96–7, 103–4, 141
motherhood

cultural scripts of contemporary
motherhood 122–3, 130–3, 150–2,
154, 175
downgrading of value of 111
and femininity 119
'motherhood penalty' 15
see also 'good mothers'
mothers' gatherings 131
Ms. Foundation 185

N

nannies 29
negative effects of having a working
mother 46–7, 53, 55, 57–71, 132,
172, 179
neoliberalism 176
Neuenfeldt, B. 99
Newman, J. 140
Nielsen, B. 114
number of children 34–5

O

O'Brien, K. M. 167
occupational choices 73–94
Office of National Statistics 160
Olivetti, C. 62, 76
Opportunity Now 99, 101, 109
Orbach, S. 75
Orgad, S. 10
Orrange, R. M. 120

P

Padfield, M. 38
parental determinism 122–3, 132–3,
154, 175
'parenting' (as verb) 122
parenting 'experts' 123, 139, 151, 154
partners
careers taking priority 126
and contemporary motherhood
132–3
difficulties between partners 69
implications for 181–2
and pragmatic attitudes 54
shared parenting 120, 157–70
working around the work hours of
107
see also fathers
part-time working
to achieve more leisure time 68
allocation of hours 142–3
attitudes to 61

'best of both worlds' discourse
127–30, 132, 133, 154, 169, 172,
174–5, 179, 187
changing to 60
combining with partners' work 157
cultural scripts 70, 119, 120–1, 127–9
daughters' aspirations for 117, 118,
119, 132, 145, 146, 153, 174–5
declining hours in the labour market
124–5
drawbacks of 128
and egalitarian parenting 166–8
versus flexible working 129
lack of opportunities for 37
long working hours 130
women disproportionately in 13
see also flexible working
Patacchini, E. 62
paternity leave 160
patriarchy 9
pay gap 12, 14
peer influence 92–3, 150
people-pleasing 100
perfectionism 42, 74, 100, 106, 113
Pew Research 61
Phipps, A. 92
policy, government 12, 101, 154, 159,
160, 182–5
politics 14, 114
postfeminism 10, 141, 176, 178
potential, reaching one's 76, 89, 110,
183
pragmatic attitudes
daughters' attitudes 146–7
and egalitarian parenting 165
and involvement of partners 158
key findings 172–3
mothers' 39–42, 44, 45, 52, 54, 66
preschool children 17, 30, 108, 129
primary carer, women's role as 8, 9,
10, 31, 107, 121–3, 126–30, 157–8,
163, 167, 169, 170
prioritisation of work over children
59, 66
Proctor, I. 38
professionalisation of motherhood 152
psychological wellbeing
of children 64
of mothers 63, 70
public scrutiny 123, 132, 133, 151,
154, 175
public sector 14, 80–1, 177
PwC 183

Q

qualitative research methodology
16–20, 189–91
quiet ambition 5, 95–116, 174

R

recession 93, 94, 112
relationships
father-daughter 50, 90, 96, 114
mother-daughter 18–19, 49, 67, 85, 94, 96–7, 103–4, 141
mothers compromise other relationships 48–9, 58
with partner 158, 159, 162, 164
women's identity based on 33, 119–20
renunciation versus repudiation of mothers 49
responsiveness, parental 65
returning to previous career 36
risk, perceptions of 122, 154
role models
daughters following 62, 69, 73
expectation of a career 76–7
gender identity 119
key findings 171, 172, 173–4
mothers as 3–5, 45–6
and quiet ambition 110, 111, 115
Rottenberg, C. 31, 43, 121, 127, 132, 178
routines, stable 48, 51, 56, 173
Rowbotham, S. 88, 103
Roxburgh, S. 63
Rudberg, M. 8, 9, 18, 32, 33, 119, 123, 140, 157

S

salary levels 82, 110
Sandberg, S. 16, 100
Scandinavia 13, 160, 185
school events, attendance at 28, 41, 48, 51, 56, 60, 61, 118–19, 173
school pick-ups 48, 60
Scott, J. L. 61
Seagram, S. 32
'second shift' 32, 159, 161, 162
self-confidence see confidence
self-efficacy 85, 91–2
self-employment 48
self-esteem 10, 11
self-respect 81
senior levels, women reaching
aiming for the top 97–9

daughters 69
and fathers 114
flexible working 179
history of 12, 13, 14–16
mothers 55, 87
quiet ambition 95–116
stalling of 171
sense of purpose 89, 119
see also social value of work
sexism 126, 176
sexual harassment 87, 101
shared parental leave 160, 185
Shipman, C. 100
siblings 67, 114
sick children 40, 49
Sigala, M. 34
Simon, H. A. 44
single, remaining 120
single mothers see lone mothers
sisterhood 132, 177
skills, interchangeable work/ family 36
skills, mothers teaching daughters 85, 103
sleep, mothers missing out on 48–9
Sluis, S. van de 100, 111
Smart, D. 168
Smith, R. 15
social media 117–18, 123, 132, 152
social networks 131
social practice, families as sites of 7
social value of work 80–1, 84–5, 92, 102
socialisation 8, 33, 62, 77, 100, 111, 180
sociology 10
sons 17, 104–5
stamina/ determination 79
Stansell, C. 178
status, careers providing 84
status shields 32
Stone, A. 141, 147, 152
Stone, P. 43, 121, 133, 143
storytelling 7–8, 32
stress 37, 62–4, 65, 69, 70, 71, 101, 109, 142–3, 165
study subjects 16–20, 192–4
success
daughters' expectations of 112
daughters' talk about 108–10, 174
definitions of 16, 63, 84, 95–6, 115, 184
mothers' talk about 105–8, 112, 115
women's view of 102, 105–8
Sullivan, S. E. 99, 108
Super, D. E. 75
Sutherland, J.-A. 54

T

teamwork, parenting as 158, 164
teenage years
  after-school period, importance of 29
  need for mother's presence 29, 46,
    179
  time spent with parents 65
Think Future 12, 14, 98
Thomson, R. 32, 36, 121, 123, 132,
    133, 140, 147, 151, 152, 154, 158,
    161, 165
time, and working motherhood 6,
    140–3, 154, 174–5
Timescapes 53
Tipping, J. 129
tiredness 48–9, 65, 142, 158
trade-offs 38, 39, 41–2, 46, 54, 107
traditional gender roles 33–4, 61, 157,
    161–6, 169
travelling away for work 46, 59
Tutchell, E. 15
Twenge, J. M. 11, 68, 125

U

United States 13, 15
university 12, 73–4, 75–6, 79, 93, 137
unsuccessful careers 105–6

V

verbal transmission of values 94, 115,
    148–9, 152, 155
Vere, J. P. 124
Vinnicombe, S. 15

W

Walkerdine, V. 75, 80, 167
weekends and holidays, making the
    most of 48, 52
Williams, J. C. 16, 62, 122, 142
Winnicott, D. 179
Wolf, A. 12, 13, 16, 17, 124, 176–7
Women in Whitehall 101
Woodfield, R. 69, 77, 98
work ethic see 'hard work' discourse
work experience, mothers arranging
    73, 83, 174
working classes 79, 82, 145
working from home 126, 132, 151
work-life
  aiming for 'balance' 6, 11, 127–30,
    132
  allocation of hours 142–3

boundaries around family life 48, 107
  and digital working 52, 153
  dislike of term 28, 32
  and domestic chores 160
  interconnectedness of work/ family
    life 36, 181
  leisure time 68
  and maternal guilt 31–2
  mothers' advice on 143–7
  mothers' concern over daughters' 138
  planning for children in career choices
    118, 125–7
  and stress 62–4
  see also 'best of both worlds' discourse
workplace cultures 15, 97, 100–2, 105,
    184

Y

Young, Z. 183
YSC 98–9, 102